The Dictionary of
Beer and Brewing

The Dictionary of Beer and Brewing

Second Edition

Compiled by Dan Rabin and Carl Forget
Preface by Gregg Smith

FITZROY DEARBORN PUBLISHERS
CHICAGO · LONDON

For information write to:

FITZROY DEARBORN PUBLISHERS
70 East Walton Street
Chicago, Illinois 60611
USA

or

FITZROY DEARBORN PUBLISHERS
310 Regent Street
London WIR 5AJ
England

Cataloging-in-Publication Data is available from the Library of Congress and the British Library

ISBN 1-57958-078-5

First published in the USA and UK 1998

Printed by Braun-Brumfield, Inc., Ann Arbor, Michigan
Cover designed by Peter Aristedes

Contents

PREFACE

Approximately 6,000 years ago, in an area between the Tigris and Euphrates rivers encompassing southern Mesopotamia and known as Sumeria, someone discovered fermentation. In all probability, the discovery involved chance.

Grain had been the principal domesticated crop for the 7,000 years since the most primitive farming began, valued for both nourishment and ease in storage. Earthen jars were fashioned to hold the annual harvest, a practice that many historians and anthropologists agree may have indirectly led to the discovery of beer. It is likely that rainfall on uncovered jars resulted in the discovery of malt. Someone unwilling to discard wet grain probably spread it out to dry; later, when the grain was cooked into bread, it was found to be especially sweet. Malting had unwittingly been discovered. Bread loaves were stored in earthenware jars as well. Rain may have again effected a fortunate disaster; windborne yeast settling on watery barley soup would have resulted in fermentation. It was not until thousands of years later, during the nineteenth century A.D., that yeast was identified as the cause of fermentation in malted barley water.

Early societies thought beer had supernatural powers because of the mood-altered state it induces; intoxication was considered divine. Some anthropologists hypothesize that ancient people were so enamored of these qualities that they inspired crop cultivation (farming), which led to settlements and what is now called civilization. It has also been postulated that the art of fashioning jars and other vessels advanced because of the need for receptacles in which to ferment beer.

An ancient engraving in the Sumerian language gives the earliest account of barley, followed by a pictograph illustrating bread being baked, crumbled into water (mash), and made into a beverage. This drink is described as making people feel "exhilarated, wonderful and blissful." Sumerians considered this brew a divine drink and offered it to their gods. A seal dated at around 4,000 years old features a Sumerian "Hymn to Ninkasi," the goddess of brewing. As brewing was considered a household art, it was the women's domain.

In one of the first great works of literature, the *Gilgamesh Epic* dating from the third millennium B.C., it is described how Enkidu, an uncivilized primitive man, is educated by a whore:

Enkidu knew not, what bread was nor how one ate it. He had also not learned to drink beer. The whore opened her mouth and spoke to Enkidu:

Eat the bread now, O Enkidu, as it belongs to life. Drink also beer, as it is the custom of the land." Enkidu drank seven cups of beer and his heart soared. In this condition he washed himself and became a human being.

Dr. Guillermo Algaze, an anthropologist from the University of California at San Diego, who specializes in the colonialism of ancient civilizations, theorized that beer was one of early civilization's most important forms of currency. His hypothesis was based upon the archaeological site of Hacinebi Tepe. Located near the Euphrates River in southern Turkey, Hacinebi Tepe was an early trading outpost of Mesopotamia, founded as a result of developments 700 miles down the river. In 3500 B.C. in the Fertile Crescent, inhabitants enjoyed larger and larger harvests resulting from improved methods of farming the rich soil. Irrigation gave them the first known grain surpluses, and they kept accounts of the amounts they reaped. This bookkeeping would be the basis of writing and hence the beginning of recorded history. As the wealth poured in, formerly remote farmers were drawn together, forming one of the first modern cities, named Uruk. As its population grew, the economy was forced to change. Although Uruk was agriculturally rich, it lacked other natural resources such as metals, semi-precious stones and timber. The solution was to set up trade with less advanced neighboring groups in possession of these resources. Such was the function of Hacinebi Tepe, an outpost for the conduct of trade. Among Hacinebi artifacts is some of the earliest evidence of beer.

Beer was a logical commodity for trading. Uruk had a surplus of grain, and while transportation of grain was difficult because of climate sensitivity, rodents and insects, alcohol remained relatively stable during shipping. Thus beer was suitable for trading throughout the region.

After the collapse of the Sumerian empire during the second millennium B.C., the Babylonians ruled Mesopotamia. Their culture had evolved from that of the Sumerians, and consequently they also mastered brewing. Clay tablets dating back more than 4,500 years tell of more than nineteen different types of ale produced by the Babylonians. Production of ale and the quality of the supply were of such importance that laws were enacted governing recipes and methods of brewing. Hammurabi (1810–1750 B.C.), a Babylonian king and founder of an empire, decreed the oldest known collection of laws, which included the establishment of a daily beer ration. The size of rations depended on an individual's social standing. Beer was not sold but was traded for barley; accepting silver for beer as well as serving low quality beer were crimes punishable by drowning.

Ancient Egyptians are also known to have produced alcoholic beverages more than 5,000 years ago. In Egyptian legend, Osiris, the god of agriculture, taught men how to make beer. They used unbaked bread dough to make beer and flavored their brew with dates, traditions that are upheld today by Egyptians living along the Nile, called Fellahs. Beer was an essential ingredient in both Sumerian and Egyptian medicine.

Drinking ale in ancient times was far different from today. Glasses had not been invented, so the custom of the Babylonians, Syrians, Hittites, Armenians, Egyptians and Greeks was to drink their unfiltered beer directly from large jars using straws or tubes; royalty was provided straws of gold for drinking. This helped strain out some of the brew residue, which was very bitter in the mouth. Pictograms frequently depict this practice. The Greek historian Xenophon also documented the custom of using straws in his *Anabasis* (c. 380s B.C.):

> For drink there was beer which was very strong when not mingled with water, but was agreeable to those who were used to it. They drank this with a reed, out of the vessel that held the beer, upon which they saw the barley swim.

Ale was a staple of all classes; poorer quality went to the unfortunate lower classes, while the royals drank premium ale from gold inlaid bowls.

Mention of brewing and ale appears repeatedly in early writing. Biblical references include the story of Noah. Assyrian tablets dating from the third century B.C. describe Noah's preparations for the great flood and catalog the ark's manifest. Noah loaded ale to sustain his family through the flood. Judg. 4:19–20 also mentions ale in a description of boiling loaves to draw a malty broth.

The origin of the word *beer* is difficult to pinpoint; it may have come from the Jewish word for grain, based on the root *bre*. Jews held captive in Babylon drank bre as a magic protection from disease; because of their widespread travels and because they always carried with them a type of starter used to begin fermenting a new batch of ale, Jews may have greatly facilitated the spread of brewing knowledge throughout the Middle East and Europe. The term *beer* may also have come from the Saxon word for barley, *bere*, or the Latin for drink, *bibere*.

Beer had been brewed for thousands of years before the Greeks became the world's most dominant civilization. Though usually associated with wine, Greeks also brewed and consumed beer, most notably before the growing of grapes for wine became common. Thereafter beer was only brewed in the outer areas of the Greek empire where wine was difficult to obtain. The Greek Herodotus (484–425 B.C.), noted as the "father of history," wrote extensively on the customs, geography and history of the Mediterranean. In 460 B.C. he produced a lengthy treatise on beer. Likewise Sophocles (496–406 B.C.), the famous Greek dramatist, was an avid promoter of beer. He publicly advocated a diet of moderation that included bread, meat, vegetables and a daily portion of beer. Extensive Greek writings ensured the continuation of brewing; their library at Alexandria served as a repository for this knowledge, which eventually passed to the Romans.

Romans considered beer a barbarous drink. Cornelius Tacitus (A.D. 56–120), when describing the ancient German Teutons, wrote: "To drink, the Teutons have a horrible brew fermented from barley or wheat, a brew which has only a very far removed similarity to wine." The Roman historian Pliny (A.D. 23–79) recorded that Romans learned brewing from the Egyptians, describing how they used corn as an adjunct. He also wrote of the extensive brewing conducted by the Gauls, Germans, Celts, Visagoths and Vandals. Romans called their ale *cerevisia*. Derived from *Ceres*, the Roman goddess of agriculture, and *vis*, Latin for strength, it implied the strength of a harvest. To this day the Latin root *cerevisia* survives in most Spanish languages as the word for beer, *cerveza*.

Until medieval times, brewing was exclusively women's work; ancient laws decreed that brewing vessels were solely a woman's property. In ancient Babylon, women were responsible for the first link between religion and brewing: women brewers were priestesses of the temple. Shortly before the end of the first millennium A.D., monasteries turned their attention to beer brewing, and women's involvement began to wane.

During the eighth century A.D., Charlemagne, Europe's greatest ruler of the time, was engaged in constructing the Holy Roman Empire according to his own vision. From his throne he laid out criteria by which towns were ruled, and he ensured that brewers occupied a prominent position among the hierarchy. Charlemagne also promoted the birth of brewing science. From his era emerged the world's first modern brewer, Saint Gall. Refining the brewing process, Gall introduced methods for mashing, fermenting, storing and caring for ale that changed the character of European ale.

The precedent established by Charlemagne combined with the power of the church enabled monks to control brewing over the next several centuries. Monks had not only the time but also the inclination to brew the most premium beer possible. Monastery meals were frugal; a pleasant tasting, nutritious brew was highly desirable as an accompaniment. Liquids were also not considered to break a fast, so beer was always permitted, and beer consumption in monasteries reached astonishing levels—it is recorded that in some monasteries monks were allowed as much as five liters per day.

Eventually monks obtained the right to sell beer, purveyed in monastery pubs. Clerics were both brewers and wholesalers, using ale as a form of currency. Monastery brews were popular and of premium quality; there were also lower strength "everyday" beers and higher strength beers reserved for special occasions. It was necessary to pay homage to the church in order to obtain a draught of ale, and predictably community ale drinking became a sanctified activity. Celebrations and feasts became known as "church ales"; spiritual leaders incorporated ale into virtually every religious ritual. Even weddings were celebrated with ale—bride ales were encouraged as a means of raising money for a new couple. A mother would brew a special batch of ale for her daughter's wedding, and at the reception the bride would dispense ale in return for wedding gifts. The modern word *bridal* is derived from the term *bride ales*.

Because the church controlled the ale supply, furnishing their congregations and sacred celebrations with ample quantities, the demand for commercial brewing was slow to materialize. Eventually a few private, part-time brewers began to operate in England, mostly people in search of some extra income. They tended to operate in the countryside, removed from the monasteries' watchful eye.

Since activities were centered around the local church, brewing remained a part-time occupation up until the fourteenth century, at which time local potentates began to introduce beer taxes. Monasteries were exempt from the taxes because of their privileged status, and as a result conditions began to change. Sovereigns closed many monastery breweries; they were undesirable because they contributed no money to the local coffers.

After the Black Plague (1347–1352), resources were concentrated in the hands of the survivors; money turned over more quickly, and the average worker of central Europe in the fifteenth century enjoyed more than double the real wages his counterpart would have earned only a century before. People had more discretionary income, and the economy burst into a frenzy of activity. Conditions were ideal to introduce full-time commercial brewing. People had both the thirst and the money for beer. Ale wives, as they were called, who formerly brewed only occasionally, now enjoyed an enormous demand for their goods. They also profited from the merchants traveling between the markets who needed a place to stay, providing the traders with accommodations that featured a steady supply of ale. The burgeoning demand for such lodging led directly to the introduction of the inn, which featured a taproom, called a tavern.

Taverns were soon a regular meeting place for traveling merchants. The comfort of an inn must have been welcome respite from the crowded, confusing open air markets. Soon it became routine to conduct business from the comfortable taproom of an inn, and by the end of the Middle Ages the inn was firmly established as a trading center. The development of this new outlet for ale caused drastic changes in the makeup of towns and cities.

Typically the inn was built on a village's main street. Four main buildings, each two stories high, formed a central courtyard, making it the most dominant structure in the town. In addition to drink, meals, lodging and entertainment, the inn provided warehouses for the merchant's goods and stables for his horses. Taverns and inns were lucrative businesses, and by the sixteenth century an inn keeper was usually counted among the wealthiest people in any town.

Expanding consumption introduced several changes in beer, mostly concerning quality. At the start of commercial brewing, beer was a rather soupy substance. Most brewers used barley, but variations included wheat, oats and millet. Worse, the brews were rarely completely fermented. To help preserve the product and to disguise faults, brewers took to flavoring ale with spices. In all it was a thick, sweet, rough-textured beverage of low alcoholic content. One thirteenth-century writer described it thus:

> muddy, foggy, fulsome, puddle, stinking;
> for all of these ale is the only drinking.

In approximately 768, Germans had first added hops to brew kettles. The bitterness of hops balanced the sweet malt flavor, and it was added for preservative reasons as well. The use of hops incited a heated debate concerning the flavoring license ("Grutrecht" in old German—grut was a combination of herbs used to flavor beer). The flavoring license was similar to a patent and ensured a monopoly over a particular essence for every brewer. The introduction of hops for flavoring, however, rendered grut obsolete and threatened these powerful positions of individual brewers.

Some of the herbs used before the advent of hops augmented beer's intoxicating properties with hallucinogens and other poisons, such as alkaloid, which was produced from the commonly used herb henbane during the brewing process. Superstitions arose from the resulting physiological phenomena, leading to persecutions and burnings of persons deemed responsible for the brewing failures, who were referred to as "brew witches" or "beer witches." The last known execution of a brew witch occurred in 1591, after which the used of hops caused hallucinations and other peculiar symptoms to cease.

The conservative English had been reluctant to embrace such a drastic change, considering the addition of hops a contamination of good ale. So strong was the British aversion that for a time hops were banned; despite some sporadic use of hops by monks, the first appearance of note in the British Isles did not occur until shortly after the Hundred Years' War between France and England (1337–1453). Then they were used by Dutch and Flemish brewers, who were exempted from the law banning hops. As late as 1524 English brewers continued to resist their use. A poem of that year read:

> Hops, Reformation, Bays and Beer
> Came to England in one bad year.

Gradually hops were accepted, and with that acceptance came a change in terminology. The great compiler of English and writer of the first notable dictionary, Samuel Johnson, defined the use of hops:

Ale: A liquor made by infusing malt in hot water, and then fermenting.
Beer: Liquor made from malt and hops.

The term *ale* virtually disappeared from use while *beer* became the new designation. Ale resurfaced centuries later when there was a new need to differentiate between the new method of brewing, cold lagering (beer), and the older method of warm fermentation (ale). But its use in describing an unhopped malt beverage had become obsolete.

With the power of the church mitigated following the Reformation in Europe, commercial brewers took over the responsibilities of brewing. The use of hops rendered beer more pure, closer to the modern beverage. In 1516, Wilhelm IV, Duke of Bavaria, proclaimed the German Beer Purity Law, decreeing that only barley, hops and pure water could be used to brew beer. This law still exists and is the oldest valid food law in the world.

Distribution and export of beer increased along with its quality. Regular brewing centers developed, such as Bremen, which supplied the Netherlands, England and the Nordic countries; and Hamburg. In 1500 Hamburg alone was home to 600 breweries. Brunswick, Einbeck and Berlin in Germany were other beer centers.

Meanwhile, the number of English inns, taverns and alehouses grew, and another factor arose which impelled more people to partake of beer: water pollution. In Europe, rivers and streams were becoming the equivalent of a flowing dump. The fouled water supply made drinking perilous, and many who partook of the fetid supply developed serious health problems. Eventually the situation became so grave that England's Parliament enacted laws against polluting. It was too late; nearly every supply was tainted. By the mid-fifteenth century the bias against drinking water was deeply ingrained. Sir John Fortescue (1385–1479) wrote of the English peasants: "They drank no water unless it be . . . for devotion." Residual fear from this problem followed English colonists across the ocean. North American settlers could not be persuaded that the streams running through the forests of the New World were uncontaminated. As Englishmen traveled to the New World, the most precious cargoes the small ships held was beer.

On 9 September 1620 the Pilgrims set sail from England. Delays in contracting passage had postponed their planned summer departure, pushing it into the bad weather of late fall. Storms forced them further north than their port of destination, in what is now New York. They settled for the most favorable spot they saw, near Plymouth, Massachusetts. Rations were running low; according to passenger William Bradford, the shortage of beer was a factor in their decision to put ashore:

> So in the morning, after we had called on God for direction, we came to this resolution—to go presently ashore . . . for we could not now take much time for further search or consideration, our victuals being much spent, especially our beer, and it now being the 19th of December.

More settlers would follow, and each group had a similar list of priorities: fertile land for farming, timber for housing, an adequate supply of clothing, and beer. Incidentally, Europeans did not introduce beer to the North American continent. In the Southwestern region, native Americans were already brewing a beer made from fermented maize.

In the eighteenth century brewing and beer drinking entered a new era. Popular fashion began dictating drinking habits. One of the first rages was porter, a mixed drink comprised of equal parts of common ale, beer and two-penny ale. Immensely popular, its preparation was, at first, inconvenient. It required three separate taps to prepare one serving. In the early eighteenth century patrons of London bars were ordering the mixture called "three threads" (thirds) or "entire" with such regularity it was running the tavern keepers ragged. One of them, Ralph Harwood, was certain there was an easier way to prepare the popular drink. He believed a brewery could replicate the taste in one keg. At the Bell Brewery in London's Shoreditch section Harwood perfected the recipe for the style called porter. It was an instant success.

The replication of "entire" became immensely popular in London. Indeed, it was immortalized in the words:

> When treading London's well-known ground
> If e'er I feel my spirits tire
> I haul my sail, look up around
> In search of Whitbread's best entire
> —unknown; *A Pot of Porter, Ho!*

There are two theories as to the origin of the name *porter*: it was popular with the porters of London's markets; or, more likely, it came from the porters who delivered kegs to the pubs. The arrival would be announced by the call, "Porter's here!" Regardless of the name, the new style had an immense impact on the world of beer. Sales of porter eventually peaked and then faded, as did the demand for its cousins in the ale family—bitters, milds, pale and brown ales. All were supplanted by yet another new style of beer.

Through the ages yeast had been the great unknown of brewing. Brewers simply called it "God is good," implying that it was a gift only God understood. During the seventeenth and eighteenth centuries, scientists uncovered the mystery of yeast. In 1680, Dutch scientist Antoni van Leeuwenhoek (1632–1723), as a result of his own pioneering work in microscopes, correctly identified tiny particles—yeast cells. George Ernst Stahl (1660–1734), a German chemist, produced the first significant work devoted to yeast. Close observation of fermentation inspired Stahl to write "Zymotechnica Fundamentalis." Presented in rather general terms, the work was the first to suggest yeast and fermentation were biologically linked. Details were inaccurate and vague, but the proposal that yeast caused fermentation was sound. Shortly after Stahl's work was published, Dutch physician Hermann Boerhaave (1668–1738) identified three distinct phases in the fermentation process.

French scientist Antoine Laurent Lavoisier (1743–1794) built upon the theories of Stahl, Boerhaave and Leeuwenhoek. He demonstrated that fermentation was a process that broke sugar molecules into alcohol and carbon dioxide (CO_2). By 1818 scientists were in agreement that yeast was a living organism, and within seven years had classified several different strains of yeast. Meanwhile, brewers put all the new discoveries to practical application.

Brewers had identified two phases of fermentation. Principal fermentation (or primary fermentation) was the process of converting saccharine to alcohol and carbon dioxide. The second phase, secondary fermentation, was described as the ripening of beers, during which the impurities were removed. Without the science of yeast, aging and its effect on beer had been a mystery. As the study of yeast revealed its characteristics, brewers were able to manipulate yeast's environment to produce specific end results in beer. Finally, a pair of brewers assembled the accumulated knowledge, and in doing so created a new style of beer.

Gabriel Sedlmayer of Munich and Anton Dreher of Vienna both believed that refinement of techniques, recording of measurements and collection of data resulted in cleaner and better beer. They visited the breweries of England to gather all the knowledge possible; credited with introducing modern brewing methods to the German states, they were pioneers in defining the process of lagering. A procedure of repeatedly warming and cooling the brew over a period of weeks to control the activity and suspension of the yeast results in a clear and bright beer. Sedlmayer was instrumental in persuading the Kaiser to establish a brewing school in 1836, and by 1840 he was, along with Dreher, Europe's foremost lager brewer. When Dreher supplied Danish scientist Christian Hansen with a sample of the yeast used in lagering, his action drastically altered the world of beer. Hansen isolated the strain of yeast known as lager and within a few short years it modified the flavor of beer the world over. After lager's introduction in the mid-1880s, an ever-growing number of brewers responded to the market demand and began lagering. Industrial developments at the beginning of the nineteenth century brought about two inventions that also revolutionized the art of brewing beer. James Watts' steam engine introduced steam power to breweries, which began calling themselves "steam beer breweries," and when Carl von Linde invented refrigeration, brewing, which requires cold temperatures, became independent of the seasons.

In the early half of the twentieth century the seemingly unrelated global factors of temperance, economic depression, drought and war combined to make lager the world's favorite type of beer. In North America the temperance movement succeeded in securing national prohibition in 1919, and over the next fourteen long years the United States was without legal beer. Prohibition was repealed in 1933, but the jubilant brewers had to contend with two new challenges: the Great Depression and the drought. Because of the Depression many Americans were without discretionary income to spend on such luxuries as alcohol; and the drought had reduced many formerly prolific grain fields into a massive dust bowl. As a result of these two hardships, brewers who were attempting to establish or re-establish themselves found alternatives; they thinned out their recipes and substituted other grains, such as corn and rice, for barley. When brewed in the lager style of pilsner the resulting beer was light in body—much lighter than German versions of the same substance. Citizens of North America, happy to have any beer at all, did not complain; rather, they quickly adapted to the new taste.

As the United States recovered financially from the Great Depression, World War II caused grain to remain in short supply. Brewers continued to make the light lager-style beers, and consumers continued to enjoy them. By the end of the war Americans had been drinking this lighter style beer for more than twelve years, and it had gained a major share of the market. Consumers shunned attempted re-introductions of the stronger old-style ales.

Ale remained popular in Europe, but was largely restricted to the traditional markets of England and Belgium. Germans had long since embraced lager. Over time the style gradually gained acceptance in Britain.

By the 1980s English pubs were serving the American-style lagers, and German brewers introduced lighter versions of their own beers to compete.

For a time light lager beer was the largest-selling style of beer the world over. Then in the mid-1980s, some beer drinkers began to show renewed interest in the older styles of beer. Porter, stout, pale ale and bitters regained a small share of beer sales. Slowly at first, the numbers of consumers of the traditional styles of beer began to grow. At the beginning of the 1990s the rate increased and the trend was labeled as "the microbrewery movement."

Throughout the beer drinking world a new diversity emerged, and pubs and bars were no longer necessarily tied to one brand of commercially brewed light lager beer. Patrons at bars now frequently enjoy a tap selection that may include these as well as perhaps an Irish stout, a Dutch lager, a microbrewery ale and an English bitter. Lager continues to dominate commercial beer sales, but the traditional styles of beer have carved out a profitable niche. Restaurants that actually contain their own microbreweries have become increasingly popular, giving patrons a selection of fresh specialty brews that may change according to season, demand, or the owner's most recent experimentation with recipes.

As the twenty-first century approaches, beer drinkers have more choices than ever before. While microbrews and darker ales have a secure place in the ranks of popularity now, one can only guess what changes the next century or even the next decade can bring in demand as well as method.

—Gregg Smith

The Dictionary of
Beer and Brewing

Key to Pronunciation

Consonants

b   voiced bilabial stop, as in English **b**eet

c   voiced palatal fricative, as in German i**ch**

ch   voiceless alveopalatal affricate, a combination of /t/ and /sh/, as in English **ch**ur**ch**

d   voiced alveolar stop as in English **d**eep

dh   voiced interdental fricative, as in English **dh**is

d: an alveolar flap, produced by many speakers of American English for both intervocalic /t/ and /d/, sounding like the /r/ in British English ve**r**y; when /t/ is the written consonant, **t** is usually an acceptable variant to **d:**, especially in careful speech

f   voiceless labiodental fricative, as in English **f**eet

g   voiced velar stop, as in English **g**reet

gh   voiced velar fricative, as in French and German /r/ in **gh**ot (red) or French **gh**oozh (red) (pronounced **kh**, but with voicing added)

h   voiceless back glide, as in English **h**eat

j   voiced alveopalatal affricate, a combination of /d/ and /zh/, as in English **j**ud**g**e

k   voiceless velar stop, as in English **k**eep

kh   voiceless velar fricative, as in German lo**ch**

l   lateral liquid, as in English **l**eap

m   bilabial nasal, as in English **m**eet

n   alveolar nasal, as in English **n**eat

ng   velar nasal, as in English si**ng**

ny   palatal nasal, as in English ca**ny**on

p   voiceless bilabial stop, as in English **p**eat

p'   palatalized /p/, as in English **p**ure

q   voiceless uvular stop, found in Arabic **q**abbala, but pronounced by most English speakers as /k/

r   (usually) alveolar liquid, as in English **r**eap

r~   trilled /r/, as in Spanish pe**rr**o

s   voiceless alveolar fricative, as in English **s**eat

sh   voiceless alveopalatal fricative, as in English **sh**eep

t   voiceless alveolar stop, as in English **t**ake

th   voiceless interdental fricative, as in English **th**rough

v   voiced labiodental fricative, as in English **v**ine

w   labio-velar glide, as in English **w**ine

y   palatal glide, as in English **y**oung

z   voiced alveolar fricative, as in English **z**eal

zh   voiced alveoplatal fricative, as in English vi**s**ion or a**z**ure

Vowels

a   back low vowel, as in English f**a**ther or b**o**x

ae   front low vowel, as in English b**a**t

e   short central vowel, often represented as a schwa and in English mostly found in unstressed syllables, as in fath**e**r; in British English it is found instead of /r/ in fath**e**, and to speakers of American English often seems to have an /r/ quality to it

ee   tense high front vowel, as in English b**ee**t or n**ea**t (often called a "long /e/")

eh   lax mid front vowel, as in English b**e**t

ei   tense mid front vowel, as in English w**ei**ght or d**a**y (often called a "long /a/")

eiy   indicates a tense mid front vowel with an off-glide that sometimes results in a short schwa sound, as in **eiy**l (pronunciation for "ale")

i   lax high front vowel, as in English b**i**t or sk**i**p

o   tense mid rounded back vowel, as in English b**o**at, d**o**te, or hell**o**

oe   mid rounded front vowel, as in German G**oe**the or French b**eu**rre (butter)

oo   tense high front vowel, as in English b**oo**t or fr**ui**t

oh   lax mid rounded back vowel, as in English f**o**rt, **a**ll, and in some pronunciations of c**au**ght; **oh** positioned at the end of a word is almost always pronounced by speakers of American English in the western United States as a low back vowel, as in f**a**ther

u   lax high rounded back vowel, as in English p**u**t or l**oo**k

ue   front rounded high vowel, as in French l**u**ne (moon)

uh   short central vowel, somewhat lower than a schwa and more often found in stressed syllables than schwa, as in English b**u**t, **o**ther, or b**u**tter

~   following a vowel (or dipthong), indicates that the preceding vowel/dipthong is nasalized, as in French b**o~** (good)

Dipthongs

aw   a low back vowel followed by a lax rounded back vowel, as in English c**ow** or b**ou**t

ay   a low back vowel followed by a lax high front vowel, as in English bite (often called a "long /i/")

oy   a lax mid rounded back vowel followed by a lax high front vowel, as in English b**oy**

(Note: An asterick (*) following a word indicates it is either (1) a foreign word the linguist was unable to translate phonetically because its country of origin was not identified; (2) an archaic word with no known pronunciation; or (3) a specific brewing term with several variants in pronunciation.)

a-acid. *(eiy ae'-sid)*
Abbreviation for alpha acid.

AAU.
Abbreviation for alpha acid unit.

abbey beer. *(ae'-bee beeyr')*
Any top-fermented beer produced by a commercial brewery that is under license from a monastery, located near an abbey, or has retained the original name and brewing style of a particular abbey. In Belgium, according to a law passed in Gand on February 28, 1962, beers brewed in Trappist monasteries or by commercial breweries under license may be labeled "Trappiste" whereas those brewed by commercial brewers in the style and manner of Trappist beers must be labeled "Bière d'Abbaye" or "Abdijbieren" (abbey beer). There are presently five Trappist abbeys brewing beer in Belgium and one in the Netherlands. In Germany and Austria, beers labeled "Klosterbräu" or "Stiftsbräu" are not distinctive in style nor are they typically brewed in abbeys. **Syn:** monastery beer. **See also:** Trappist beer.

abdijbieren. *(ab'-dee-bee-ghen)*
See: abbey beer.

absolute alcohol. *(aeb-suh-loot' ael'-kuh-hohl)*
1. Pure, water-free ethyl alcohol. Specific gravity: 0.79359; boiling point: 173.12 °F (78.4 °C). The American standard is 200 proof whereas the British standard is 175.1 proof. **Syn:** anhydrous alcohol. **2.** The total amount of alcohol contained in a beverage.

aca. *(a'-ka)*
A type of maize beer brewed in Peru since at least 200 BC. It was consumed

by the common people and the Sapa-Inca; it also was offered to the gods and poured over the graves of the deceased *mojicas*. The *aca* of the Sapa-Inca could only be prepared by the Sun Virgins of the palace in Cuzco. **See also:** *chicha*.

acerbic. *(uh-suhr'-bik)*
Describes a bitter and somewhat astringent taste in beer, less pronounced than acidic.

acetaldehyde. *(ae-suh-tael'-d:uh-hayd)*
A volatile compound derived from the degradation of sugars during fermentation through decarboxylation of pyruvic acid. **Syn:** ethylaldehyde. **See also:** aldehyde; carbonyls.

acetic. *(uh-see'-d:ik)*
Imparting a smell of acetic acid or ethyl acetate.

acetic acid. *(uh-see'-d:ik ae'-sid)*
Formula: CH_3COOH. A weak, monocarboxylic acid found in vinegar. It is the first member of the fatty acid series and also belongs to the larger group of carboxylic acids. This acid is a natural by-product of yeast metabolism and is formed via the Krebs cycle during aerobic respiration. In beermaking, it forms through oxidation of alcohols during the fermentation process when the beer is exposed to air (oxygen), giving the beer a vinegar taste and smell.

acetification. *(uh-si-d:e-fuh-key'-shen)*
The changes brought about by the production of acetic acid, generally as spoilage by aerobic bacteria but also by the pH adjustment in the mash.

Acetobacter. *(uh-see'-d:oh-baek-ter)*
A microorganism, a genus of aerobic bacteria (Bacteriaceae family), that turns ethyl alcohol to acetic acid during fermentation.

achroödextrins. *(aek-ro-o-dehk'-strinz)*
Simple "border" dextrins, from the reduction of starch (amylopectin) by alpha-amylase; alpha-limit dextrins that have a negative reaction with iodine.

acid. *(ae'-sid)*
1. Any compound that yields hydrogen ions (H^+) in a solution or chemical that reacts with alkalis to form salts. **2.** Describes a solution having a pH lower than 7. **See also:** pH. **3.** Describes a beer exhibiting a sour acidic smell or flavor.

acidic. *(uh-si'-d:ik)*
Describes a beer having a biting, sour, or pungent aroma and flavor reminiscent of vinegar or acetic acid. **Syn:** sour.

acidification. *(uh-si-d:uh-fuh-kei'-shen)*
The process of lowering the pH of a solution until it falls below 7.

acidity. *(uh-si'-d:uh-d:ee)*
1. The state of being acid or the extent to which a solution is acidic. **See also:** pH. **2.** In beer tasting, the degree of sharpness to the taste.

acid malt. *(ae'-sid mohlt')*
A type of malt prepared by various methods and used mainly at a proportion of 10 percent or less to lower the pH in the mash tun. One method consists of spraying the growing malt with 10 percent lactic acid followed by steeping in a solution of lactic acid prior to kilning.

acid rest. *(ae'-sid rehst)*
A stage of the mashing process that allows the enzyme phytase to convert phytic acid to phosphoric acid to acidify the mash. During this rest, the mash is held at 95–100 °F (35–40 °C) for fifteen to thirty minutes.

acrospire. *(ae'-kro-spayr)*
The shoot contained within the embryo of the barley grain that, during germination, is allowed to grow up to two-thirds or three-fourths the length of the corn kernel beneath the husk before kilning. **Syn:** plumule.

activator. *(aek'-tuh-vei-d:er)*
A substance that increases the effectiveness or activity of an enzyme.

Adam's ale. *(ae'-d:emz eiyl')*
A misnomer for water.

Adam's wine. *(ae'-d:emz wayn')*
A misnomer for water.

additive. *(ae'-d:uh-d:iv)*
Any chemical, natural or synthetic, intentionally added to beer for a specific purpose in the course of production, packaging, or storing. Most legislation pertaining to beermaking exempts the labeling of food ingredients (nutritive

materials) such as salt, sugar, vitamins, minerals, amino acids, spices, seasonings, flavorings, food enhancers, and others, which fall into other categories covered by food regulations. **Syn:** food additive.

ad-humulone. *(aed-hyoo'-myuh-lon)*
The third (or sometimes second) most prevalent of the three alpha acids, which, when isomerized during boiling of the wort, becomes iso-ad-humulone, providing most of the bittering characteristic that comes from hops.

adjunct. *(ae'-juhngkt)*
Any substitute unmalted cereal grain or fermentable ingredient added to the mash in order to reduce costs by producing more, usually cheaper fermentable sugars, and/or to produce paler, lighter bodied, and less malty beers or, as in the case of wheat, to produce special beers or to correct the composition of the extract. Oats, wheat, corn, tapioca flour, flaked rice and maize, inverted sugar, and glucose are used for this purpose. Most cereal adjuncts saccharify very slowly in the mash and must first be gelatinized by boiling before they can be attacked by amylases. To avoid pre-boiling, maize and a few other cereals are added in the form of flakes. In Belgium the amount of unmalted cereals added to the grist varies from 10–50 percent whereas French and U.S. lager beers may contain 30–40 percent adjuncts. In Germany the use of adjuncts was prohibited by law until the Reinheitsgebot was repealed. **Syn:** malt adjunct; cereal adjunct.

Adriaan Brouwer Bierfesten. *(a'-dghee-an bghau'-wer beegh'-feh-sten)*
An annual beer festival held June 25–27, in Oudenaarde, Belgium, to commemorate the famous painter Adriaan Brouwer, born in that city in 1605.

adsorption. *(aed-zohrp'-shen)*
The surface retention of solid, liquid, or gas molecules by another surface without any chemical reaction with the adsorption material. Adsorption substances are used for fining and filtration. They include activated charcoal, silica gel, albumin, bentonite, kieselguhr, and similar substances.

aerating. *(eiy'-[e]-rei-d:ing)*
The action of providing aeration.

aeration. *(eiy-[e]-rei'-shen)*
1. The action of impregnating with or exposing to air at various stages of the brewing process. Aerating the cooled wort, for example, favors the growth

and multiplication of yeast cells before fermentation begins. **2.** An operation introducing air into a mass of barley grains at a rate of flow adequate to achieve and maintain levels of temperature and humidity required for satisfactory storage.

aerobic. *(eiy-[e]-ro'-bik)*
   Occurring in the presence of air (oxygen), such as the lag phase of fermentation when yeast cells require oxygen to grow and multiply. **See also:** aerobic fermentation; anaerobic.

aerobiosis. *(eiy-[e]-ruh-bay-o'-sis)*
   Life existing in the presence of air and oxygen. **See also:** anaerobiosis.

aftersmell. *(aef'-ter-smehl)*
   An odor that lingers after swallowing the beer, which may possibly be caused by remaining volatiles.

aftertaste. *(aef'-ter-teist)*
   The lingering taste, odor, and tactile sensations after the beer has been swallowed.

agar. *(a'-ger)*
   See: agar-agar.

agar-agar. *(a'-ger-a'-ger)*
   A colloidal gel obtained from the dried, putrefied stems of a red seaweed growing in Japanese waters and used for fining or as a culture medium for bacteria and yeasts. **Syn:** agar; Madagascar gum; vegetable gelatin.

aged flavor. *(eijd' flei'-ver)*
   Off-flavors due to oxidation.

agglutination. *(uh-gloo'-ti-ney'-shen)*
   The grouping of cells by adhesion.

aging. *(ei'-jing)*
   Synonym for maturation.

airing. *(eh'-ring)*
   The action of ventilating the barley between steeps. **Syn:** ventilation.

airlock. *(ehyr'-lak)*
Synonym for fermentation lock.

air rest. *(ehyr' rehst')*
An interruption in the steeping process to allow oxygen to get through and stimulate growth and uniform germination. This technique, now regarded as traditional, was first developed in the early 1960s to overcome dormancy in water-sensitive types of barley. **See also:** airing; steeping.

airspace. *(ehyr'-speys)*
Synonym for ullage.

airtight. *(ehyr'-tayt')*
So constructed or sealed as to prevent the inlet and outlet of air.

albumen. *(ael-byoo'-mehn)*
1. Orthographic variant for albumin. **2.** The starchy content of the barley grain.

albumin. *(ael-byoo'-min)*
A name for a certain group of water-soluble proteins that coagulate when they are heated. Albumins are hydrolized to peptides and amino acids by proteolytic enzymes.

alcohol. *(ael'-kuh-hohl)*
A synonym for ethyl alcohol or ethanol. Etym: From the Arabic *al kohl,* meaning like kohl (a cosmetic eye paint) because the method of distillation by vaporizing native brew was similar to that for producing kohl.

alcohol beverage. *(ael'-kuh-hohl beh'-vrij)*
Synonym for alcoholic beverage.

alcohol by volume. *(ael'-kuh-hohl bay val'-yoom)*
A measurement of the alcohol content of a solution in terms of the percentage volume of alcohol per volume of beer. To calculate approximately (margin of error ± 15 percent) the volumetric alcohol content, subtract the terminal gravity from the original gravity and divide the result by 7.5. Abbrev: v/v. **See:** appendices C and E.

Formula: $\% \text{ v/v} = (OG - TG) / 7.5$
Example: $50 - 12 = 38 / 7.5 = 5\% \text{ v/v}$

alcohol by weight. *(ael'-kuh-hohl bay weit')*

A measurement of the alcohol content of a solution in terms of the percentage weight of alcohol per volume of beer. (Example: 3.2 percent alcohol by weight equals 3.2 grams of alcohol per 100 centiliters of beer.) The percent of alcohol by weight figure is approximately 20 percent lower than the alcohol by volume figure because alcohol weighs less than its equivalent volume of water. Abbrev: w/v. **See:** appendices C and E.

alcohol content. *(ael'-kuh-hohl can'-tehnt)*

The amount of ethyl alcohol that is contained in a beverage. In beer, it is related to the specific gravity of the wort prior to its fermentation (called original gravity), which usually varies from 1.030–1.060 but may reach 1.100. Beer fermentation is self-limiting because beyond 12–16 percent alcohol by volume, yeast cells are killed by the alcohol. Alcohol tolerance depends on yeast strain. **Syn:** alcoholic strength.

alcoholic. *(ael-kuh-ha'-lik)*

Warming taste of ethanol and higher alcohols.

alcoholic beverage. *(ael-kuh-ha'-lik beh'-vrij)*

Any potable beverage containing ethyl alcohol produced by fermentation of sugars such as beer, wine, mead, cider, and others or by distillation of these products. Fermented beverages may contain up to 16 percent alcohol by volume at which point the yeast is killed.

alcoholic strength. *(ael-kuh-ha'-lik strehngkth')*

In the United States and Germany the alcoholic strength of beers is measured, in percent alcohol by weight whereas Canada and the United Kingdom refer to volumetric content. In the United Kingdom the specific gravity (or density) method is used. This measurement system attributes the number 1.000 to water, and the density of beers is measured in comparison to that standard. An approximate formula for converting beer densities to alcohol by weight consists of dividing the last two figures of the density by 13. (Example: specific gravity 1.052 equals 52 / 13 equals 4 percent alcohol by weight.) Other systems such as degrees Plato (°P), derived from the Balling system, measure the concentration of solids in unfermented worts. An approximate formula for converting degrees Plato to percent alcohol by weight is obtained by dividing the former by 3. (Example: 12 °P / 3 equals 4 percent alcohol by weight.) **See also:** Belgian degrees; Régie.

alcoholimeter. *(ael-kuh-hoh-li'-muh-d:er)*
Orthographic variant for alcoholometer.

alcoholmeter. *(ael'-kuh-hohl-muh-d:er)*
Orthographic variant for alcoholometer.

alcoholometer. *(ael-kuh-hoh-la'-muh-d:er)*
An instrument, such as a densimeter or hydrometer, for measuring the amount of ethyl alcohol in a solution. It consists of a graduated stem that rests on a spindle-shaped float, which expresses the percentage of alcohol by weight or volume. Also spelled: alcohometer; alcoholimeter; alcoholmeter.

alcoholometry. *(al-kuh-hoh-la'-muh-tree)*
The quantitative determination of ethyl alcohol in aqueous solutions, usually by measuring the specific gravity of the solution at a standard temperature with an alcoholometer.

alcohols. *(al'-kuh-hohlz)*
See: higher alcohols.

alcohometer. *(al-kuh-hohl'-muh-d:er)*
Orthographic variant for alcoholometer.

aldehyde. *(al'-duh-hayd)*
Any of a large class of organic compounds derived from alcohols through dehydrogenation (oxidation) and containing the grouping (or radical) –CHO. When aldehydes are oxidized further, acids are produced. Some aldehydes contribute to the bouquet of beer. Etym: From *alcohol* and *dehydrogenation.*

aldehyde dehydrogenase. *(al'-duh-hayd dee-hay-dra'-juh-neis)*
An enzyme that catalyzes the oxidative conversion of an aldehyde to its corresponding acid in the metabolism of ethanol.

ale. *(eiyl')*
1. Historically, a nonhopped malt beverage (also called spiced ale) as opposed to hopped beer. **2.** A generic name for beers produced by top fermentation, usually by infusion mashing, as opposed to lagers produced by bottom fermentation, usually by decoction mashing. Ales tend to have a higher alcoholic content, more robust flavor, and deeper hue than lagers—the predominant style in the British Isles. Ales constitute a category including alt, barley wine, bitter, brown ale, *kölsch,* mild ale,

pale ale, porter, stout, Trappist beer, and others. **3.** In the United States, some state legislations prohibit the use of the name *lager* or *beer* for malt beverages containing more than 5 percent alcohol by weight, and such beverages are *often* labeled as ales although they are bottom-fermented (lager) beers. Etym: Derived from the Norse *oel* (Danish and Swedish *öl*; Finnish *olut*), a nonhopped malt beverage. The Vikings called their barley beer *aul*. The Anglo-Saxon word for ale was *ealu*. **Syn:** top-fermented beer. **See also:** lager; top fermentation; top-fermenting yeast.

ale barrel. *(eiyl' bae'-rel)*
In England, a barrel containing 32 imperial gallons (146.47 liters), not to be confused with a beer barrel that contains 36 imperial gallons (163.65 liters).

aleberry. *(eiyl'-beh-ree)*
An old-fashioned drink popular in England in the 1600s consisting of oatmeal, ale, lemon juice, nutmeg, and sugar served hot with sops of toast. It also was known as alebrue and alemeat.

ale bowl. *(eiyl' bol')*
An early drinking vessel for ale.

ale brewer. *(eiyl' broo'-wer)*
One who brews ales. In fifteenth-century England, when hops were beginning to be accepted for beermaking, there was a clear distinction between ale brewers, who brewed unhopped spiced ales, and beer brewers, who brewed hopped beers. Beer brewers were persecuted at every opportunity, but luckily for them their brew was considered by many as superior to ale. In 1436 the king issued a writ to the sheriffs of London, ordering them to protect the beer brewers. **Syn:** ale maker.

ale bush. *(eiyl' bush')*
Synonym for ale garland.

ale conner. *(eiyl' ca'-ner)*
In Old England, an official appointed by the authorities of the city or borough to inspect and judge newly brewed ale to be sold by the ale makers. In the fourteenth century the ale conner wore leather breeches and tested the ale by pouring it on a bench, and sitting in the puddle for half an hour. If upon rising the breeches stuck to the bench, the ale was sugary and imperfect; otherwise, it was fit for consumption. Shakespeare's father was an ale conner in Stratford-on-Avon in 1557. Also spelled: aleconner.

alecost. *(eiyl'-cast)*
An obsolete name for costmary (*Tanacetum balsamica, Balsamita vulgaris,* or *Chrysanthemum balsamita*), once used to flavor ales in England.

ale draper. *(eiyl' drei'-per)*
An ale-house keeper.

Ale Flip. *(eiyl' flip')*
A cocktail consisting of 1 or 1/2 of a pint of ale mixed in a shaker with crushed ice and 1 egg.

alegar. *(a'-li-ger)*
An obsolete word for spoiled, sour ale.

ale garland. *(eiyl' gar'-lend)*
An ivy bush or garland of evergreens hung at the top of a pole called an ale stake and placed outside an ale house. **Syn:** ale bush.

ale gill. *(eiyl' gil')*
A type of ale once flavored with ground ivy.

ale glass. *(eiyl' glaes')*
A long- and narrow-stemmed glass for serving old ale.

alehoof. *(eiyl'-huf)*
An early name given to ground ivy used to flavor ales.

ale house. *(eiyl' haws)*
A public house where beer is sold. In early England, the term *brewery* referred to both the brew house and the room in which the ale was sold, which later became known as an ale house. Licenses to operate ale houses have been issued as early as the fourteenth century. In 1305 one William Saleman was fined two shillings for operating a brewery on Cornwall without a license. Later such licenses were issued by the justice of the peace. Also spelled: alehouse. **Rare syn:** bush house. **See also:** Brewster Sessions.

ale jug. *(eiyl' juhg')*
Synonym for beer jug.

ale knight. *(eiyl' nayt')*

An obsolete term referring to a person who frequents ale houses and whose knighthood comes from conquering ale glasses.

ale maker. *(eiyl' mei'-ker)*

Synonym for ale brewer.

Ale Nog. *(eiyl' nag')*

A cocktail. One recipe suggests 1 liter of ale, 4 coffeespoons of milk, 100 grams of sugar, 8 egg yolks, and nutmeg. The egg yolks and sugar are mixed and beaten; the ale is poured in slowly while still beating; and last the nutmeg is added for flavor.

ale passion. *(eiyl' pae'-shen)*

A slang term for a headache caused by ale drinking.

ale pole. *(eiyl' pol')*

Synonym for ale stake.

ale posset. *(eiyl' pa'-sed:)*

See: posset.

ale post. *(eiyl' post')*

Synonym for ale stake.

ale stake. *(eiyl' steik')*

In Old England, a branch, stick, or pole placed outside a house to indicate that ale had been freshly brewed there. The practice dates back to Saxon times when wayside taverns or ale houses erected on Roman roads were identified by means of a long pole. If wine was sold along with mead and ale, an ivy bush was hung atop the pole. In the fourteenth century the same bush or ivy plant was a sign for the ale conner and customers that a fresh brew was ready. In London, in 1375, a city ordinance prescribed that such poles should not extend higher than 7 feet. **Syn:** ale pole; ale post.

aleurone. *(ael'-yuh-ron)*

The protein reserve in the form of granules or grains contained within the aleurone layer.

aleurone layer. *(ael'-yuh-ron lei'-yer)*

The single, outer layer of large cells containing the starchy endosperm. It is situated just below the surface of the grain and constitutes 2–3 percent of its weight. **Syn:** proteinaceous layer.

ale warmer. *(eiyl' wohr'-mer)*

A conical vessel with a handle made of thinned brass or copper and formerly used to warm ale over a fire in a grate. **Syn:** ass's ear.

ale wife. *(eiyl' wayf')*

In medieval England, a woman who brewed ale or who kept a tavern or both. The term sometimes refers to a woman who simply sold ale on the premises where it was made as opposed to a hukster. From 1300 onward, ale wives found guilty of overcharging or pitching a mug were severely punished, apparently more so than male brewers. Punishment could be a fine or the ducking stool (or cucking stool). The practice of ducking persisted well into the eighteenth century. Also spelled: alewife. **Syn:** brewster; breweress. **See also:** hukster.

ale yard. *(eiyl' yaerd')*

Synonym for yard of ale. Also spelled: aleyard.

ale yeast. *(eiyl' yeest)*

Synonym for top-fermenting yeast.

algin. *(ael'-jin)*

An insoluble colloidal substance obtained from a brown marine algae (*Phaophyceae*) and sometimes used for clarifying beer. **Syn:** alginic acid.

alginic acid. *(ael-ji'-nik ae'-sid)*

Synonym for algin.

algarroba beer. *(al-ga-r~o'-buh beeyr')*

A type of beer brewed in both Central and South America from the sweet ripe beans of the carob, mesquite, or other leguminous trees, especially those of the genus *Prosopis*. It is the sacred drink of the Chaco tribes and is forbidden to women. **Also spelled:** *algorobo*.

alixone. *(a-leek-so'-ne)*

An Old French name for a type of beer made in the Middle Ages.

alkali. *(ael'-kuh-lay)*

Any compound that yields hydroxyl (OH⁻) ions in a solution or chemical that reacts with acids to form salts.

alkaline. *(ael'-kuh-layn)*

1. Describes a solution having a pH greater than 7. **See also:** pH. **2.** Describes a beer that has retained traces of an alkali from the brewing liquor.

alkalinity. *(ael-kuh-li'-nuh-d:ee)*

The extent to which a solution is alkaline.

all-extract beer. *(ohl'-ehk'-straekt beeyr')*

A beer made entirely from malt extract as opposed to one made from barley, or from malt extract and barley.

all-grain beer. *(ohl'-grein beeyr')*

A beer made entirely from malt as opposed to one made from malt extract, or from malt extract and malted barley.

all-malt beer. *(ohl'-mohlt' beeyr')*

A beer made entirely from barley malt and without the addition of adjuncts or sugars.

Alost. *(a-lohst')*

A variety of hops grown in Flanders, Belgium.

alpha acid. *(ael'-fuh ae'-sid)*

One of the two soft resins in hops. It consists of a mixture of three closely related chemical compounds—humulone, co-humulone, and ad-humulone—and forms 2–14 percent of the total weight of hop cones and approximately 45 percent of their soft resins. Although the relative proportion of ad-humulone is fairly constant at 15 percent, the proportion of humulone and co-humulone varies from one hop variety to another. For example, the co-humulone content of Northern Brewer is close to 40 percent whereas that of Fuggles is about 30 percent. Alpha acids have a low wort solubility, and about 90 percent of beer bitterness is caused by compounds that form during boiling, the most important of which are iso-alpha-acids (iso-humulones), which account for most of the bitterness. The conversion of alpha acids to iso-alpha-acids takes from one half to one and a half hours; however, this may vary because the solubility of alpha acids decreases with increasing wort gravity. In commercial brewing, iso-humulones are sometimes added in the form of isomerized extracts, usually after fermentation. During aging, alpha acids oxidize and lose approximately 30 percent of their bittering power after one year and about 40 percent after two years. Abbrev: a-acid. **Syn:** humulon(e); alpha resin. **See also:** beta acid; soft resins.

alpha acid unit. *(ael'-fuh ae'-sid yoo'-nit)*
    A measurement of the potential bitterness of hops expressed in terms of their percentage of alpha acid content. Low equals 2–4 percent, medium equals 5–7 percent, high equals 8–12 percent. Abbrev: AAU. **See also:** bittering units; bitterness units; homebrew bittering units; hop bitterness coefficient; hop bitterness units.

alpha-amylase. *(ael'-fuh ae'-muh-leis)*
    A diastatic enzyme produced by malting barley, also known as liquefying enzyme because it converts soluble malt starch into complex carbohydrates called dextrins during mashing. Alpha-amalyses work best at a high pH (5.6–5.8) and at a high temperature (150 °F, 65.6 °C). They can withstand temperatures in excess of 163 °F (73 °C) but are destroyed at 176 °F (80 °C). **Syn:** liquefying enzyme; dextrinogenic amylase. **See also:** amylase; beta-amylase.

alpha resin. *(ael'-fuh reh'-zin)*
    Synonym for alpha acid.

alt. *(alt' or aelt')*
    Synonym for *altbier.*

altbier. *(alt'-beegh)*
    A traditional style of beer brewed mainly in Düsseldorf but also in Münster, Korschenbroich, Krefeld, Issum, and a few other cities of North Rhineland– Westphalia. The German word *alt* means old or ancient and refers to the fact that these beers are brewed by the traditional method of top fermentation, predating the relatively new method of bottom fermentation introduced in the mid eighteenth century and now predominant throughout Germany. Alt beers have a deep, luminous, copper color. They are brewed from dark malts, are well hopped, and display a slightly fruity, bittersweet flavor. Their alcohol content varies from 3.5–4 percent by weight (4.4–5.0 percent by volume) and are brewed from an original gravity of about 12.5 °Balling. Those from Düsseldorf have "Echte Düsseldorfer Altbier" written on the label. **Syn:** Düsseldorfer *altbier; alt.*

amasaké. *(a-ma-za-kei)*

In Japan, a sweet, nonalcoholic, sakélike beverage flavored with ginger. The term means sweet *saké*. Also spelled: *amazaké*.

amateur brewer. *(ae'-muh-chur broo'-wer)*

Synonym for homebrewer.

amazaké. *(a-muh-za'-keh)*

Orthograhic variant for *amasaké*.

amber beer. *(aem'-ber beeyr')*

A general name for any top- or bottom-fermented beer displaying an amber color, halfway between pale and dark. *Copper colored* or *coppery* are sometimes synonyms, but these words suggest a more reddish hue.

amber malt. *(aem'-ber mohlt')*

Malt prepared from well-modified malt containing 3–4 percent moisture that is dried rapidly at high temperature, usually around 200 °F (93.3 °C), for fifteen to twenty minutes and then gradually to 280–300 °F (138–149 °C) for a long period during which time the embryo and some enzymes are killed, thus imparting a slightly toasted or biscuity flavor to beer.

ambient temperature. *(aem'-bee-yent tehmp'-[e]-ruh-choor)*

The surrounding temperature.

amines *(uh-meenz')*

Volatiles found in beer, most of which are derived from ammonia originating from malt and hops through replacement of one or more hydrogen atoms by organic radicals. Amines form during the germination process. It has been suggested that they are responsible for the characteristic aroma of germinated barley. The concentration of volatile amines is greater in hops than in malt, and Fuggles has the highest concentration followed by Alsace, Backa, and Hallertau.

amino acid. *(uh-mee'-no ae'-sid)*

Any of the organic acids whose molecules contain one or more acidic carboxyl groups (COOH) and one or more amino groups (NH_2) and that polymerize to form peptides and proteins. Proteins are macromolecules composed of combinations of large numbers of the twenty different natural amino acids. During the beermaking process, amino acids are formed by the enzymatic degradation of such proteins. During kilning, amino acids combine with simple sugars to form colored compounds called melanoidins. Of the twenty amio acids found in nature, eight are considered to be essential in the diet (essential amino acids are identified by an asterick in the following table); the other twelve are considered nonessential. The crucial issue associated with amino acids is their rate of uptake by yeast and the role they play in metabolism. Others are essential in the sense that can come only from malt. All amino acids are used by yeast as nutrients at different parts of the fermentation process.

Essential and Nonessential Amino Acids

Amino Acids	Abbrev.	Molecular Weight	Solubility in Water
Alanine	Ala	89.09	High
Arginine	Arg	174.14	High
Aspartic acid	Asp	133.07	Low
Cystine	Cys	240.30	Almost insoluble
Glutamic acid	Glu	147.08	Low
Glutamine	Gln	146.15	Low
Glycine	Gly	76.07	High
Histidine	His	155.09	Medium
Hydroxylysine	Hyl	162.19	High
Hydroxyproline	Hyp	131.08	High
Isoleucine*	Ile	131.11	Low
Leucine*	Leu	131.11	Low
Lysine*	Lys	146.19	High
Methionine*	Met	149.15	Medium
Phenylalanine*	Phe	165.19	Medium
Proline	Pro	115.08	High
Threonine*	Thr	119.08	High
Tryptophane*	Trp	204.11	Very low
Tyrosine	Tyr	181.19	Almost insoluble
Valine*	Val	117.09	Medium

amyl acetate. *(ae'-mil ae'-suh-d:eit)*
    Formula: $CH_3COOC_5H_{11}$. An amylic ester derived from acetic acid and responsible for the fruity or bananalike odor in beer. **Syn:** banana oil, banana ester. **See also:** butyl acetate.

amylase. *(ae'-muh-leis)*
    A generic name for alpha- and beta-amylase, which are enzymes that hydrolize starch into maltose. Alpha-amylase converts insoluble and soluble starch into dextrins and maltotriose, then beta-amylase hydrolizes the dextrins into glucose, maltose, maltotriose, and alpha-limit dextrins. The complete

degradation of starch requires both alpha- and beta-amylase. Amylases are also present in saliva, which accounts for the practice of mastication in primitive times to induce fermentation in beery substances. **See:** alpha-amylase; beta-amylase; diastase.

amylodextrin. *(ae-muh-lo-dehk'-strin)*
A very complex dextrin produced by the amylolytic hydolysis of starch.

amyloglucosidase. *(ae'-muh-lo-gloo-ko'-suh-d:eis)*
1. A type of amylase available commercially. **2.** A typical fungal enzyme with temperature optimal at 104–122 °F (40–50 °C). When added to fermenting wort, it splits dextrins into fermentable sugars, thus producing a highly alcoholic and low-calorie (diatetic) beer devoid of dextrins. **Syn:** glucoamylase.

amylolysis *(ae-muh-la'-luh-sis)*
The enzymatic hydrolysis of starch into glucose, maltose, and dextrins.

amylolytic. *(ae'-muh-loh-li'-d:ik)*
A characteristic applied to enzymes that convert starch to soluble substances. **Syn:** diastatic.

amylolytic enzyme. *(ae'-muh-loh-li'-d:ik ehn'-zaym)*
An enzyme that converts starch into soluble substances, mainly sugars. **See also:** proteolytic enzyme.

amylopectin. *(ae'-muh-loh-pehk'-tin)*
The branched-chain fraction of starch that is relatively insoluble in water. Barley contains about 73 percent amylopectin, 75 percent wheat, 83 percent rice, and 78 percent maize. The other fraction is amylose.

amylose. *(ae'-muh-los)*
The straight-chain fraction of starch that is relatively soluble in water. Barley contains about 27 percent amylose, 25 percent wheat, 17 percent rice, and 22 percent maize. The other fraction is amylopectin.

anaerobic. *(aen-nuh-ro'-bik)*
Occurring in the absence of air (oxygen).

anaerobiosis. *(aen-uh-ro-bay-o'-sis)*
Life existing in the absence of air, or oxygen. **See also:** aerobiosis.

analyte. *(ae'-nuh-layt)*
A chemical compound that is the target of a particular assay or test system.

anhydrous alcohol. *(aen-hay'-druhs ael'-kuh-hohl)*
Synonym for absolute alcohol.

anion. *(aen'-ay-en)*
A negatively charged ion.

antelmann. *(an'-tel-man)*
An instrument for measuring the length of the acrospire of germinating barley. The maltster uses the growth of the acrospire as a rough guide to estimate the progress of the germination process, which is usually stopped by kilning before the acrospire grows beyond the end of the grain.

anthocyanogens. *(aen[t]-the-say-ae'-nuh-jenz)*
Phenolic compounds that, depending on their degree of condensation or polymerization, influence the colloidal stability of beer.

antifreeze. *(aen'-ti-freez)*
A substance that is added to an aqueous solution to lower its freezing point. In brewing, calcium chloride and glycol are sometimes added to beer for this purpose.

antioxidant. *(aen-tay-ak'-si-dent)*
A reducing agent added in small amounts to bottled beer to delay or prevent oxidation. Antioxidants are commonly used to retard the oxidative rancidity of fats. I-ascorbic acid (vitamin C) and the sulfites sulfur dioxide, potassium metabisulfite, and bisulfite are used for this purpose.

antiseptic. *(aen-ti-sehp'-tik)*
A substance that is used to destroy or prevent growth of infectious microorganisms or bacteria.

Apache beer. *(uh-pae'-chee beeyr')*
See: *tiswin.*

apparent attenuation. *(uh-peh'-rent uh-teh-nyuh-wei'-shen)*
A simple measure of the extent of fermentation that a wort has undergone in the process of becoming beer. Using either gravity units (GU),

Balling (B), or Plato (P) units to express gravity, apparent attenuation is equal to the original gravity minus the terminal gravity divided by the original gravity. The result is expressed as a percentage and equals 65–80 percent for most beers.

appealing. *(uh-pee'-ling)*
Descriptive of a pleasant, easy-drinking beer, containing no off-flavors or odors.

appetizing. *(ae'-puh-tay-zing)*
Describes a beer suitable for serving as an apéritif because it whets the appetite.

aqueous. *(ei'-kwee-uhs)*
Consisting of or comprising water; dissolved in water.

Armstrong rake. *(arm'-strohng reyk)*
A rotating arm that is fitted to the bottom of the mash tun for mixing the grist with the liquor prior to mashing, and also used for loosening a set mash. Also called: porcupine.

aroma. *(uh-ro'-muh)*
The pleasant fragrance of beer that originates from the natural odors of its ingredients—barley, malt, and hops. **See also:** bouquet.

aroma hops. *(uh-ro'-muh haps')*
Synonym for finishing hops.

aromatic hops. *(ae-ruh-mae'-d:ik haps')*
Synonym for finishing hops.

aromatic malt. *(ae-ruh-mae'-d:ik mohlt')*
A specialty malt lending strong malt aroma to a beer. Also called: Belgian aromatic.

artificial saturation. *(ar-d:uh-fi'-shel sae-chuh-rei'-shen)*
Carbon dioxide gas dissolved into beer by pressure, usually to compensate for a lack of it at the end of secondary fermentation.

asbestos filter. *(aez-beh'-stuhs fil'-ter)*
A type of filter consisting of layers of asbestos fiber sheets through which beer is pumped.

ascorbic acid. *(uhs-kohr'-bik ae'-sid)*

Formula: $C_6H_8O_6$. A water-soluble vitamin occurring naturally in many plants, especially citrus fruits, or made synthetically from glucose. It has mild reducing properties and is added to finished beer to prevent or delay oxidation and partly to clear the beer of dissolved oxygen. **Syn:** l-ascorbic acid; vitamin C; L-xyloascorbic acid.

ash. *(aesh)*

The residue left behind after all the organic matter of a substance has been incinerated. It consists of mineral matter and serves as a measure of the inorganic salts that were in the original substance.

ass's ear. *(ae'-sez eeyr')*

Synonym for ale warmer.

astringency. *(uh-strin'-jin-see)*

A characteristic of beer taste mostly caused by tannins, oxidized tannins (phenols), and various aldehydes (in stale beer) that cause the mouth to pucker.

astringent. *(uh-strin'-jint)*

In beer, a harsh, mouth-puckering sensation. **Syn:** harsh; tannic; austere.

attemper. *(uh-tehm'-per)*

To regulate or moderate process temperature, as by maintaining ambient temperature cooler than the fermentation temperature.

attemperating coil. *(uh-tehm-puh-rei'-d:ing coyl)*

A type of heat exchanger consisting of a series of spiral-coiled pipes into vats to heat or cool the solution within. **Syn:** attemperator.

attemperator. *(uh-tehm'-puh-rei-d:er)*

A small, ice-filled container immersed in bottom-fermenting beer to maintain a constant temperature of 43–45 °F (6–7 °C). It was replaced in the 1970s by attemperating coils. **Syn:** swimmer; attemperating coil.

attenuation. *(uh-teh-nyuh-wei'-shen)*

The percentage of reduction in the wort's specific gravity caused by the transformation of contained sugars into alcohol and carbon dioxide gas through fermentation. The fermentable sugars in the wort (which have a higher specific gravity than water) are converted into alcohol (which has a lower specific gravity than water) and carbon dioxide gas (which escapes as gas or goes into the solution):

$$C_6H_{12}O_6 \longrightarrow 2\,C_2H_5OH + 2\,CO_2$$

The percentage drop in gravity is measured with a saccharometer and is calculated as follows:

Formula: $A = (B - b) / B \times 100$
Example: $(12 - 4) / 12 \times 100 = 66.6\%$
A = attenuation: % of sugar of the original wort converted into alcohol and carbon dioxide after or during fermentation
B = original gravity in °Balling (or °Plato) prior to fermentation
b = specific gravity in °Balling (or °Plato) after or during fermentation

See also: apparent attenuation; final degree of attenuation; primary attenuation; real attenuation; secondary attenuation.

attenuation final. *(uh-teh-nyuh-wei'-shen fay'-nel)*
Synonym for final degree of attenuation.

attenuation limit. *(uh-teh-nyuh-wei'-shen li'-mit)*
Synonym for final degree of attenuation.

audit ale. *(oh'-did: eiyl')*
A strong ale formerly brewed at Trinity College, Cambridge, for the day of audit. At Oxford College a similar beer was called brasenose ale.

austere. *(oh-steeyr')*
Synonym for astringent.

autolysis. *(oh-ta'-luh-sis)*
The process of self-digestion of the body content of a cell by its own enzymes. The slow disintregration and breakdown of the membrane of yeast cells in the fermenting medium allows for the passage of nitrogen into the wort. If too pronounced the autolysis process gives a yeasty flavor to finished beer.

automatic carbon dioxide injector. *(oh-d:uh-mae'-d:ik kar'-ben day-ak'-seid in-jeh'k-ter)*
A type of carbon dioxide injector fitted on pressure barrels and containers to maintain a constant cover of carbon dioxide so as to keep the beer fresh and take up the pressure in the container during use.

auxiliary finings. *(ag-zil'-[e]-yuh-ree fay'-ningz)*

Finings that are sometimes used in conjunction with isinglass under special circumstances.

awn. *(ohn)*

Long bristle fibers at the end of glumes on oats, barley, and some wheat and grasses or, more often, such fibers collectively. **Syn:** beard. **See also:** glume.

awn cutter. *(ohn' kuh'-d:er)*

A machine that is used in maltings to remove the awns on kilned-dried malted barley.

Bb

B.

Abbreviation for Balling (°B).

b-acid. *(bee ae'-sid)*

Abbreviation for beta acid.

B & B. *(bee end bee)*

In England, a mix of equal parts of Burton ale and bitter.

baby. *(bei'-bee)*

In England, a quarter bottle with a capacity of 1 imperial gill (0.1355 liter) of beer.

back. *(buhk)*

A holding vessel. Derived from the word *bucket*.

bacteria. *(baek-ti'-ree-uh)*

A group of unicellular microorganisms that lack chlorophyll and reproduce rapidly by simple fission. They are classed according to their shape or on the basis of their oxygen requirements. Bacilli (singular: bacillus) are rod shaped; cocci (singular: coccus) are spherical or ovoid; vibro are comma shaped; and spirillum are curved and rodlike. Aerobic bacteria require atmospheric oxygen whereas anaerobic bacteria cannot live in the presence of oxygen. Bacteria develop under strict conditions of pH, temperature, and humidity (above 90 percent) and may be killed by disinfectants. They are responsible for certain diseases and for the degradation and spoilage of food.

bacterial. *(baek-ti'-ree-[y]el)*
A general term covering off-flavors such as moldy, musty, woody, lactic, acetic, or other flavors resulting from microbiological spoilage.

bacteriostatic. *(baek-ti-ree-[y]o-stae'-d:ik)*
Bacteria inhibiting.

bail. *(bey[e]l)*
Metal wire used to secure the ceramic cap of a swing-top bottle.

balance. *(bae'-luhn[t]s)*
The proportion of malt to hops in a beer. Brewers strive for a seamless balance of the two.

balché. *(bal-chey')*
Mayan hallucinogenic mead made with *balché* bark.

Ball. *(bohl)*
A shot of whiskey chased with a glass of beer.

Balling. *(bohl'-ling)*
1. A type of saccharometer devised by Carl Joseph Napoleon Balling in 1843. Balling noticed that the extract in wort increased the density of the wort in almost the same proportion as saccharose increased the density of water. He prepared solutions of saccharose and computed tables giving the extract content based on the density of the wort. The Balling saccharometer is graduated in grams per hundred (or percent) so as to give a direct reading of the percentage of extract by weight per 100 grams of solution and is calibrated for use at 63.5 °F (17.5 °C). (Example: 10 °B equals 10 grams of sugar per 100 grams of wort.) Pale ales commonly tend to be around 13.5 °B and porters around 12.5 °B. On the specific gravity scale, 1 °B equals 3.8 points. Because the reading gives the percentage extract by weight, it must be multiplied by the specific gravity to obtain the percentage weight per 100 milliliters. The tables computed by Balling were slightly erroneous but were corrected by Plato around 1900. Balling also devised the following formula to calculate the original extract of a beer from its alcohol content and terminal (or true) gravity:

$$E = [(2.665 \times A + n) \times 100] / (100 + 1.0665 \times A)$$
$$E = \text{original extract}$$

n = true extract of the beer
A = percent weight of alcohol

2. Balling (degree). A measure on the Balling saccharometer. Abbrev: °B. **See also:** Brix; Plato.

balm. *(bohlm)*
An old brewing term for yeast.

Bamberg beer. *(bam'-behrg beeyr')*
Synonym for *rauchbier.*

Bamberger rauchbier. *(bem'-behrg-ger ghawkh'-beeyr')*
Synonym for *rauchbier.*

banana ester. *(buh-nae'-nuh eh'-ster)*
Synonym for isoamyl acetate.

banana oil. *(buh-nae'-nuh oyl)*
Synonym for isoamyl acetate.

Bang. *(baeng)*
A mixed drink of warm spiced ale, cider, and whiskey.

Bantu beer. *(baen'-too beeyr')*
Synonym for *kafir* beer.

barley. *(bar'-lee)*
A cereal plant (*Hordeum vulgare*) of the grass family (Gramineae) that also includes wheat, rye, oats, maize, rice, millet, and sorghum. There are two varieties of barley classed according to the number of rows of grain on each of the ears of the plant: two- and six-rowed barley. Barley is the cereal grain preferred for brewing because the corn (or grain) is covered by a strawlike husk that protects the embryo (or germ) during malting and helps to filter the wort during lautering by forming a filter bed. The essential qualities for brewing barley are high starch content, sufficient diastatic power to transform the starch into sugar, low protein content, and germinative power close to or above 98 percent. Because carbohydrates, especially starch, constitute the bulk of the extract, a high nitrogen content of the barley automatically means a reduced amount of starch and sugars; hence, the higher the nitrogen content of the barley,

the lower the extract that can be obtained from its malt. The average weight of the barley grain is 35 milligrams. Substitute cereal grains used in brewing are called adjuncts.

barley broth. *(bar'-lee brath')*
Colloquialism for strong ale. Also called: whiskey. **Obsolete syn:** barley bree; barley broo.

barley corn. *(bar'-lee cohrn')*
A grain of barley. Also spelled: barleycorn.

barley island. *(bar'-lee ay'-lend)*
An Old English name for an ale house.

barley malt. *(bar'-lee mohlt')*
See: malt.

barley wine. *(bar'-lee wayn')*
1. Historically, the name given by ancient Egyptians and Greeks to "wine made from barley," which is translated in modern English texts as barley wine. **2.** In England, the name given to any top-fermented beer of unusually high, winelike, alcohol content prepared from worts of 1.065–1.120 original gravity yielding as much as 12 percent alcohol by volume. Barley wines are usually copper colored or dark brown, strongly flavored, fruity, bittersweet, and sometimes fermented with wine or champagne yeast. Because of their unusual strength they have little head retention and require long aging periods ranging from six months to many years. They are often brewed for special events. Russian stout, although slightly less alcoholic (10.5 percent alcohol by volume), is often classed as a barley wine, yet there are those who consider it a style unto itself. Also spelled: barleywine. **See also:** Russian stout.

barm, to. *(barm, too)*
To pitch, that is, add yeast.

barm. *(barm)*
1. Liquid yeast appearing as froth on fermenting beer. **Syn:** barm beer.
2. Synonym for brewer's yeast, especially from the strain *Saccharomyces cerevisiae*.
3. The foam on a glass of beer.

barm beer. *(barm beeyr')*
See: barm.

baron. *(ba-gho~')*
In Belgium, a beer glass with a capacity of 50 centiliters. **See also:** formidable.

barrel. *(bae'-rel)*
1. A large cylindrical container of greater length than breadth and with bulging sides once made of wood coated with tar (pitch) to prevent infection, now made of aluminum or stainless steel. **2.** A standard liquid measure in the United States that is 31.5 gallons (119.2369 liters), although federal tax laws are based on a 31-gallon (117.344-liter) capacity.

1 (full) barrel = 31 U.S. gal = 117.344 l
1/2 (half) barrel = 15.5 U.S. gal = 58.672 l
1/4 (quarter) barrel = 7.75 U.S. gal = 29.336 l
1/8 barrel (or pony) = 3.875 U.S. gal = 14.668 l

In Britain, a beer barrel has a capacity of 36 imperial gallons (163.65 liters) whereas an ale barrel has a capacity of 32 imperial gallons (146.472 liters). Abbrev: bbl.

barreling. *(bae'-ruh-ling)*
The action of transferring beer into barrels.

barrique. *(ba-gheek')*
1. The French name for a hogshead, the official capacity of which varies with region and commodity. **2.** In Britain, a cask containing 50 imperial gallons (227.495 liters).

basi. *(ba-see)*
The traditional alcoholic drink of the Ilocanos of the Philippines prepared by fermenting sugarcane juice and flavored with herbs.

batch fermentation. *(baech' fuhr-mehn-tei'-shen)*
Traditional fermentation where each batch is fermented separately.

batch sparging. *(baech' spar'-jing)*
A technique during mashing in which the total volume of sparge water is added to the tun at one time.

Baudelot cooler. *(bo'-de-loh koo'-ler)*
A type of wort cooler consisting of a series of horizontal copper pipes laid in a vertical plane and activated by cold water or brine. The wort is poured over the

pipes and gradually reaches the fermentation temperature of 57–77 °F (14–25 °C) for ales and 41–54 °F (5–12 °C) for lagers.

Baumé hydrometer. *(bo-mei' hay-dra'-muh-d:er)*
A hydrometer used mainly in France to determine the percentage of alcohol obtainable after complete fermentation in average cellar conditions.

Bavarian Northern Brewer. *(buh-veh'-ree-en nohr'-dhern broo'-wer)*
A seedless variety of hops grown in Bavaria that contains 7 percent alpha acids. It is more resistant to disease than the Hallertau variety, which is gradually being wiped out by disease.

Bayerischer weize. *(bay'-e-ghi-shegh vay'-tse)*
See: *weizenbier.*

Bayerisches Reinheitsgebot. *(bay'-e-ghi-shegh ghayn'-hayts-ge-bot')*
See: Reinheitsgebot.

B. B.
See: B & B.

bbl.
Abbreviation for barrel.

bead. *(beed)*
1. The bubbles rising to the surface of a glass of beer. **2.** The ring of bubbles adhering to the glass once the foam collar has collapsed.

beard. *(beeyrd)*
Synonym for awn. **See also:** glume; malt comes; malt tails.

beer. *(beeyr')*
1. A generic name for alcoholic beverages produced by fermenting a cereal or a mixture of cereals. **2.** An alcoholic beverage made by fermenting malt with or without other cereals and flavored with hops. Etym: From the Latin *bibere*, meaning to drink.

Composition

Water	75–92%
Alcohol	2–13%
Albuminoids	3–6%

Dextrins	3–6%
Mineral salts	0–2%
Carbon dioxide	0.1–0.4%

Nutrients (12 fl oz)

Water	92%
Food energy	150 kcal
Protein	1.1 g
Carbohydrate	14 g
Calcium	18 mg
Sodium	28 mg
Thiamine	0.01 mg
Riboflavin	0.11 mg
Niacin	2.2 mg

beer barrel. *(beeyr' bae'-rel)*
1. In the United States, a beer barrel has an official capacity of 31 gallons (117.344 liters). **2.** In England, a beer barrel has a capacity of 36 imperial gallons (163.65 liters) whereas an ale barrel contains 32 imperial gallons (146.472 liters). **See also:** barrel. **3.** Slang for a drunkard.

beer blast. *(beeyr' blaest')*
Slang among students in the United States for a party where large quantities of beer are consumed. **Syn:** beer bust.

beer brewer. *(beeyr' broo'-wer)*
One who brews beer. **See also:** ale brewer.

beer bust. *(beeyr' buhst')*
Synonym for beer blast.

Beer Buster. *(beeyr' buh'-ster)*
A mixed drink served in a highball glass consisting of beer, 0.5 ounce (14.8 milliliters) of vodka, and a dash of Tabasco sauce.

beer can. *(beeyr' kaen')*
1. Historically, a pail-like vessel to carry beer from the tavern to the home. **2.** Today, in the United States, a sealed aluminum container in which beer is sold with a capacity of 12 fluid ounces (355 milliliters), sometimes one-third larger (1 pint) or one-half smaller (a split or nip).

beer engine. *(beeyr' ehn'-jin)*
A pumplike tap for drawing beer from the cask or cellar to the bar. **Syn:** beer pump. **See also:** beer pull.

beer festivals. *(beeyr' feh'-sti-velz)*
See: Adriaan Brouwer Bierfesten; Bergkirchweih; Canstatter Wasen; Carnaval de Binche; Frühjahrsbierfest; Kermesse de la Bière de Marbeuge (Julifest Maubergeoise); Leuven Bier Festival; Oktoberfest; Poperinge Hoppefeesten.

beer from the wood. *(beeyr' fruhm dhuh wud')*
Draft beer.

beer garden. *(beeyr' gar'-den)*
A terrace area adjoining a tavern where beer is served. Sometimes called: beer hall. A term and tradition borrowed from Germany where it is called *biergarten,* or *bierkeller,* if the beer casks are kept in a cellar. There are more than one hundred beer gardens in Munich alone and the largest, Hirschgarten, can seat seven thousand people.

beer gardener. *(beeyr' gard'-[e]-ner)*
Slang for a beer garden owner.

beer hall. *(beeyr' hohl')*
A large room in an establishment where only beer is sold to customers. **See:** beer garden.

beer house. *(beeyr' haws')*
In England, a public house where only malt liquors are sold. Also spelled: beerhouse.

beer-house. *(beeyr' haws)*
A place licensed to sell beer only.

beer jug. *(beeyr' juhg')*
A name given by antique dealers and collectors to a type of eighteenth-century glass engraved with hops and/or barley and with a capacity of approximately 1 quart. **Syn:** ale jug.

beer life. *(beeyr' layf')*
Synonym for shelf life.

beer on tap. *(beeyr' ohn taep')*
Draft beer. **Syn:** beer from the wood.

beer parlor. *(beeyr' par'-ler)*
In Canada, an establishment where only malt liquors are sold.

beer pull. *(beeyr' pul')*
The handle of a beer engine.

beer pump. *(beeyr' puhmp')*
Synonym for beer engine.

beer saloon. *(beeyr' suh-loon')*
An establishment where draft beer was sold prior to Prohibition in the United States.

beer scale. *(beeyr' skeiyl')*
Synonym for beerstone.

beer stein. *(beeyr' stayn')*
A cylindrical or slightly tapered ceramic mug usually covered with a hinged metal lid. **See also:** stein.

beerstone. *(beeyr'-ston)*
Technically, calcium oxylate acid, which is precipitated by the addition of calcium. In homebrewing, beerstone is evident when the same vessel is used repeatedly; a hard film forms through the combination of calcium oxylate, protein, and sugar. Also spelled: beer stone. **Syn:** beer scale.

Beer-Wine Revenue Act. *(beeyr' wayn' reh'-vuh-noo aekt')*
Another name for the Cullen Act.

beery. *(bi'-ree)*
Pertaining to beer or resembling it in taste, aroma, or composition.

beet sugar. *(beet' shu'-ger)*
Sucrose obtained from sugar beets.

Belgian degrees. *(behl'-jin di-greez')*
In Belgium, the density of the wort is derived from the value of the specific

gravity by subtracting 1 and moving the decimal point two digits to the right. Hence, a specific gravity of 1.069 equals 6.9 °Belgian; 1 °Belgian equals approximately 2.5 °Plato.

Belgian lace. *(behl'-jin leys')*
　　See: lace.

belied measure. *(beh'-leed meh'-zher)*
　　An early English baluster-shaped ale measure.

bench capper. *(behnch' kae'-per)*
　　A freestanding or table-mounted bottle-crimping device.

bentonite. *(behn'-tuh-nayt)*
　　A clay mined in the United States, natural aluminum silicate of the monmorillonite group, used industrially at a rate of 20–60 grams per hectoliter to clarify beer through the adsorption of colloidal substances. If the contact period is too long, bentonite will affect foam retention and taste. However, if too short, the treatment is ineffective. **Obsolete syn:** Wyoming clay.

Bergkirchweih. *(behgh'-kighc-vay)*
　　A beer festival that is held annually during Whitsuntide in Erlangen, Franconia (Germany).

Berliner weisse. *(behgh-lee'-ner vay'-se)*
　　A regional beer of northern Germany, principally Berlin; a very pale (but not white) top-fermented beer of low-density (7–8 °B) made from a 1:3 or 1:4 wheat-to-barley ratio. It is lightly hopped and mildly alcoholic at 2–3 percent alcohol by weight (2.5–3.7 percent alcohol by volume). A secondary fermentation induced by the addition of a lactic acid culture *(Lactobacillus delbrueckii)* at 68 °F (20 °C) is responsible for its dry, sharp flavor, its thick white foam, and the deposit of yeast in the bottle. It is traditionally served in large bowl-shaped stemmed glasses with a dash of green essence of woodruff (Schultheiss Berliner Weisse) or red raspberry syrup (Kindl Berliner Weisse). Its popularity dates back to Imperial Germany (962–1806), and is mentioned in texts as early as 1572. It is also known as champagne of the spree, and was nicknamed *champagne du nord* by Napoleon's troops in 1809. **Syn:** *weissbier* or *weisse bier*. **See also:** *weissbier; weizenbier;* wheat beer.

Berliner weisse mit Schuss. *(behgh-lee'-ner vay'-se mit shus')*
　　Berliner *weisse* served with a dash of syrup in a tall glass.

Berliner weisse mit Strippe. *(behgh-lee'-ner vay'-se mit shtghi'-pe)*
Berliner *weisse* served in a tall glass with a proportionately tall head and accompanied by a chaser of Kummel spirits in a smaller glass.

best bitter. *(behst' bi'-d:er)*
Bitter ale prepared from an original wort gravity of 1.038–1.045. It tends to be medium-bodied, dry, and hoppy. **See also:** bitter.

beta acid. *(bei'-d:uh ae'-sid)*
One of the two soft resins in hops; it consists of a mixture of three closely related chemical compounds—lupulone, co-lupulone, and ad-lupulone. Contrary to alpha acid, it contributes very little (10 percent) to the bitterness of beer and accounts for approximately one-third of its preservative quality. Beta acids constitute about 25 percent of soft resins. They are present in larger quantities than alpha acids, but because of their low solubility (soluble in water only if oxidized) their content level is usually insignificant. Abbrev: b-acid. **Syn:** lupulon(e); beta resin. **See also:** alpha acid; lupulin; soft resin.

beta-amylase. *(bei'-d:uh ae'-muh-leis)*
A diastatic enzyme produced by malting barley, also known as saccharifying enzyme because it converts dextrins and soluble starches into maltose, maltotriose, glucose, and alpha-limit dextrins. Beta-amylase works best at low pH (± 5–5.2) and at temperatures ranging from 135–150 °F (57–66 °C) and is destroyed at 167 °F (75 °C). **Syn:** beta resin; saccharifying enzyme; maltogenic amylase. **See also:** alpha-amylase; amylase.

beta glucan. *(bei'-d:uh gloo'-kaen)*
A gummy substance found in the aleurone layer of barley. Unmalted grains are rich in these gums. In moderation beta glucan aids beer foaming, but an excess can cause runoff problems.

beta resin. *(bei'-d:uh reh'-zin)*
Synonym for beta acid.

bevel. *(beh'-vel)*
The outer surface at the head of a cask or barrel.

beverage. *(beh'-vrij)*
1. Any potable liquid. **2.** More often applied to an artificially prepared drink of pleasant taste and aroma.

beverage(d) alcohol. *(beh'-vrij[d] ael'-kuh-hohl)*
The ethyl alcohol content of a beverage. **Syn:** alcoholic beverage.

bicarbonate. *(bay-car'-buh-neit)*
A salt formed by neutralization of one hydrogen in carbonic acid. Calcium bicarbonate is used in the treatment of water to render it hard.

bier. *(beegh)*
German for beer. German beers are classed in three legal categories: (1) *starkbiers* are brewed from an original gravity of 16 °B or more and contain at least 5 percent alcohol by weight (6.2 percent alcohol by volume); (2) *vollbiers* are medium-strength beers prepared from original gravities of 11–14 °B and contain 3.5–4.5 percent alcohol by weight (4.4–5.65 percent alcohol by volume); and (3) *schankbiers* are brewed from original gravities of 7–8 °B and contain 2–3 percent alcohol by weight (2.5–3.7 percent alcohol by volume).

bierbauch. *(beegh'-bawkh)*
German for beer belly.

bière. *(byehgh)*
1. French for beer. 2. French legislation distinguishes three categories of beers based on the original gravity of the wort expressed in degrees Régie (°R): *bière de table,* 2–2.2 °R; *bière bock,* 3.3–3.9 °R; and *bière de luxe,* 4.4 °R or higher. The latter category also comprises, since 1971, two subcategories: *bière de choix* (4.4–4.6 °R) and *bière spéciale* (5–7 °R). The term *petite bière* (small beer) refers to low alcoholic beers brewed from an original gravity of 2 °R or less. **See also:** Régie. 3. In Belgium, there are four historical categories for beer based on the original gravity expressed in degrees Plato (°P): Category S, 15 °P or higher; Category I, 11–13.5 °P; Category II, 7–9 °P; and Category III, 1–4 °P. **See also:** Belgian degrees. Etym: The earliest mention of this word dates back to 1345 in a legal document signed by King Jean le Bon to regulate the trade rules and prices of beer; it appears again in 1489 in a decree signed by Charles VIII concerning the corporation des brasseurs de paris (corporation of brewers of paris).

bière blanche de Hoegaarden. *(byehgh' blan~sh' de o-gar-deh~')*
See: blanche de Hoegaarden.

bière bock. *(byehgh' bohk')*
In France, one of the three legal categories for beers comprising those prepared from medium-gravity worts of 3.3–3.9 °Régie. It should not be confused

with German bock beers, which are strong beers brewed from a wort of 16 °P (about 6.5 °Régie). **See also:** *bière; bock.*

bière d'abbaye. *(byehgh' da-bay'-[e])*
French for abbey beer.

bière de couvent. *(byehgh' de koo-vae~')*
  See: *biére des péres.*

bière de Diest. *(byehgh' de dyehst')*
  A very dark, sweet, highly nutritious beer brewed in Belgium from a mix of barley, caramelized malt, and 30 percent wheat. It contains 511 calories per liter as opposed to 400 calories in ordinary beers. **Syn:** *gildenbier.*

bière de garde. *(byehgh' de gaghd')*
  1. Any beer that has matured in casks for a long period of time. **2.** A regional style of beers from the north of France, so named because they spend long aging periods in casks. These amber-colored beers of 4.4–4.8 percent alcohol by weight (5.5–6 percent by volume) are produced by top fermentation (occasionally by bottom fermentation) to form a blend of pale and dark malts in a single-mash system; they are sold in corked and wired champagnelike bottles.

bière de luxe. *(byehgh' de lueks')*
  In France, the legal nomenclature for beers, based on the specific gravity of the original wort expressed in degrees Régie, stipulates that the strongest beers, *bière de luxe*, must be brewed from original wort gravities of 4.4 °R or higher. **See also:** bière; Régie.

bière de malt. *(byehgh' de malt')*
  A rich-flavored, low-alcoholic malt beverage once given to children and nursing mothers. It was brewed by adding malt extract to the wort followed by a very light fermentation. **Syn:** *bière de nourrice.* **See also:** malt beer; *malzbier.*

bière de mars. *(byehgh' de maghs')*
  A special beer brewed in France by a few breweries to renew the traditional practice of March beers. Before the advent of artificial cold (end of the nineteenth century), it was in March that beer was at its best. The barley had been harvested in August, malted in November, brewed in December, and lagered until March. **See also:** *Märzen(bier).*

bière de moine. *(byehgh' de mwa~n')*
French for abbey beer.

bière de nourrice. *(byehgh' de noo-ghees')*
Synonym for *bière de malt*.

bière des pères. *(byehgh' dei pehgh')*
A strong monastery beer brewed in France in the sixteenth century; a weaker brew was called *bière de couvent*.

bière de table. *(byehgh' de ta'-ble)*
In France, this is the legal nomenclature for beers, stipulating that low-strength table beers must be prepared from original wort gravities of 2–2.2 °Régie. **See also:** *bière*.

bierkieser. *(beegh'-kee-zegh)*
The name given in Alsace in 1723 and 1763 to sworn beer assayers. The role of these experts consisted of tasting the newly tapped beer to ensure that its quality was up to the standards set by the magistrate of that city, who had decreed that only malt, water, and hops could be used for its production. The addition of any other ingredients was a punishable offense. In the neighboring regions of Artois and Flanders, people with similar functions were called *eswarts, égards,* or *coeuriers.*

Biersteuergesetz. *(beegh-stoy'-er-guh-sehts)*
The beer tax law of Germany that governs not only the taxation of beer but the methods and processes of malting and brewing.

Big Six. *(big' siks')*
Refers to Britain's six largest brewing companies: Courage, Allied Breweries, Scottish & Newcastle, Watneys, Bass Charington, and Whitbread. The Big Six produce more than 80 percent of all the beer sold in Britain and own more than half of all the outlets.

bi-kal. *(bee-kal)*
The name given to a heavy beer in ancient Sumer.

bilbil. *(bil-bil)*
A type of beer once brewed in Upper Egypt from durra(h), a type of sorghum also known as Indian millet. The durrah grains were germinated

between leaves of *onna oskur* (*Calotropis procera*), sundried, and milled into a fine flour. The flour was mixed with water in large earthenware pots, and the wort was boiled for six to eight hours over open fires. After cooling, a yeasty preparation was added to induce fermentation. This first brew was called *merissa*; if boiled a second time, filtered, and refermented, it was called *bilbil*. Etym: From *bülbül*, mother of the nightingale, because it caused drinking men to sing. **Syn:** *omm bilbil.*

bilge. *(bilj)*
The wide, bulging part of a cask or barrel located in the middle where the circumference is greatest. Once called: bouge.

bilge water. *(bilj' wa'-d:er)*
British slang for an inferior beer.

billet. *(bi'-lit)*
Synonym for thumbpiece.

bine. *(bayn)*
Synonym for hop bine.

biochemical pathway. *(bay-o-keh'-mi-kuhl paeth'-wei)*
A sequence of chemical reactions, each of which is catalyzed by enzymes supplied by microorganisms. **See also:** chemical pathway.

biochips. *(bay'-o-chips)*
Sterilized sawdust sprayed with pitch and used to assist clarification during secondary fermentation or maturation.

birch beer. *(buhrch' beeyr')*
A nonalcoholic, usually carbonated beverage flavored with oils of wintergreen, sweet birch, or sassafras.

biscuit malt. *(bis'-kit mohlt')*
A lightly roasted specialty malt that imparts a bready or biscuity flavor and aroma to beers.

bi-se-bar. *(bee-sei-bar)*
The name given to a light barley beer in ancient Sumer.

Bismark. *(biz'-mark)*
In the United Kingdom the German name given to a mix of champagne and stout called Black Velvet.

bit-sikari. *(beet-si-ka-ree)*
The name given to a brew house in ancient Sumer.

bitter. *(bi'-d:er)*
A sharp and tangy taste in beer associated with hops.

bitter. *(bi'-d:er)*
In Britain, the draft equivalent of pale ale, a golden-brown or copper-colored top-fermented beer usually highly hopped, dry, and lightly carbonated. Bitter accounts for about 80 percent of draft beer sales in English pubs. It is slightly more alcoholic (3–5.5 percent alcohol by volume) and more heavily hopped than mild. It is usually available in three strengths although there are regional variations: ordinary bitter, original gravity 1.033–1.038; best bitter, original gravity 1.038–1.045; and special or strong bitter, original gravity 1.045–1.060. Traditionally, bitter is unpasteurized and cask-conditioned in the pub cellar. In the 1960s the large brewing companies introduced kegged beer, a filtered, pasteurized, chilled, and artificially carbonated bitter. A consumer campaign initiated by Campaign for Real Ale in the 1970s opposed this new trend, and naturally conditioned casked bitter is again available as real ale. **Obsolete syn:** slight beer. **Syn:** bitter beer; bitter ale. **See also:** best bitter; ordinary bitter; special bitter.

bitter ale. *(bi'-d:er eiyl')*
Synonym for bitter.

bittering hops. *(bi'-d:uh-ring haps')*
Synonym for flavoring hops.

bittering units. *(bi'-d:uh-ring yoo'-nits)*
A formula devised by the American Homebrewers Association® to measure the total amount of bitterness in a given volume of beer, multiplying the alpha acid content (in percent) by the number of ounces.

Example: 2 ounces of hops at 9 percent alpha acid for five gallons
Formula: $2 \times 9 = 18$ BU per 5 gallons

See also: alpha acids units; bitterness units; homebrew bittering units; hop bitterness coefficient; hop bitterness units.

bittern. *(bi'-d:ern)*

A very bitter mixture of equal parts of quassia and other drugs formerly used for adulterating beer. Ross-Mackenzie (*Brewing and Malting*, London, 1935) gives the following formula: equal parts of quassia extract and sulphate of iron, 2 parts of extract of *Cocculus indicus*, 8 parts of treacle, and five parts of Spanish juice.

bitterness. *(bi'-d:er-nis)*

The quality or state of being bitter. In beer, the bitter flavor is caused by the tannins and the iso-humulones of hops. When tasting beer a distinction is made between the first bitterness, when the liquid touches the tastebuds, and the postbitterness felt at the back of the mouth when the beer is swallowed. **See also:** alpha acid; beta acid.

bitterness units. *(bi'-d:er-nis yoo'-nits)*

An international system of units for measuring and expressing the bitterness in beer based on the parts-per-million content (or milligrams per liter) of alpha acids. Note: this formula is an approximation that can be off by as much as 20 percent, depending on hop utilization in the brew kettle and iso-alpha-acid loss during fermentation and aging.

Formula: $BU = H \times (a - a + b - a / 9) / 0.3$
Where:
H = weight of hops in grams per liter (H g/l)
$a\%$ = alpha acid percent
$b\%$ = beta acid percent
9 = a constant; the flavoring power of alpha acids is about nine times greater than that of beta acids
0.3 = a constant that represents an approximate 30 percent rate of efficiency in hop extraction caused by vaporization or precipitation (boiling, skimming, racking, and fining)

Conversely, to calculate the amount of hops in grams per liter required to obtain a specific bitterness unit, the formula is rearranged:

$H\ g/l = BU / (a\% + b\% / 9) \times 0.3$

(Example: If a beer is to reach 25 BU using Hallertau hops containing 5 percent alpha/beta acids, $H = (25 / 5) \times 0.3 = 1.5$ g/l.) **Abbrev:** BU. **Syn:** units of bitterness; International Bitterness Units (IBU). **See also:** alpha acid units; bittering units; homebrew bittering units; hop bitterness units; hop bitterness coefficient.

bitter orange peel. *(bi'-d:er o'-renj pee[e]l)*
A spice and key ingredient in Belgian white beers. Also called: Curaçao orange peel. **See also:** sweet orange peel.

bitter resins. *(bi'-d:er reh'-zinz)*
Synonym for soft resins.

bitter stout. *(bi'-d:er stawt)*
See: stout.

bitter wort. *(bi'-d:er wuhrt)*
Sweet wort made bitter by boiling with hops for one to two hours. The boiling process extracts and dissolves the bitter resins and aromatic oils contained in the hops in the wort, giving it its characteristic bitterness.

Black and Tan. *(blaek' end taen')*
A mix of equal parts of dark and pale beers such as porter and Pilsener, stout and mild, or stout and bitter.

black beer. *(blaek' beeyr')*
A general term for very dark-colored beers. **Syn:** spruce beer.

black champagne. *(blaek' shaem-peiyn')*
The name given to imported English ale under Louis XIV. According to historians, a rich brewer named Humphrey Parsons, twice mayor of London, visited the French court of Louis XIV. During a steeplechase he accidentally dropped the reins of his black horse, which had the impudence to overrun the king's mount. Upon inquiring as to the identity of the culprit, the king was told that Lord Parsons was a *chevalier de malte* and a brewer. Lord Parsons had the diplomatic sense of giving the horse to Louis who in turn asked the brewer to provide the court of Versailles with his stout, which the courtiers called black champagne.

black jack. *(blaek' jaek')*
A large tankardlike drinking vessel made of leather and internally waterproofed with black pitch or resin common in England in the sixteenth and seventeenth centuries. Also spelled: black jack; blackjack.

black malt. *(blaek' mohlt')*
Partly malted barley of moderate nitrogen content (1.5 percent), germinated for four to six days and kiln dried down to 2–5 percent moisture, then roasted at

high temperature (± 450 °F, 232 °C) for two to two and a half hours in a coke or gas-heated rotating drum. It is used in small amounts in stouts and dark beers to which it contributes a dark color and a burnt or carbonized flavor. Because it contains no fermentable sugar, all the solids extracted from it remain in the finished beer. **Syn:** black patent malt; patent malt; carbonized malt; chocolate malt. **See also:** chocolate malt.

black mead. *(blaek' meed)*
A variety of melomel prepared by fermenting a must of honey, black currants, and water.

Black Velvet. *(blaek' vehl'-vuht)*
A cocktail mix of equal parts of stout and champagne (or sparkling wine) usually prepared in a champagne glass by slowly pouring the stout on the side of the glass so that it does not mix with the champagne. **See also:** Bismark.

blanche de Hoegaarden. *(blan-sh' de o-gar-deh~')*
A traditional wheat beer brewed in one of the oldest brewing towns—and once the largest—Flanders, in Belgium (thirty breweries for two thousand people in 1745). An old document states that "in Hoegaarden, only animals drink water." The *bière blanche* is prepared from a mash of 50 percent barley malt and 50 percent wheat, sometimes with the addition of 10 percent oats (or oat flakes). Originally, it was fermented by wild yeasts and lactic bacteria and sold to wholesalers only a few days after primary fermentation, or it was buried in March to be unearthed the following year and was then an occasion for celebrations. The brewery, closed in the 1950s after five hundred years of operation but reopened in the 1960s by Pierre Celis, is once again brewing its traditional style of beer by top fermentation in aluminum vats. **Syn:** Hoegaardse *wit*.

blanche de Louvain. *(blan~sh' de loo-vae~')*
A traditional, top-fermented wheat beer brewed in the Flemish town of Louvain in Belgium. The mashing process, from a mix of malt and raw wheat in a ratio of 60:40, 50:50, or 45:45 with 10 percent oats, is very long, up to seventeen hours, and only about one-third of the wort is boiled with hops. The original wort density ranges from 1.040–1.048 (4–4.8 °Belgian). **Syn:** Leuvense *wit*.

blend, to. *(blehnd, too)*
To mix products of the same nature or varieties of the same product.

blend. *(blehnd)*
A product obtained by mixing substances of the same nature.

blenders. *(blehn'-derz)*
Companies that contract or buy *lambic* beers, which they ferment, mature, and blend.

blending. *(blehn'-ding)*
The action of mixing two or more products of the same nature.

blind pig. *(blaynd' pig')*
During Prohibition, an illegal drinking saloon. The term originated in Maine in the 1850s when saloon owners attempted to evade the prohibitory law of that state by charging admission to view a "blind pig," which entitled the customer to a free drink. **Syn:** blind tiger.

blood heat. *(bluhd' heet')*
An empirical method of ascertaining or expressing the temperature of a liquid by dipping a finger or an elbow, which should feel neither hot nor cold. In homebrewing this constitutes a test to determine the appropriate time for pitching the yeast. **Syn:** blood temperature; blood warm.

blowby. *(blo'-bay)*
In homebrewing, a single-stage fermentation method using a glass or plastic carboy into the mouth of which a plastic hose is fitted, curving down over the edge into a pail of sterile water. This method allows the primary fermentation to blowout all the froth and carbon dioxide while preventing air from coming into contact with the fermenting beer, thus avoiding contamination. After one to three days the beer is either transferred to a second carboy or left in the first one for the secondary fermentation process.

blowoff. *(blo'-af)*
See: blowby.

blowout tube. *(blo'-awt toob')*
A 1-inch plastic tube fitted into the mouth of a carboy in the blowby method.

bock(bier). *(bohk'[beegh])*
1. A very strong beer originally brewed by top fermentation in the Hanseatic League town of Einbeck in Lower Saxony where it is still brewed

and known as Ur-Bock, the original *bock*. It was once a heavy dark beer brewed in winter for consumption in spring. German bock beers are now brewed by bottom fermentation and are usually dark brown, but pale bocks are increasing in popularity and a distinction is sometimes made between light bock beer and dark bock beer. Modern *bockbiers*, according to German law, must be fermented from an original wort gravity of at least 16 °P (1.064), resulting in an alcoholic content of 6 percent by weight or higher (7.5 percent alcohol by volume). They are full-bodied, malty, and well hopped. Etym: From the town of Einbeck (circa 1250) in northern Germany. This beer was later exported to Munich and was one of the first beers to be brewed by the Hofbraü, the brewery of the dukes of Bavaria. In the eighteenth century, the name became Oanbock and was later shortened to bock. According to one legend, bock was once made from the dregs of barrels and vats at spring cleaning. This is obviously untrue, for such a beer would have been weak, to say the least. Because the word *bock* also means male goat or billy goat in German, such an animal is often represented on the labels of bottles containing bockbier. **See also:** *doppelbock; eisbock*. **2.** In the United States, bock beers made their first appearance around 1840 and were seasonal beers available at springtime. After Prohibition was repealed (December 1933), bars proclaimed the good news with a sign saying "Bock is back," but in fact the sales of bock beers dwindled and production was discontinued until the 1970s when a few bock beers were revived. American bock beers are usually light-bodied and mildly hopped. The name of these so-called bock beers comes not from their strength but rather from their dark color and artificial flavoring (caramel). **3.** In France, bock refers to a medium strength beer of medium density ranging from 3.3–3.9 °Régie. **See also:** *bière bock*. **4.** In France, a beer glass with a capacity of either 33 centiliters or 1/4 of a liter (25 centiliters).

body. *(ba'-d:ee)*
   The consistency, thickness, and mouth-filling property of a beer. The sensation of palate fullness in the mouth ranges from full-bodied to thin-bodied. Lack of body is the opposite. **Syn:** mouthfeel; fullness.

boggle. *(ba'-gel)*
   A pitcher- or juglike drinking vessel of Scottish origin shaped in the likeness of a man.

boiler. *(boy'-ler)*
   A large vessel in which to boil the wort.

boiler hopping. *(boy'-ler ha'-ping)*

The addition of finishing hops near the end of the boiling process or ten to thirty minutes after boiling has stopped for the purpose of increasing the aromatic character of the finished beer.

Boilermaker. *(boy'-ler-mei-ker)*

1. A jigger of whiskey chased with a glass of beer. Etym: From the expression "head of steam" used to describe the heady feeling that this drink generates.
2. Sometimes, salted beer.

boiling. *(boy'-ling)*

An operation in which the sweet wort is transferred to the brew kettle (or copper) for boiling for one to two and a half hours. During that time, flavoring (or bittering) hops will be added at the beginning of the process, and finishing (or aromatic) hops will be added near the end to produce the bitter wort. The objective of boiling is to stabilize the composition of the final wort, to clarify it through the coagulation and precipitation of tannins and proteins, to sterilize it by killing bacteria, and to extract the desirable principals of the hops that give beer its characteristic flavor and aroma. Boiling also contributes to the color through the caramelization of sugars and the formation of melanoidins. At the end of the boiling stage the hops are removed and the wort is quickly cooled to further clarify the brew. **Syn:** brewing.

boiling copper. *(boy'-ling ka'-per)*

Synonym for brew kettle.

boiling hops. *(boy'-ling haps')*

Synonym for flavoring hops.

bolt, to. *(bolt, too)*

In British maltings, the term refers exclusively to separating the flour from the products of grinding. **Syn:** sieve.

bomber. *(ba'-mer)*

A 22-ounce longneck bottle.

booza(h). *(bo'-zuh)*

Orthographic variant for *boza*.

botte. *(boht)*

A French beer glass with a capacity of 1 liter. **See also:** *demi; distingué; lion.*

bottle. *(ba'-d:el)*
A glass container with a narrow neck for holding liquids.

bottle-aged. *(ba'-d:el eijd)*
Synonym for bottle-conditioned.

bottle capper. *(ba'-d:el kae'-per)*
See: capper.

bottle-conditioned. *(ba'-d:el kuhn-di'-shend)*
   1. Describes beer that is aged in the bottle. **Syn:** bottle-aged. **2.** Describes a beer carbonated naturally by priming or re-yeasting. **See also:** carbonation; conditioning.

bottled beer. *(ba'-d:eld beeyr')*
Beer sold in bottles as opposed to casks or cans. Bottled beer is frequently chilled, filtered, carbonated, pasteurized, and sterilized by the addition of inhibitory materials.

bottled draft beer. *(ba'-d:eld draeft' beeyr')*
A mislabeled product consisting, like draft, of unpasteurized beer.

bottled goods. *(ba'-d:eld goudz)*
Alcoholic beverages sold in bottles.

bottled mild. *(ba'-d:eld may[e]ld')*
Synonym for brown ale.

bottle opener. *(ba'-d:el op'-[e]-ner)*
A device for levering (prying off) bottle caps.

bottle pressure. *(ba'-d:el preh'-sher)*
U.S. brewers bottle beer at about 2.5 atmospheric pressure (± 37 pounds per square inch, or 2.58 kilograms per square centimeter). Bottle pressure at a given carbon dioxide level varies dramatically with temperature. For example, if a beer contains 2.5 volumes of carbon dioxide, then a bottle pressure of 37 pounds per square inch will occur at 79 °F (26.11 °C); however, at 45 °F (7.22 °C) the pressure will be approximately 15 pounds per square inch. Homebrewers can produce such pressure by priming with 1.5 ounces of dextrose per gallon of beer (1.8 ounces per imperial gallon) prior to bottling. **Syn:** bottling pressure.

bottlery. *(ba'-d:el-ree)*
Synonym for bottling department.

bottle washer. *(ba'-d:el wa-sher)*
An automatic machine for washing bottles.

bottle works. *(ba'-d:el wuhrts)*
Synonym for bottling department.

bottling. *(bat'-ling)*
The action of filling bottles manually or automatically. Because bottled beer is often stored for longer periods and at warmer temperatures than draft beer, it is usually pasteurized to prevent any further fermentation.

bottling department. *(bat'-ling duh-part'-ment)*
The area of the brewery where bottles are washed, sterilized, filled, capped, labeled, and packaged. **Syn:** bottlery; bottling hall; bottle works.

bottling fleet. *(bat'-ling fleet')*
The total amount of bottles owned by a brewery.

bottling hall. *(bat'-ling hohl')*
Synonym for bottling department.

bottling line. *(bat'-ling layn')*
An automated U- or L-shaped production line where bottles are examined, washed, rinsed, sterilized, filled, labeled, and corked.

bottling pressure. *(bat'-ling preh'-sher)*
Synonym for bottle pressure.

bottom fermentation. *(ba'-d:em fuhr-mehn-tei'-shen)*
One of the two basic methods of fermenting beer, during which time dead yeast cells sink to the bottom of the fermentation vessel. The maximum growth temperature for *Saccharomyces carlsbergensis* is 88.9–93.2 °F (31.6–34.0 °C). Primary fermentation requires temperatures of 41–50 °F (5–10 °C) usually over a three-stage cycle of 41–48–41 °F or 45–54–45 °F (5–9–5 °C or 7–12–7 °C), and secondary fermentation takes place at 34–36 °F (1–2 °C). Beers brewed in this fashion are commonly called lagers or bottom-fermented beers.

bottom-fermentation yeast. *(ba'-d:em fuhr-mehn-tei'-shen yeest')*
Synonym for bottom-fermenting yeast.

bottom-fermented beer. *(ba'-d:em fuhr-mehn'-ted beeyr')*
Synonym for lager.

bottom-fermenting lager yeast. *(ba'-d:em fuhr-mehn'-ting la'-ger yeest')*
Synonym for bottom-fermenting yeast.

bottom-fermenting yeast. *(ba'-d:em fuhr-mehn'-ting yeest')*
One of the two types of brewer's yeast so named because the majority of the yeast cells flocculate and sink to the bottom of the wort toward the end of fermentation. Lager yeasts work best at 41–50 °F (5–10 °C) but can ferment at temperatures as low as 34 °F (1 °C), and they have the ability to ferment melibiose sugar because of the presence of melibiose enzymes in their cells. Lager yeast is thought to have been first isolated by a German monk named Benno Scharl, who operated a small brewery near Munich around 1810. It was later used by the Spatenbrauerei (Spaten brewery). Samples of this yeast were taken from Munich to Copenhagen by Jacob Christian Jacobsen in 1845–46, a five-hundred-mile journey by stagecoach. Here they were analyzed by the microbiologist Emil Hansen of the Carlsberg Labs, who isolated the first single-cell culture of this yeast, which he named *Saccharomyces carlsbergensis*. *Saccharomyces uvarum* is another well-known fermenting yeast. **Syn:** lager yeast; bottom-fermenting lager yeast; bottom fermentation yeast; bottom yeast.

bottoms. *(ba'-d:emz)*
Yeast sediments that have collected at the bottom of a fermentation vessel or conditioning tank.

bouge. *(booj)*
An obsolete synonym for bilge.

bouquet. *(boo-keiy')*
The overall smell of beer caused by odors that originate during fermentation and maturation. **See also:** aroma.

boutique brewery. *(boo-teek' broo'-[e]-ree)*
A small brewery with a production of less than 15,000 barrels per year.

bousa. *(bo'-zuh*)*
Orthographic variant for *boza*.

box malting. *(baks' mohl'-ting)*

A type of pneumatic malting process carried out in germination boxes.
Syn: compartment malting.

boza. *(bo'-zuh*)*

1. In ancient Babylonia and Egypt (3000–2000 BC), a type of beer usually
fermented from millet (*Panicum miliaceum*). Until recently, an archaic method of
preparing *boza*, practiced by desert nomads (*fellaheen*), was steeping and partially
germinating millet. Afterward, the grains were crushed into a dough and baked
into dehydrated cakelike masses. Once in the desert, the cakes where broken into
pieces, steeped in water, and fermented. **2.** In Ethiopia, a wheat beer. **3.** In
Turkey, a nonalcoholic beer prepared from corn. Also spelled: *bosa; bousa; bouza;
booza(h)*. The term *booze* is probably derived from *boza*.

bracteole. *(braek'-tee-ol)*

The overlapping petals that constitute the strobile (hop cone). **Syn:** breact.

braga. *(bra'-guh*)*

1. A mild mead made in Russia during the Middle Ages. **2.** In Romania, it is
known as millet beer.

bragget. *(brae'-git)*

Honey-sweetened spiced ale or a mix of mead and ale. Etym: From Bragget
Sunday, the fourth Sunday in Lent, in nineteenth-century England, on which the
ale was drunk continuously.

braggot. *(brae'-git)*

Mead made with malt (but not to exceed 50 percent of fermentables).
Sometimes called: bracket.

bragot. *(bra'-guht)*

An ancient Welsh drink consisting of beer, honey, cinnamon, and
"galingale." Also called: hero drink.

Brambling Cross. *(braem'-bling kras)*

A variety of hops cultivated in the United Kingdom and containing 5–6
percent alpha acids. Also called: Bram Cross.

brasenose ale. *(breiz'-noz eiyl')*

Synonym for audit ale.

brassage. *(brae'-sij)*
From *brace*, grain used to prepare malt and *bracis* (steeped, softened grain).

brasserie. *(bgha-se-ghee')*
A bar where food and drink are served. From *brasser,* to brew. **See also:** brassage.

breact. *(bree'-aekt*)*
Synonym for bracteole.

break. *(breik)*
The coagulation and precipitation of protein and polyphenol complexes during the boiling stage (hot break) and cooling stage (cold break).

breakage. *(brei'-kij)*
Synonym for flocculation.

Brettanomyces lambicus. *(breht-[e]-no-may'-seez lam'-bik-us)*
A type of yeast used in Belgium for brewing *lambic* beers. It produces more esters than other yeasts and imparts a characteristic leathery or horse-blanket aroma to beer.

brew, to. *(broo, too)*
1. Generally speaking, to make beer. **2.** The infusion and boiling stages of the beermaking process, that is, preparing the bitter wort.

brew. *(broo)*
1. Synonym for beer. **2.** The wort (or the quantity of it) in preparation.

brewer. *(broo'-wer)*
A person or industrialist who makes beer. Etym: From the Gallic word *brai* (or *brace*), originally meaning barley, and later barley mixed with water. **See also:** master brewer.

breweress. *(broo'-[e]-riss)*
Synonym for brewster.

breweriana. *(broo-[e]-ree-ae'-nuh)*
The collecting of beer-related artifacts by enthusiasts.

Brewer's Gold. *(broo'-werz gohld')*
A variety of hops cultivated in Kent, England, and in Washington and

Oregon in the United States, containing 8.5–11 percent alpha acids and 4.5–5.5 percent beta acids.

brewer's grains. *(broo'-werz greynz')*
Synonym for spent grains.

brewer's gravity. *(broo'-werz grae'vi-d:ee)*
Specific gravity in brewer's pounds, which is calculated by the following formula: $(SG - 1{,}000) \times 0.36$. **See also:** brewer's pounds.

brewer's grits. *(broo'-werz grits')*
Coarsely crushed barley, corn, or rice grains that have to be treated in a converter prior to mashing.

brewer's paddle. *(broo'-werz pae'-d:el)*
A long-handled wooden or polypropylene paddlelike instrument used to stir (or rouse) the beer at various stages of production. **Syn:** rouser; stirring spoon.

brewer's pounds. *(broo'-werz pawndz')*
The excess weight of a barrel (36 imperial gallons) of wort over that of a barrel of water (360 pounds) at 60 °F (15.5 °C). This figure represents the extract in brewer's pounds. Hence, the specific gravity of the wort is calculated by the following formula: (excess brewer's pounds + 360) / 360. **See also:** brewer's gravity; extract.

brewer's yeast. *(broo'-werz yeest')*
Yeast specifically prepared for beer brewing. Two main types of yeast are used for beermaking: one ferments primarily at the top of the brew (ale yeast), and the other ferments primarily at the bottom (lager yeast). Brewer's yeast may be gathered from the lees of the previous brew or it may be purchased in dry or liquid form. **Syn:** brewing yeast.

brewery. *(broo'-[e]-ree)*
1. A building in which beer is made. **2.** A place were beer is served.

brew house. *(broo' haws)*
The section of a brewery where the actual brewing or mashing takes place. Also spelled: brew-house. **Obsolete syn:** brewery.

brewing. *(broo'-wing)*
1. The art (or science) of making beer. Commercial brewing is divided into nine basic steps: steeping, germinating, kilning, milling, mashing, lautering, boiling, fermenting, and bottling (canning or casking). All nine stages can be accomplished in two weeks to four months. **2.** The mashing and boiling stages of beermaking. **3.** Pertaining to the beermaking process.

brewing copper. *(broo'-wing ca'-per)*
Synonym for brew kettle.

brewing liquor. *(broo'-wing li'-ker)*
Synonym for brewing water.

brewing water. *(broo'-wing wa'-d:er)*
Water of suitable quality and quantity that was historically often supplied to breweries from nearby wells. Some brewing centers became famous for their particular type of beer, and the individual flavors of their beer were strongly influenced by the brewing water used. Burton is renowned for its bitter beers, Edinburgh for its pale ales, Dortmund for its pale lager, and Plzen for its Pilsner Urquell, also a pale lager. **Syn:** liquor; brewing liquor.

Ionic Concentrations of Salts in Typical Brewing Liquors
(in millivals*)

Ions	Burton[†]	Edinburgh	London[‡]	Dortmund	Munich	Plzen
Sodium	1.3	4.0	4.3	3.0	0.1	0.1
Magnesium	5.2	3.0	1.6	1.9	1.6	0.1
Calcium	13.4	7.0	2.6	13.0	4.0	0.4
Nitrate	0.5	0.5	—	—	0.1	—
Chloride	1.0	1.7	1.7	3.0	0.1	0.1
Sulfate	13.7	4.8	1.6	5.9	0.1	0.1
Carbonate	4.7	7.0	5.2	9.0	5.5	0.3
Total salts (ppm)	1,226.0	800.0	463.0	1,011.0	273.0	30.8

* Millivals are the equivalent weight in milligrams per liter, or N/1000, or 0.001 Normal; 1 millival equals 1 milligram equivalent per liter. Water with less than 2.5 millivals is considered soft; 2.5–5 is moderately soft; 5–7.5 is slightly hard; 7.5–12.5 is moderately hard; 12.5–17.5 is hard; above 12.5 is very hard.
  †Burton-on-Trent
  ‡deep-well water

Source: A.J.B. Schofield, *The Treatment of Brewing Water.* Privately published, in Liverpool, England, 1956.

brewing yeast. *(broo'-wing yeest')*
Synonym for brewer's yeast.

brew kettle. *(broo' keh'-d:el)*
One of the vessels used in the brewing process in which the wort is boiled. Also called: boiling kettle; copper.

brewmaster. *(broo'-maes-ter)*
Synonym for master brewer.

brewpot. *(broo'-pat)*
Synonym for brew kettle.

brewpub. *(broo'-puhb)*
Pub that makes its own beer and sells at least 50 percent of it on the premises. Also known in Britain as a homebrew house and in Germany as a house brewery.

brewster. *(broo'-ster)*
A female brewer. **Syn:** ale wife.

Brewster Sessions. *(broo'-ster seh'-shinz)*
In Old England, by a law of 1729, special sessions of the justice of the peace to consider the issue or renewal of licenses to operate ale houses.

bridal. *(bray'-d:el)*
See: bride ale.

bride ale. *(brayd' eiyl')*
In Old England, a wedding feast where the bride prepared a special batch of her finest ale for friends and attendants who contributed money according to their purse. The tradition dates back to the Middle Ages, and the words *bridal* and *bridale* were derived from it.

bright. *(brayt)*
Effervescent. **Syn:** brilliant.

bright tank. *(brayt' taengk)*
A tank used to carbonate beer.

brilliance. *(bril'-yuhn[t]s)*
An expression of the quality of beer in terms of clearness, limpidity, brightness, and sparkle. To retain its brilliance a beer must have good biological and colloidal stability. Sometimes called: purity; brilliancy.

brilliancy. *(bril-yuhn-see)*
Synonym for brilliance.

brilliant. *(bril'-yuhnt)*
Describes a beer showing good clarity, brightness, and sparkling qualities. **Syn:** bright.

brim. *(brim)*
The upper edge of a cup, bowl, or plate.

brine. *(brayn)*
An aqueous solution of calcium chloride or sodium chloride used in the brewing industry as a freezing medium in coolers and refrigerators. **Syn:** saltwater or salt-water.

British champagne. *(bri'-d:ish shaem-peiyn')*
A sobriquet for porter.

Brix. *(briks)*
A specific gravity scale based on the Balling scale but designed for use at 59 °F (15 °C).

broach, to. *(broch, too)*
To insert a tap in a cask for the purpose of drawing its contents.

broc. *(brohk*)*
An Old French capacity measure for liquids.

bromelain. *(bro'-muh-lin)*
An enzyme that breaks down protein. It is prepared by the precipitation of pineapple juice for use in the brewing industry as a chillproofing agent. Also spelled: bromelin.

bromelin. *(bro'-muh-lin)*
Orthographic variant of bromelain.

brother bung. *(bruh'-dher buhng')*
British slang for a brewer or a drinking partner.

brown ale. *(brawn' eiyl')*
In Britain, a dark-colored top-fermented beer considered by many as the bottled equivalent of mild ale, although it is somewhat sweeter and fuller bodied. Brown ales are lightly hopped and are flavored and colored with roasted and caramel malts. They are brewed with soft water from original wort gravities ranging from 1.035–1.050, resulting in an alcohol content of about 3.5 percent or more. Sometimes called: bottled mild.

brown beer. *(brawn' beeyr')*
A general name for dark-hued, slightly coppery beers. **See also:** brown ale; brune d'Aarschot.

Brown Betty. *(brawn' beh'-d:ee)*
In Old England, a hot or warm drink made of brandy and ale served with spiced toasts.

brown cow. *(brawn' kaw')*
British slang for a cask of ale.

Brown Velvet. *(brawn' vehl'-vit)*
A mix of equal parts of stout and port.

brown water. *(brawn' wa'-d:er)*
Australian slang for beer.

Bruheater. *(broo'-hee-d:er)*
Trade name for a multipurpose wort boiler, masher, and sparger thermostatically controlled by a rheostat. Invented in England, it has a 6-gallon capacity and is designed for a single infusion mash at 160 °F (71 °C).

brumalis canna. *(broo-ma'-lees ka'-nuh)*
A foamy aromatic beer made from ginger and fruit in medieval France.

brumalt. *(broo'-mohlt*)*
A very dark, sugar-rich malt prepared in Europe from highly steeped, eight-day malt placed under a cover in layers of 20 centimeters for twenty-four hours, causing the temperature to rise sharply to about 122 °F (50 °C) where it levels

briefly and then drops sharply when the oxygen under the cover is consumed and carbon dioxide starts to accumulate. This is followed by kilning at temperatures of no more than 212 °F (100 °C).

brune d'Aarschot. *(bghuen'-[e] dagh-sho')*
A brown beer once brewed in Belgium from a mix of 60 percent malt and 40 percent wheat, flavored with old hops and fermented in large, 230-liter vats called *poensels*.

brush, to. *(bruhsh, too)*
To mechanically clean the surface of barley grains by means of a brush.

brutolé. *(bghue-toh-lei'*)*
A medicinal beer once brewed by dissolving medicinal or curative herbs and spices into beer. For example, an Egyptian prescription dated 1600 BC recommends mixing half an onion with beer foam to guard against death.

bubbler. *(buh'-bler)*
Synonym for fermentation lock, so named because of the bubbles of carbon dioxide gas that rise in the water-filled lock.

budding. *(buh'-d:ing)*
The most common form of yeast cell reproduction. The cell increases in size, forming a rounded outgrowth that eventually separates into a daughter cell.

BU:GU ratio. *(bee yoo jee yoo rey'-shee-o)*
The ratio of bitterness units to gravity units for a specific beer or group of beers. International bitterness units (IBU) are used for bitterness, and gravity units (GU) are used for the gravity component. For most beers and beer styles the resulting ratio has a value between 0.3 and 1.

buffer. *(buh'-fer)*
A substance capable of resisting changes in the pH of a solution.

buire. *(bweegh')*
An Old French drinking vessel similar in shape to a flagon.

Bullion. *(bul'-yen)*
A variety of very bitter hops grown in England and in Washington and Oregon in the United States, containing 8.5–11 percent alpha acids and 4.5–5.5 percent beta acids.

bung, to. *(buhng, too)*

To plug the bung hole of a cask hermetically, thus preventing carbon dioxide gas from escaping and allowing the beer to saturate naturally. A safety valve is sometimes used for this purpose to ensure a maximum pressure of 300 grams per square centimeter.

bung. *(buhng')*

1. A sealing stopper, usually a cylindro-conical piece of wood, fitted into the mouth of a cask. A safety valve is sometimes used during secondary fermentation to maintain pressure at a maximum of 300 grams per square centimeter. **See also:** spile. **2.** In homebrewing, the rubber or plastic seal into which the fermentation lock is fitted for secondary fermentation in carboys. **3.** British slang for a publican. **Syn:** bung hole.

bung hole. *(buhng' hol)*

The round hole in the bilge of a cask used for filling. **Syn:** bung.

bunging. *(buhng'-ing)*

Sealing a cask with a bung.

bunging apparatus. *(buhng'-ing ae-puh-rae'-d:uhs)*

A safety valve fitted on a storage cask.

bung juice. *(buhng' joos')*

British slang for beer.

bung stave. *(buhng' steiv)*

Synonym for cant.

burnt sugar. *(bernt shu'-ger)*

Synonym for caramel.

burou. *(bee-roo')*

Japanese for beer.

Burton ale. *(ber'-ten eiyl')*

1. A pale or bitter ale made from gypsum-rich water in the town of Burton-on-Trent in England where beer has been brewed since 1004 and where William Bass opened his first brewery in 1776. **2.** A beer similar in style and taste to those brewed in Burton-on-Trent.

burtonization. *(ber-te-nay-zey'-shen)*
The addition of mineral salts to water such as calcium or magnesium sulfate and sodium or calcium chloride.

Burton soda. *(ber'-ten so'-duh)*
A cocktail mix of equal parts of ale and ginger beer.

Burton Union System. *(ber'-ten yoo'-nyuhn sis'-tem)*
A system of twenty-four interconnecting 153-gallon (7-hectoliter) oak casks arranged in two parallel rows in which a yeasty circulatory fermentation takes place. Each cask is fitted with an internal tubular attemperator (heating and cooling tubes) and an external swan-neck pipe at the top. The pipes are connected to a long inclined trough leading to a feeder vessel. During active fermentation, fobbing causes yeast and beer to rise up the pipes and fall into the trough. The yeast tends to sediment, and the beer collected in the feeder is returned to the casks through side rods. After thirty-six hours of fermentation, the wort is transferred to "unions" (4-barrel capacity) where it clarifies for five days. The yeast and barm ale works out through the neck, purges itself into a barm back (or yeast trough), and is brought back automatically into the fermenters. This traditional system, unique to Burton-on-Trent, is called "the quiet process." It was shut down by Bass in 1981 and is now used only in the Marston brewery.

Burton water. *(ber'-ten wa'-d:er)*
Hard water from the famous brewing town of Burton-on-Trent in England. An analysis published in an encyclopedia by Lamirault in 1880 (*Inventaire Raisonné des Sciences, des Lettres et des Arts*) gave the following composition in grams per liter: 0.143 carbonate of lime, 0.791 lime sulfate, 0.013 magnesium sulfate, and 0.188 calcium chloride. **See also:** brewing water.

bush house. *(bush' haws)*
Historically, a temporary ale house for making beer on the spot such as at a county fair. Etym: So named because a bush was placed in front of it to mark its location. Also spelled: bushhouse. **Syn:** ale house.

buska. *(boos'-kuh*)*
The name given by early Germans, the Goths, to beer.

butt. *(buht)*
A large cask of varying capacity for holding beer, water, or wine. In Britain, a butt for beer contains 2 hogsheads, or 108 imperial gallons (490.86 liters).

buttenmann. *(bu'-ten-man)*
Synonym for tanzeman.

buttered ale. *(buh'-d:erd eiyl')*
In Old England, an unhopped beverage consisting of sugar, cinnamon, butter, and ale.

butterfly valve. *(buh'-d:er-flay vaelv)*
Lever-operated valve often found on large commercial brewing vessels.

buttery. *(buh'-d:uh-ree)*
Displaying a taste of butter or butterscotch, which is caused by the presence of diacetyl.

button handle. *(buh'-d:en haen'-del)*
Button- or knob-shaped handle.

butyl acetate. *(byu'-d:el ae'-suh-d:eit)*
Formula: $CH_3COOC_4H_9$. A butylic ester derived from acetic acid, responsible for fruity odors in beer.

Cc

C.

Abbreviation for centigrade (C).

cabbagelike. *(kae'-bij-layk)*

Aroma and taste of cooked vegetables; often a result of spoilage bacteria in the wort killed by alcohol later in fermentation.

Calandra granaria. *(ka-lan'-druh gruh-na'-ree-uh)*

The scientific name of the grain weevil.

calcium bicarbonate. *(kael'-see-uhm bay-kar'-buh-neyt)*

The principle substance causing temporary hardness in our water supplies. A substantial quantity can be precipitated by boiling the water for a short period and then racking off the sediment after allowing it to cool.

calcium chloride. *(kael'-see-uhm kloh'-rayd)*

Formula: $CaCl_2$. A powder, soluble in water and ethanol, used for the treatment of water to make it hard.

calcium disodium EDTA. *(kael'-see-uhm day-so'-dee-uhm [eh'-thuh-leen-day'-uh-meen-teh-truh-ae'-suh-d:eit])*

A foam-stabilizing additive used in commercial beers at a rate of about 10 parts per million (0.0010 percent). EDTA stands for ethylenediaminetetraacetate.

calcium sulfate. *(kael'-see-uhm suhl'-feit)*

Formula: $CaSO_4$. The technical name for gypsum, a mineral salt that imparts hardness to soft water.

Calichal. *(ka-lee-chal'*)*
A drink prepared in Mexico by mixing 1 part beer and 4 parts pulque.

calorie. *(kal'-uh-ree)*
The unit of heat equal to the amount of heat required to raise the temperature of 1 kilogram of water by 1 °C at atmospheric pressure. Also called: kilocalorie (kcal).

cambier. *(ka~-byei')*
The name given in medieval times to a brewer in the north of France.

Campden tablet. *(kaemp'-den taeb'-lit)*
A commercial name for potassium metabisulfite, a source of sulfur dioxide used to prevent oxidation and growth of wild yeasts and bacteria in beer.

Campaign for Real Ale. *(kaem-payn' fohr reeyl' eiyl')*
In Britain, a campaign launched originally by four concerned beer drinkers for the protection and return of nonpasteurized cask-conditioned "real ale." It was originally called Society for the Preservation of Beers from the Wood, later known as the Campaign for the Revitalization of Ale, and in 1973 the present name was adopted. Similar consumer campaigns were launched in the Netherlands such as PINT (Promotion Information Traditional Beer) and Campaign for Better Beer in the United States. Abbrev: CAMRA.

Campaign for Better Beer. *(kaem-payn' fohr beh'-d:er beeyr')*
A campaign launched by the American Homebrewers Association and modeled after the British CAMRA.

CAMRA.
Abbreviation for Campaign for Real Ale.

candi sugar. *(kaen'-dee shu'-ger)*
Sugar traditionally used in certain Belgian beer styles. Available in light, amber, and dark varieties.

cane sugar. *(kein' shu'-ger)*
Sucrose obtained from sugarcane.

canette. *(ka-neht'-[e])*
1. A German and Swiss drinking mug of tall, conical, or cylindrical form popular in the sixteenth century. **2.** An Old French measure for liquids, principally beer.

can. *(kaen)*
   1. A drinking vessel shaped like a mug but standing on a molded base and having a single- or double-scroll handle. **2.** A liquid capacity measure holding 1 pint. Also spelled: cann.

canned beer. *(kaend' beeyr')*
   Beer sold in cans. An enameled can suitable for packaging beer was first introduced by the American Can Company in 1934–1935, which tested it with the Gottfried Krueger Brewing Company in Richmond, Virginia. It met with immediate success, and Pabst and Schlitz came out with canned beer the following year.

canning. *(kae'-ning)*
   Transferring fermented beer from the maturation vat to sterilized beer cans.

Canstatter Wasen. *(kan-shta'-tegh va'-zen)*
   An autumn fair held annually in the riverside district of Cannstatt in Stuttgart (Germany). The fair was started in 1818 by the king of Württemberg originally as an agricultural show but it is now the prime rival of the Oktoberfest.

cant. *(kaent)*
   The piece of wood, at the head of a cask, in which a tap hole is pierced. **Syn:** bung stave.

cap. *(kaep)*
   Short for bottle cap or crown cap.

capper. *(kae'-per)*
   1. A general name for instruments used for capping (sealing) beer bottles, usually with crown seals. **Syn:** bottle capper. **2.** Often refers to a hand tool used with a hammer as opposed to a two-handled capper or hand-lever capper. **See also:** hammer capper.

capping. *(kae'-ping)*
   Synonym for capsuling.

capping machine. *(kae'-ping muh-sheen')*
   An automated machine for capping bottles by pressing and closing crown stoppers around the mouth of the bottles.

capsicumel. *(kaep-si'-kyoo-mehl)*
Mead made with chili pepper.

capsule. *(kaep'-s[y]ool)*
A metallic object of various shapes used to close bottles. **Syn:** seal.

capsuling. *(kaep'-s[y]oo-ling)*
The action of closing a bottle with a capsule. **Syn:** capping.

Carafa chocolate malt. *(kuh-ra'-fuh chak'-luht mohlt')*
Similar to chocolate malt but darker in color. Also called: German Carafa.

caramel. *(kae'-ruh-mel)*
An amorphous brown mass formed by heating saccharose or dextrose with an acid or alkali. It is used for flavoring and coloring beer. **Syn:** burnt sugar.

caramelization. *(kaer-muh-lay-zey'-shen)*
The heat-induced browning of sugars, different from the Maillard reactions in malt kilning.

caramelized malt. *(kaer'-muh-layzd mohlt')*
Synonym for caramel malt.

caramel malt. *(kae'-ruh-mel mohlt')*
Malt prepared from fully modified sugar-rich barley that is lightly steeped, kiln dried, re-steeped, and heat dried again at temperatures of 150–170 °F (65.5–76.7 °C) for one to two hours, thus converting the soluble starches within the grain into sugar as in mashing. The temperature is then increased to about 250 °F (120 °C) with frequent checks for color. Caramel malt is available in pale (CaraPils) to dark (as high as 160 °L) colors and is used in small amounts (12–15 percent) to impart sweetness, aroma, and a coppery color to beer. **Syn:** caramelized malt; crystal malt. **See also:** pale crystal malt.

CaraMunich malt. *(kae-ruh-myoo'-nik mohlt')*
Crystal malt that produces a subtle toasted flavor and some residual caramel sweetness in beers. Darker and more robust than CaraVienna malt. Also called: Belgian CaraMunich.

CaraPils. *(kae'-ruh-pilz)*
The name given in Europe to pale crystal malt.

carastan malt. *(kae'-ruh-staen mohlt')*
Similar to dextrin malt, it adds body to a beer without imparting residual sweetness. Also called: British carastan.

CaraVienna malt. *(kae-ruh-vee-[y]eh'-nuh mohlt')*
Similar to CaraMunich malt but lighter in color and less intensely flavored. Also called: Belgian CaraVienna.

carbohydrate. *(kar-bo-hay'-dreit)*
Any of a group of compounds composed of carbon, hydrogen, and oxygen (with two atoms of hydrogen for every one atom of oxygen) including sugars, starches, and celluloses.

carbonate, to. *(kar'-buh-neit, too)*
To inject or dissolve carbon dioxide gas in a liquid such as beer. **Syn:** to saturate. **See also:** carbonation.

carbonated. *(kar'-buh-nei'-d:id)*
A beer in which carbon dioxide has been injected artificially.

carbonates. *(kar'-buh-neyts)*
Alkaline salts whose anions are derived from carbonic acid.

carbonation. *(kar'-buh-nei'-shen)*
The process of injecting or dissolving carbon dioxide gas in a liquid to create an effervescence of pleasant taste and texture. In beermaking, one of three methods is used: (1) injecting the finished beer with the carbon dioxide collected for this purpose during primary fermentation; (2) kraeusening, or adding young fermenting beer to finished beer to induce a renewed fermentation; or (3) especially in homebrewing, priming (adding sugar) to fermented wort prior to bottling or to each bottle prior to capping to create a secondary fermentation within the bottle. Fermentation in a sealed bottle or container creates carbon dioxide gas that dissolves in the beer. The adjective *carbonated* usually refers to beers artificially injected with carbon dioxide; when caused by priming, the expression "bottle-conditioned" is more common. Beers intended to be consumed at low temperatures are usually highly carbonated to compensate for the low temperature, and vice versa for beers to be drunk at high temperatures. Bottled beer is always carbonated; U.S. draft beers are usually carbonated, and British draft ales are for the most part cask-conditioned. **Syn:** saturation. **See also:** conditioning.

carbonator. *(kar-buh-nei'-ter)*
An apparatus used in the carbonated beverage industry for introducing carbon dioxide gas into water or sugared water. The efficiency of this apparatus is measured by comparing the quantity of carbon dioxide injected into a liquid to the amount absorbed by that liquid; this ratio should be as close as possible to 95 percent. **Syn:** saturator. **See also:** regulator-carbonator.

carbon dioxide. *(kar'-ben day-ak'-seid)*
Formula: CO_2. An inert gas responsible for the effervescence in beer. **See also:** carbonation; fermentation.

carbonic acid. *(kar-ba'-nik ae'-sid)*
1. Formula: H_2CO_3. A weak and unstable acidic compound formed by the combination of carbon dioxide gas and water. It reacts with bases to form salts called carbonates and bicarbonates, and with alcohols and other compounds to form esters such as diethyl carbonate. **2.** In brewing literature this term is often synonymous with carbon dioxide.

carbonyls. *(kar'-buh-nilz)*
A generic name for a group of volatiles that contribute to the flavor of beer. A carbonyl is a radical made up of one atom of carbon and one atom of oxygen, connected by a double bond. In beer, the important carbonyls are aldehydes, ketones, and oxidation products. These volatiles form by reactions during malting, mashing, fermentation, and aging. Boiling results in a decrease of some volatiles whereas fermentation increases the concentration of some and decreases that of others.

carboy. *(kar'-boy)*
A large, narrow-necked glass, plastic, or earthenware bottle sometimes encased in wicker or in a plastic or wood frame. Glass carboys, such as those used in homebrewing for secondary or single-stage (blowby) fermentation, should never be filled with hot wort (210 °F, 98 °C) because they cannot withstand thermal shock.

cardamom seed. *(kar'-duh-muhm seed)*
An herb with a spicy cola flavor used in some Belgian beers.

carmi. *(kar-mee*)*
In ancient Egypt, diluted *zythum*. **See also:** zythum.

Carnaval de Binche. *(kagh-ne-val' de bae~sh')*
A beer festival held annually in Binche, Belgium, on Shrove Sunday, Monday, and Tuesday. The carnival dates back to the fourteenth century; gallons of beer are tapped, oranges are thrown, and dancing is allowed in the streets.

carrageen. *(kae'-ruh-geen)*
Synonym for Irish moss. Also spelled: carragheen.

carte. *(kaght')*
Orthographic variant of *quarte*.

caryophylline. *(kae-ree-[y]o-fi'-leen)*
A secondary component of hop oil found in varying proportions in different varieties of hops.

Cascade. *(kaes-keid')*
A variety of hops grown in the Pacific Northwest and containing 5–6.5 percent alpha acids and 5–6 percent beta acids.

cask. *(kaesk)*
A barrel-shaped container for holding beer. It was originally made of iron-hooped wooden staves but is now commonly found in stainless steel and aluminum. In England, casks are made in seven sizes: butt (108 gallons, 491 liters), puncheon (72 gallons, 327.3 liters), hogshead (54 gallons, 246 liters), barrel (36 gallons, 164 liters), kilderkin (18 gallons, 84 liters), firkin (9 gallons, 42 liters), and pin (4.5 gallons, 21 liters). **Syn:** barrel.

casked ale. *(kaeskt' eiyl')*
See: real ale.

casked-conditioned. *(kaeskt' kuhn-di'-shind)*
In Britain, ale conditioned in the cask as is real ale. Casks of ale are delivered to the pubs where they spend two to three days in cool cellars at a temperature of about 56 °F (13 °C) while conditioning is completed. **See also:** cellar; cellarman.

casking. (kaes'-king)
The action of racking beer into casks.

cask washer. *(kaesk wa'-sher)*
A machine for washing casks at the brewery.

cask wood. *(kaesk wud')*
Boards of wood, usually oak, used for making casks. Also spelled: caskwood. **Syn:** stavewood.

cassava beer. *(kuh-sa'-vuh beeyr')*
Synonym for manioc beer.

cassis. *(ka-see')*
A fruit derivative of *lambic* made by macerating black currants in a blend of young lambics.

cast. *(kaest)*
As in "the wort is cast from the kettle"; this is the running off of the wort after processing.

casting. *(kae'-sting)*
The act of emptying a vessel.

cast-out wort. *(kaest-awt wuhrt')*
Hot wort that has been cast out from the brew kettle after the boiling process has been completed.

catalyst. *(kae'-d:uh-list)*
Any substance that speeds up a chemical reaction, such as in the conversion of starch into sugar, without being changed itself in the process. Enzymes, for example, are natural, organic catalysts.

cation. *(kaet'-ay-en)*
A positively charged ion.

caudle. *(koh'-del)*
A sort of fortifying soup consisting of wine or ale, eggs, bread, sugar, and spices and formerly given to the sick.

celia. *(seel'-yuh)*
Synonym for *prima melior.*

cellar. *(seh'-ler)*

1. Originally, an underground room for storing beer. Now, any thermostatically controlled room, above or below ground, for storing beer. **2.** In English pubs, the cool cellar (55–65 °F, 12.8–18.3 °C) where casked ale undergoes further conditioning and maturation before being sold.

cellarage. *(seh'-le-rij)*

Storing beer in cool cellars or refrigerated rooms after fermentation for conditioning and maturation. By extension, any treatment applied to beer during storage such as fining, racking, filtration, polishing, bottling, or blending.

cellarman. *(seh'-ler-men)*

1. At the brewery, the person responsible for the care of beer while it is in the storage room or cellar. **2.** In English pubs, the person who receives, stacks, and prepares the casks of freshly brewed beer for consumption.

cellulase. *(sehl'-yuh-lais)*

An enzyme contained in barley that contributes to the dissolution of the cellulosic protective layer of the granule and allows fermentation to proceed. **Syn:** cytase.

cellulose. *(sehl'-yuh-los)*

Formula: $(C_6H_{10}O_5)_n$. A polysaccharide that forms the structural cell walls of living plants including barley and yeast.

Centennial. *(sehn-tehn'-[ee]-yel)*

A variety of hops cultivated in the United States containing 9.5–11.5 percent alpha acids.

centigrade. *(sehn'-tuh-grayd)*

Thermometer scale in which the freezing point of water is 0°, the boiling point 100°, and the interval in between is divided into 100 degrees. Abbrev: C. To convert degrees centigrade to degrees Fahrenheit and vice versa:

$$°C = (°F - 32) \times 5/9 \text{ or } (°F - 32) / 1.8$$
$$°F = (°C \times 9/5) + 32 \text{ or } (°C \times 1.8) + 32$$

centiliter. *(sehn'-tuh-lee-d:er)*

One-hundredth of a liter. Abbrev: cl.

centrifugation. *(sehn-tri-fyuh-gei'-shen)*
A clarification method using centrifugal force. In brewing, such a force is used to strain and clarify the wort during its cooling stage and the finished beer prior to racking. Essentially, beer is whirlpooled in such a way that suspended solids can be removed.

centrifuge. *(sehn'-tri-fyooj)*
1. An apparatus generating centrifugal force. **2.** A filter using centrifugal force to remove suspended matter.

cereal. *(si'-ree-el)*
Any edible grain of the grass family (Gramineae). Includes barley, wheat, oats, maize, millet, rice, rye, and sorghum.

cereal adjunct. *(si'-ree-el ae'-juhngkt)*
Synonym for adjunct.

cereal cooker. *(si'-ree-el ku'-ker)*
A vessel in which cereal adjuncts (wheat, rye, oats, rice, and maize) are boiled prior to being added to the mash.

cerevisia. *(sei-rei-vee'-see-uh)*
The Latin name for a strong beery drink mentioned by Pliny the Elder (AD 23–79) in his *Natural History* as the national beverage of the Gauls. The Gallic spelling, *cere visia*, was apparently adapted from Ceres, the goddess of harvest, or *cere* meaning grain and *vise* meaning strength. In 400 BC the Gauls are said to have prepared *cerevisia* by boiling barley in a caldron and adding rye, millet, buckwheat, oats, or maize, according to what was available. The brew was said to be flavored with herbs and spices such as cumin, coriander, absinth, cinnamon, cockle, or even hops, although this has not been clearly established. After primary fermentation the beer was stored in wooden casks (which they invented) until ready to drink. The alcohol content of this beverage is said to have been much higher than that of present-day beer. Julius Caesar prefered cerevisia to wine. The spelling later evolved into *cervesia, cervisia, cerudise, cervoise* (French), *cerveza* (Spanish), *cerveja* (Portuguese), and *cervogia* (Italian) and formed such words as *Saccharomyces cerevisiae*. **See also:** *cervesia humulina*.

cerevisaphile. *(sei-rei-vee'-suh-fiyl)*
Beer enthusiast, lover, or fan.

cervesariis feliciter. *(sehr-vei-sa'-ree-ees fei-lee'-cee-tehr)*
An inscription on a clay goblet dating back to the Roman wars. Translated into modern English it would read: "Long live the beermakers."

cervesia humulina. *(sehr-vei'-see-uh hyoo-myuh-lee'-nuh)*
A hopped-flavored *cervesia* mentioned in the charter of the Abbey of St. Denis dating back to AD 768.

cerveza. *(sehr-vei'-sa)*
Spanish for beer.

cervisia mellita. *(sehr-vee'-see-uh meh-lee'-tuh)*
1. The Latin name for mead, not to be confused with *cerevisia*. **2.** A type of honey-sweetened beer.

cervoise. *(sehgh-vwaz')*
An early French name given to nonhopped beer, the equivalent of ale in Old England. In the fourteenth and fifteenth centuries, when hops were introduced, a distinction was made between *cervoise*, a nonhopped beer, and *bière*, which contained hops.

cervoise de miel. *(sehgh-vwaz' de myehl')*
The French name for *cervisia mellita*.

chafer house. *(chei'-fer haws)*
In Old England, an ale house. Etym: Probably from chefer, a saucepan.

chalk. *(chak)*
A common name for calcium carbonate, an alkaline salt sometimes used for brewing dark beers.

Challanger. *(chae'-len-jer)*
A variety of hops cultivated in the United Kingdom and containing 6.5–8.5 percent alpha acids.

champagne du nord. *(shaem-pa'-nye due nohgh)*
A sobriquet given by Napoleon's occupying troops to German wheat beer, especially Berliner *weisse*.

champagne mead. *(shaem-peiyn' meed)*
A misnomer for sparkling mead.

champagne of the spree. *(shaem-peiyn' uhv dhuh spree'*)*
A fancy name for Berliner *weisse*.

Chancelor ale. *(chaen[t]s'-ler eiyl')*
A strong ale once brewed at Queen's College, Oxford, on special occasions.

chang. *(chaeng*)*
A beer brewed from barley in Nepal and Tibet, and it was consumed in ceremonial vessels.

chaser. *(chei'-ser)*
A long mild drink, such as beer, taken immediately after a short strong one to soften its effect.

chateau collapse-o. *(sha-to' coh-laep'-so)*
British slang for old ale.

cheesy. *(chee'-zee)*
Possessing a smell or taste of cheese caused by the presence of isovaleric acid, which is produced through the oxidation of isoamyl alcohol.

chemical pathway. *(keh'-mi-kuhl paeth'-wei)*
A sequence of chemical reactions, each of which is catalyzed by an enzyme not supplied by microorganisms. (Examples: those that naturally occur in malting and mashing.)

cherry beer. *(cheh'-ree beeyr')*
See: *kriek.*

chevalier. *(she-va-lyei')*
In France, a beer glass with a capacity of 2.5 liters.

Chevalier barley. *(sheh-vuh-leeyr' bar'-lee*)*
Synonym for two-rowed barley. Etym: Named after the English botanist, the Reverend J. B. Chevallier, who first selected that variety at Debenham, Suffolk, in 1820. Also spelled: Chevallier barley.

chi. *(chee*)*

A beer brewed from millet by the Lepchas of India.

chicha. *(chee'-cha)*

The name given to *aca*, the maize beer of the Incas, by the Spanish Conquistadores. The term was borrowed from the Taino language, spoken by ancient Hispaniola tribes of Costa Rica, Panama, and Colombia, who drank large quantities of this beer. *Chicha* was made by fermenting maize with or without the addition of fruit juices. In the nineteenth century chicha was produced commercially. *Chicha flor,* the best quality, was followed by *chicha de segunda,* the common man's drink, prepared by mixing chicha flor with *mitaca* (sediments of chicha flor well diluted with water and honey). A third, very poor variety, called *runchera,* was given to hard laborers and was made by adding more water and honey to chicha de segunda. Also spelled: *chichia.* See also: aca; *sora.*

chiew. *(cheew*)*

Orthographic variant of *chiu.*

chill haze. *(chil' heiz')*

Haziness caused by a combination and precipitation of protein matter and tannin molecules during the secondary process of fermentation. It becomes visible when beer is refrigerated too fast, too cold, or too long, and soon disappears once the beer warms up. It appears around 32 °F (0 °C) and disappears around 68 °F (20 °C). It should not be confused with condensation, which is a film of water forming on the exterior of the glass when the glass and the beer are cold and the ambient air is warm and moist. In homebrewing, proteins can be removed by the addition of Polyclar, and tannins can be removed with silica gel. **Syn:** haze. **See also:** chillproofing; colloidal stability.

chilling. *(chil'-ing)*

The action of cooling the wort after boiling to cause nitrogenous matter to flocculate and precipitate.

chillproof(ed) beer. *(chil'-prooft' beeyr')*

A beer treated by one or many chemical substances, usually protein-digesting enzymes, to enable it to withstand low temperatures without clouding. Also called: nondeposit beer.

chillproofing. *(chil'-proo'-fing)*

A treatment applied to finished beer to prevent the formation of chill haze when the beer is chilled. Substances are added to provoke one of three reactions:

precipitation (as with tannic acid), adsorption (as with bentonite), or hydrolysis (as with proteolytic enzymes). In homebrewing, chillproofing is achieved by adding Polyclar and/or silica gel during the second stage of the fermentation process.

Chinook. *(shi-nuk')*
A variety of hops cultivated in the United States containing 11–13 percent alpha acids.

chips. *(chips)*
Synonym for clarifying chips.

chit, to. *(chit, too)*
To sprout.

chit. *(chit)*
The white coleorhiza (or root sheath), which breaks through the pericarp and testa and protrudes from the base of the barley corn during steeping. These chits constitute the first indication of germination after casting. **See also:** rootlets.

chitting. *(chi'-d:ing)*
The appearance of root sheaths (or rootlets) at the base of the barley corn during steeping.

chiu. *(cheew*)*
A type of wheat beer made in China during the Han dynasty (200 BC) and later. *Chiu* eventually became the predominant beer style of China and it is presently a generic word for beer. Also spelled: *chiew; kiu.* **See also:** *p'ei; shu; t'ien tsiou.*

chlorine. *(klo'-reen)*
Symbol: Cl. An element used in both commercial and homebrewing in its pure form or as household Javel water as a disinfecting and sanitizing agent. To avoid killing the yeast cells and producing chlorophenols, chlorine-treated equipment must be thoroughly rinsed.

chlorophenolic. *(klo-re-fee-no'-lik)*
Tasting of chlorophenols. Caused by chemical combination of chlorine and organics. Detectable in parts per billion. Aroma is unique, but similar to plasticlike phenolic.

chlorophenols. *(klo-re-fee'-nohlz)*
Strong and unpleasant-tasting chemical compounds formed by the combination of chlorine with a phenolic compound. Some are carcinogenic.

chocks. *(chaks)*
Wooden wedges that are used to prevent beer casks from moving. Also called: scotches.

chocolate malt. *(chak'-luht mohlt')*
Similar to black malt but roasted to a lesser, chocolate-brown color.
Syn: black malt.

Chondrus crispus. *(kan'-druhs kris'-puhs)*
The scientific name for Irish moss, a red seaweed used for clarifying the wort.

Christmas ale. *(kris'-muhs eiyl')*
A special beer brewed in certain countries for yuletide consumption, usually amber colored or dark hued, full-bodied, creamy, and high in alcohol. Examples include: Aass Jule in Norway, Noche Buena in Mexico, and Our Special Ale in San Francisco.

chung. *(chuhng*)*
A Tibetan beer made from *grim,* a type of native barley.

cidery. *(sei'-duh-ree)*
Having an undesirable taste and smell reminiscent of cider, usually due to elevated levels of acetaldehyde.

cistern. *(sis'-tern)*
In traditional malting, the vessel in which barley is steeped in water.

citric. *(si'-trik)*
Possessing a taste or smell reminiscent of citrus fruits—lemon, lime, orange, or grapefruit.

citric acid. *(si'-trik ae'-sid)*
Formula: $C_6H_8O_7H_2O$. An organic tricarboxylic acid (containing three carboxyl groups: COOC) occurring in plants, especially citrus fruits, produced through a complex series of enzymatic reactions known as the Krebs cycle or citric acid cycle.

citric acid cycle. *(si'-trik ae'-sid say'-kel)*
A complex series of enzymatic transformations of elementary sugars (glucose and fructose) that are broken down to acetate (active acetate or acetyl coenzyme A) and the degradation of acetyl that results in the transformation of a molecule of citric acid into oxaloacetate. **Syn:** Krebs cycle; tricarboxylic acid circle; TCA cycle.

cl.
Abbreviation for centiliter.

clarification. *(klae'-ruh-fi-kei'-shen)*
The process of removing suspended particles from the cloudy wort or the finished beer through mechanical (filtration, centrifugation) or chemical means (by adding proteolytic or pectolytic enzymes or fining agents).

clarifier. *(klae'-ruh-fay-er)*
A long and shallow panlike fermentation vessel used in the brewing of certain styles, such as steam beer.

clarifying chips. *(klae'-ruh-fay-ing chips')*
Thin chips of wood cut so as to present maximum surface with minimum volume or weight and used to assist clarification during secondary fermentation. **Syn:** chips; wood chips; wood strips.

clarifying tub. *(klae'-ruh-fay-ing tuhb)*
A large, cylindrical, dome-covered vessel fitted with a false bottom to retain spent grains while allowing the wort to flow. **See also:** decoction mashing.

Clark degree. *(klark' di-gree')*
A unit of water hardness equal to 1 part calcium carbonate ($CaCO_3$) to 70,000 parts water; equivalent to 1 grain (0.0648 gram) of $CaCO_3$ per imperial gallon of water (10 pounds of water at 62 °F, or 4.54 kilograms at 17 °C). In England, water is said to be soft when its hardness is less than 5 °Clark (70 parts per million) and very hard when its hardness is greater than 15 °Clark (210 parts per million). Etym: Named after T. Clark (1801–1867), who devised a hardness test for water in 1840. **Syn:** English degree.

$$1 \text{ °Clark} = 14.3 \text{ ppm}$$
$$= 0.833 \text{ gr per U.S. gal}$$
$$= 143 \text{ mg/l calcium ion}$$

= 0.7 millival

= 0.8 German degree

clean. *(kleen)*
Devoid of off-flavors.

closed fermentation. *(klozd' fuhr-mehn-tei'-shen)*
A method of anaerobic fermentation (sometimes under pressure) in closed containers.

cloth filter. *(klath' fil'-ter)*
A type of filter consisting of cloth stretched between opposing frames.

cloudy. *(klaw'-dee)*
Characteristic of a beer showing turbidity caused by unsettled particulate matter. **Syn:** hazy.

clovelike. *(klov'-layk)*
Spicy character reminiscent of cloves; characteristic of some wheat beers or, if excessive, may be derived from wild yeast. Derived from the compound 4-vinyl-guaiacol.

Cluster. *(kluh'-ster)*
A variety of hops cultivated in the United States containing 5.5–8 percent alpha acids and 4.5–5.5 percent beta acids.

coarse sludge. *(kors' sluhj')*
Flocculation caused by coagulation of soluble and nonsoluble nitrogenous substances and constituting the first stage of the clarification process of the wort. **See also:** cooler tun.

cobra head faucet. *(ko'-bruh hehd fa'-sit)*
Picnic-style beverage dispenser with spring-pressured thumb lever.

cock ale. *(kak' eiyl')*
A seventeenth- and eighteenth-century concoction mentioned in American and British cookbooks such as Eliza Smith's *The Compleat Housewife* (1736). One recipe calls for the following ingredients: 10 imperial gallons (or 12 U.S. gallons) of ale, 1 large and elderly cock, raisins, mace, and cloves.

coeurier. *(koe-ghee-ei')*
   See: *bierkieser.*

co-humulone. *(ko-hyoo'-myuh-lon)*
   The second (or sometimes third) most prevalent of the three alpha acids, which, when isomerized during boiling of the wort, becomes iso-co-humulone, providing most of the bittering characteristic that comes from hops.

coirm. *(kwaerm*)*
   An early Irish name for beer.

cold break. *(kold' breik')*
   1. The precipitation of protein and tannin material to a fine coagulum during the cooling stage. It starts around 140 °F (60 °C) and increases as the temperature drops. **Syn:** cold trub. **2.** Haziness caused by protein matter that must be strained after the cooling process. **See also:** hot break.

cold conditioning. *(kold' kuhn-di'-shen-ing)*
   See: lagering.

cold lagering. *(kold' la'-ger-ing)*
   Synonym for lagering.

cold trub. *(kold' troob)*
   Synonym for cold break.

cold trub flotation. *(kold' troob flo-tey'-shen)*
   The process of removing cold trub from cooled wort by subjecting it to an excessive amount of air. Cold trub particles accumulate on the surface of the air bubbles as they rise from the bottom to the top of the flotation vessel, building a layer of foam at the surface of the wort. The wort is then drained from the bottom of the vessel, leaving behind the foam layer and, with it, the cold trub particles. The process may take place in pitched or unpitched wort.

coliform. *(ko'-li-fohrm)*
   Waterborne bacteria, often associated with pollution.

collar. *(ka'-ler)*
   The layer of foam on a glass of beer. **Syn:** head; cream; suds.

colloid. *(kuh'-loyd)*
A gelatinous substance dispersed throughout a solution.

colloidal stability. *(kuh-loy'-del stuh-bi'-luh-d:ee)*
The ability of a beer to resist turbidity or haziness when it is exposed to cold temperatures. The two main compounds responsible for colloidal stability are the protein fractions as well as the polyphenolic compounds. **See also:** EBC test.

colored beer. *(kuh'-lerd beeyr')*
Beer with a color of up to 3,000 SRM units (8,000 EBC units) that are added to wort or beer for color adjustment. It is made using a grist composition of roughly three-fifths pale malt and two-fifths color or black malt.

Columbus. *(coh-luhm'-bis)*
A variety of hops cultivated in the United States containing 14–16 percent alpha acids.

comb. *(kom)*
A utensil to skim away excess foam on a glass of beer.

Comet. *(ka'-mit)*
A variety of very bitter hops grown in Washington and containing 9.5–10.5 percent alpha acids.

compartment malting. *(kuhm-part'-ment mohl'-ting)*
Synonym for box malting.

condenser. *(kuhn-dehn[t]s'-er)*
In a cooling system, a heat-transfer device that reduces the thermostatic fluid (ammonia, freon 12, freon 22) from a vapor to a liquid state after being in contact with water.

condition, to. *(kuhn-di'-shen, too)*
To subject beer to conditioning.

condition. *(kuhn-di'-shen)*
The amount of carbon dioxide in a beer.

conditioning. *(kuhn-di'-shen-ing)*

Inducing a secondary fermentation in a closed container for the purpose of creating carbon dioxide gas, which dissolves in the beer. Conditioning can be achieved by kraeusening or priming. **See also:** carbonation. **Syn:** maturation; aging.

conditioning tank. *(kuhn-di'-shen-ing taengk)*

An airtight tank into which the brewer pumps carbon dioxide gas under high pressure.

congelation. *(kan-juh-lei'-shen)*

A method for producing stronger beers by freezing the water, which can then be removed. **See also:** *eisbock;* ice beer.

congener. *(ko'-juh-ner)*

Any of the natural products that form during the fermentation process, including furfurals and aldehydes, and which impart flavor and aroma to beer.

continuous fermentation. *(kuhn-ti'-nyoo-uhs fuhr-mehn-tei'-shen)*

A method of fermentation used commercially since 1957. Two methods are presently in use: (1) The stirred tank method consists of a cascade system of two or more interconnected stirred fermentation vessels. The yeast is separated by centrifugation and part of it is fed back into the first fermenter. In the first systems of this type the turnover for ale was sixteen hours whereas that for lagers was thirty hours. This method is used mostly in New Zealand and in a few breweries in Britain. (2) The tower method consists of a cylindrical tower 26 feet high into which wort is pumped through a plug of highly flocculent yeast. In newer methods, such as the bioreactor systems, fermentation is reduced to two hours. **See also:** batch fermentation.

contract beer. *(kan'-traekt beeyr')*

Beer made by one brewery and then marketed by another company. The latter hires the brewery to produce beer to its specifications.

conversion. *(kuhn-vuhr'-zhin)*

The enzymatic transformation of starches into various fermentable and unfermentable sugars during the mashing process.

cooler tun. *(kool'-er tuhn)*

A flat, open tun placed immediately after the hop strainer and into which the hot wort cools naturally and loses its coarse sludge. **Syn:** coolship.

cooling. *(kool'-ing)*
The process of lowering the temperature of the boiled wort prior to fermentation. In top fermentation, the wort is cooled down to 57.2–60.8 °F (14–16 °C) whereas in bottom fermentation it must reach 42.8 °F (6 °C).

coolship. *(kool'-ship)*
Synonym for cooler tun.

coombs. *(koomz*)*
Synonym for culms.

cooper. *(koo'-per)*
1. One who makes or repairs wooden barrels and casks. **2.** In England, a drink containing equal parts of porter and stout.

cooperage. *(koop'-[e]-rij)*
1. The craft of the cooper. **2.** The place where a cooper makes or repairs casks and barrels. **3.** A cooper's fee.

copper. *(ka'-per)*
Synonym for brew kettle.

copper finings. *(ka'-per fay'-ningz)*
A substance, usually Irish moss, added to the copper during the boil to aid the protein break and improve the stability of the finished beer.

copus. *(ko'-puhs)*
A drink once made of hot beer, wine, and spices.

coriander seed. *(koh-ree-[y]aen'-der seed)*
The aromatic dried fruit of the cilantro plant. A key component of the white beer style originating in Belgium.

corker. *(kohr'-ker)*
Any device used to insert a cork into a bottle neck.

corn. *(kohrn')*
1. In the United States, maize. Corn is often used as a malt adjunct and is cooked to a gelatinized form before being added to the mash. Corn contributes additional starch without adding any particular character or flavor to the beer.

Some U.S. brewers use up to 40 percent corn in their mash. **2.** In Britain, a generic term for certain cereals, especially wheat.

corn cutter. *(kohrn' kuh'-d:er)*
    An instrument used by the maltster to cut the barley corn in half and examine its interior. Approximately fifty grains from a harvest are cut to estimate the proportion of grains that have hard and glassy (steely) endosperms as compared to those having the more desirable opaque, mealy appearance. Glassy corns usually have a higher nitrogen content than mealy ones and do not malt as well. Mealy corns, however, take up moisture more rapidly than steely ones during steeping. **Syn:** farinator.

Cornelius keg. *(kor-neel'-[e]-yuhs kehg)*
    A 2.5–5 U.S. gallon (occasionally 10-gallon) stainless steel canister, usually with ball locks, favored by homebrewers as serving tanks and sometimes as fermenting vessels.

corn sugar. *(kohrn' shu'-ger)*
    Sugar converted from cornstarch and refined. **Syn:** glucose; dextrose.

couch. *(kawch)*
    In traditional floor malting, the layer of germinating barley spread on the malt floor after steeping and draining. The first couches are thick (23–76 centimeters), and after twenty-four hours or so, the barley is spread more thinly, either by hand or mechanically, to lower the temperature, which is then maintained at 59–77 °F (15–25 °C), depending on the nature of the malt being produced. In England, prior to 1880, the couch first rested on wooden frames because tax was levied on the volume of steeped grain. Once germination had started, the grain was spread on the malting floor. **See also:** floor malting; mat plow; matted couche; piece; pneumatic malting; radicle; turner.

couching. *(kawch'-ing)*
    1. In traditional floor malting, the action of spreading the steeped barley on the malting floor first in heaps and later, after ploughing, in layers of 10–15 centimeters where it germinates. **See also**: floor malting. **2.** In modern pneumatic malting, the procedure of levelling the piece in a compartment to allow the temperature to rise to a specific level, usually around 65–70 °F (18–21 °C).

counter pressure. *(kawn'-ter preh'-sher)*
    The pressure of air or carbonic gas applied to packaged beer to prevent the

escape of carbon dioxide gas from the solution, to maintain a constant pressure and guard against the negative effects of oxygen.

courni. *(koogh-nee'*)*
An alelike beverage made by the Britons and the Hiberni (or Irish) in the first century BC and mentioned in the works of Dioscorides.

cracking. *(krae'-king)*
The act of lightly crushing grain in order to expose the endosperm to the liquor during mashing.

craft beers. *(kraeft' beeryz')*
Generally, all-malt (or barley malt and wheat malt) beers. In the market, these more flavorful beers are distinguished from traditional U.S. and Canadian brands that tend to be lighter bodied, lighter flavored, and lighter colored due to the use of a high ratio of adjunct (usually corn or rice) as fermentable substitutes for barley malt.

Cranston Bill. *(kraen'-sten bil')*
See: homebrewing.

crate. *(kreit)*
A wood, plastic, or cardboard box for packing and transporting bottles or cans.

crater. *(krei'-d:er)*
A machine for putting newly filled bottles or cans of beer into crates.
Syn: recrating machine.

crawler. *(krohl'-er)*
In Britain, a person who visits every pub in a district and samples a drink in each and every establishment. This beer enthusiast's activity is known as the "pub crawl."

cream. *(kreem)*
The froth or foam on beer. **Syn:** head; collar; suds.

cream ale. *(kreem eiyl')*
A blend of top- and bottom-fermented beers, usually more of the second, resulting in a sweet and lightly hop-flavored drink.

creamy. *(kree'-mee)*
1. Describes a well-carbonated beer producing a thick, persistent head.
2. Describes a full-bodied beer possessing a rich, smooth texture.

crock. *(krak)*
Wide-mouthed ceramic fermenter used for open fermentation.

crop. *(krap)*
The yeasts that are skimmed off the surface of top-fermenting ale during primary fermentation. **Syn:** outcrop.

crown cap. *(krawn' kaep')*
Synonym for crown cork.

crown capped. *(krawn' kaept')*
Said of a bottle closed with a crown cork. **Syn:** crown closed; crown sealed.

crown closed. *(krawn' klozd')*
Synonym for crown capped.

crown cork. *(krawn' kohrk')*
A metal cap with a cork or plastic lining and a crown-shaped contour (skirt) that is crimped around the mouth of a bottle to form an airtight seal that retains carbon dioxide gas. The first crown stopper was invented in 1892 by William Painter, founder of the Crown Cork and Seal Company. In 1920 the cork lining was replaced by pressed cork and later by plastic. **Syn:** crown seal; crown cap; crown stopper.

crowner. *(krawn'-er)*
An automatic machine or hand tool for pressing crown corks on bottles. A pressure of approximately 250 kilograms per square centimeter is required to press the plastic lining and close the skirt.

crown seal. *(krawn' seeyl')*
Synonym for crown cork.

crown sealed. *(krawn' seeyld')*
Synonym for crown capped.

crown stopper. *(krawn' stap'-er)*
Synonym for crown cork.

crush. *(kruhsh)*

A procedure used to break grain into small pieces while maintaining the integrity of the barley husk.

crushing. *(kruhsh'-ing)*

An operation that mills the malt so as to reduce its interior to a powder form while leaving the husk intact.

Crystal. *(kris'-tel)*

A variety of hops cultivated in the United States containing 2–4.5 percent alpha acids.

crystal malt. *(kris'-tel mohlt')*

Synonym for caramel malt.

cubitainer. *(kyoo-bi-tei'-ner)*

1. A commercial name for a 1- or 5-gallon, cube-shaped, semi-rigid, plastic container used by homebrewers for secondary fermentation. **2.** In England, brewers supply take-home draft beer in cubitainers called polypins.

cuitje. *(koyt'-yeh*)*

A light beer brewed in Belgium in the fifteenth century. The *double cuitje*, a stronger brew, gave its name to the French expression *double cuite*, meaning splitting headache.

Cullen Act. *(kuhl'-en aekt')*

An amendment to the Volstead Act passed in March 1933 and effective on April 7, of the same year. It authorized the production and sale of beer not exceeding 3.2 percent alcohol by volume. **Syn:** Cullen-Harrison Act; Beer-Wine Revenue Act.

culm. *(kuhlm)*

Dusty or inferior anthracite coal; a poor fuel for kilning.

culms. *(kuhlmz)*

The name given to rootlets after they have been removed from germinated barley. **Syn:** rootlets. Also spelled: kaulms.

cummins. *(kuh'-minz*)*

Synonym for rootlets.

cyser. *(say'-zer*)*

1. A variety of melomel prepared by fermenting a must of honey, apple juice, and water. **2.** Honey-sweetened cider.

cytase. *(say'-teis)*

Synonym for cellulase.

cytolysis. *(say-ta'-luh-sis)*

The partial disintegration of the cell walls of germinating barley by enzymes. This process begins in the embryo and spreads progressively through the starchy endosperm toward the apex of the grain. Cytolysis reduces the barley's strength, rendering it friable and easy to mill. **See also:** modification.

DAB.
Abbreviation for Dortmunder Aktien Brauerei. **See also:** Dortmunder.

dagger ale. *(dae'-ger eiyl')*
An Old English expression for strong ale.

dalla. *(tuh-luh*)*
Orthographic variant for *talla*.

Damson hop aphid. *(daem'-zen hap' ae'-fid)*
An insect (*Phorodon humuli*) that infects the underside of hop leaves and growing points and eventually, if not destroyed, the cones. **Syn:** hop fly.

Danzig spruce beer. *(daen'-zig sproos' beeyr')*
See: spruce beer.

dark beer. *(dark' beeyr')*
A general name for dark-colored beers. The color of caramelized or roasted malt. The ingredient licorice is sometimes responsible for the blackish color of some ales, such as porter.

dead mash. *(dehd' maesh')*
Synonym for set mash.

debitterized chocolate malt. *(dee-bi'-d:uh-rayzd chak'-luht mohlt')*
Chocolate malt that has been processed to reduce harsh flavors in beers.

decantation. *(dee-kaen-tei'-shen)*
Drawing off or pouring out without disturbing the sediments.

decanter. *(dee-kaen'-ter)*
A glass bottle with a stopper for holding and serving decanted wine and other beverages.

decarbonate. *(dee-kar'-buh-neit)*
To remove carbonate and bicarbonate ions from water, either by boiling or by adding chemicals.

deciliter. *(deh'-suh-lee-d:er)*
One-tenth of a liter. Abbrev: dl.

deckelpokal. *(deh'-kel-po-kal')*
The German name given to a type of covered cup made of metal or glass.

decoction. *(dee-kak'-shen)*
Boiling to extract the flavor and facilitate the degradation of starches and proteins, the part of the mash that is boiled.

decoction brewing method. *(dee-kak'-shen broo'-wing meh'-thuhd)*
Synonym for decoction mashing.

decoction mashing. *(dee-kak'-shen mae'-shing)*
One of the three mashing methods that is often used for bottom-fermenting beers. The process requires three vessels: a mash tun for mash mixing, a mash kettle (or copper or mash copper) for boiling, and a lauter tun (or clarifying tun) for straining. Mashing is carried out in a mash tun, and starts at a low temperature while portions of the mash are taken out and boiled in the mash kettle and later returned to the mash tun, thus gradually raising the temperature of the entire mash. The process is usually repeated two or three times, taking five to six hours. The mash temperature may start as low as 95 °F (35 °C) but more often at 113–122 °F (45–50 °C) to reach 158–169 °F (70–76 °C). The mash is then filtered in a separate vessel known as a lauter tun. **Syn:** decoction brewing method. **See also:** infusion mashing; mashing.

decrating machine. *(dee-krei-ding muh-sheen')*
An automatically operated machine that removes the empty bottles of beer from crates.

degerminate, to. *(dee-juhr'-muh-neit, too)*
    To remove the rootlets (radicles) from the malted barley after kilning.

degree. *(di-gree')*
    In hydrometry, a unit on an arbitrary scale that measures the concentration of solids or alcohol in a solution, equivalent to percent. Equations are available to convert the readings into actual values of specific gravity. The Balling, Baumé, Brix, and Plato scales are used to measure the sugar content in aqueous solutions. Sikes degrees, obsolete since 1912, once referred to the alcohol content of a solution. **See also:** Balling; Baumé hydrometer; Belgian degrees; brewers' pounds; Brix; Clark; Gay-Lussac; Plato; Régie.

degree of modification. *(di-gree' uhv ma-duh-fi-kei'-shen)*
    In malting, the extent of growth of the acrospire. **See also:** modification.

degrees Plato. *(di-greez' plei'-d:o)*
    See: Plato.

deionized water. *(dee-ay'-uh-nayzd wa'-d:er)*
    Water that has had ions removed by a series of ion-exchange columns; may contain noncharged contaminants.

delabel, to. *(dee-lei'-bel, too)*
    To remove the label on bottles prior to or during washing.

demi. *(de-mee')*
    In France, a beer glass with a capacity, originally, of 1/2 a liter but now more often 33 centiliters. **See also:** *botte; distingué; lion.*

demi-john. *(de-mee'-jan)*
    A 15-gallon fermentation vessel.

demion. *(de-mee-o~')*
    An Old French liquid measure with a capacity of one quarter of a *pinte.*

demi-posson. *(de-mee' poh-so~')*
    An Old French capacity measure for liquids equal to 1/64 of a *quarte,* or 0.029 liter.

demi-setier. *(de-mee'-seh-tyei')*
    An Old French capacity measure for liquids equal to 1/4 of a *pinte.*

demistier. *(de-mee-styei'*)*
An Old French wine measure equal to 25.5 cubic inches.

densimeter. *(dehn-si'-muh-d:er)*
An instrument for measuring the density or specific gravity of liquids. Like the hydrometer, it consists of a graduated stem resting on a spindle-shaped float weighted with lead, mercury, or pitch. The densimeter is plunged vertically into the liquid and levels off. The density is then read on the graduated stem.

density. *(dehn'-si-d:ee)*
The ratio of the mass of a given volume of liquid to that of an equal volume of water at the same temperature.

depitching. *(dee-pi'-ching)*
Synonym for unpitching.

Depth Charge. *(dehpth' charj')*
A bar drink consisting of immersing a shot glass full of schnapps into a glass of beer. **See also:** Submarino.

devil's chapel. *(deh'-velz chae'-pel)*
The name given to an ale house in medieval England.

dextrin(e). *(dehk'-strin)*
A complex, unfermentable, and tasteless carbohydrate produced by the partial hydrolysis of starch through the action of alpha-amylases during mashing. Dextrins contribute to the final gravity and body of beer; some dextrins remain undissolved in the finished beer, giving it a malty sweetness. **See also:** amylase.

dextrinization. *(dehk-stri-ni-zei'-shen)*
The enzymatic process by which alpha-amylase degrades soluble starch molecules into dextrin molecules.

dextrin malt. *(dehk'-strin mohlt')*
Malted barley with a higher dextrin content and a lower fermentable sugar content than other malts, thus contributing more to the body, sweetness, and head retention of beer.

dextrinogenic amylase. *(dehk'-stri-no-jeh'-nik ae'-muh-leis)*
Synonym for alpha-amylase.

dextrose. *(dehk'-stroz)*
Formula: $C_6H_{12}O_6$. **1.** A dextrorotatory monosaccharide, member of the class of carbohydrates, occurring naturally in corn and grapes and also found in the blood or formed by the hydrolysis of starch through the action of amylases. **2.** The commercial form of refined glucose. **Syn:** corn sugar; grape sugar; glucose.

diacetyl. *(day-ae'-suh-tel)*
A volatile compound produced in beer by the oxidative decarboxylation of acetohydroxyl acids (2-acetalactate and 2-acetohydroxybutyrate) produced by yeasts. Diacetyls contribute a butterscotch flavor to beer. **See also:** carbonyls.

diammonium phosphate. *(day-uh-mo'-nee-en fas'-feyt)*
An additive used as a yeast nutrient.

diastase. *(day'-uh-steis)*
A vegetable amylase enzyme, occurring in the seed of grains and malt, capable of changing starches into maltose and later into dextrose. **See also:** amylase.

diastatic. *(day-uh-stae'-d:ik)*
Describes an enzyme capable of converting starch to sugar. **Syn:** amylolytic.

diastatic power. *(day-uh-stae'-d:ik paw'-[w]er)*
A measurement in degrees Lintner of the starch conversion enzymes present in a malt sample.

diätbier. *(dee-eit'-beegh)*
German for diet beer.

diatomaceous earth. *(day-ae-d:uh-mey'-shuhs erth)*
The refined, fossilized skeletons of ancient marine organisms called diatoms, which are frequently used as a filtration medium.

Diest beer. *(deest' beeyr')*
See: *bière de Diest.*

diet beer. *(day'-it beeyr')*
1. Any beer low in sugar or carbohydrates but not necessarily low in calories (± 400 calories per liter). In Germany *"diet bier"* is designed for diabetics and has a relatively high alcoholic content of about 4.75 percent alcohol by weight or 6 percent by volume. They are called *diätbier* in Germany, where the

trend originated, and are now produced in other Euopean countries including Britain. **Syn:** diabetic beer. **2.** The same term often refers to low-calorie beers brewed for weight-conscious dieters. These beers are not designed for diabetics. **Syn:** light beer.

dik-dik. *(dik'-dik)*
Lees or sediments.

diketone. *(day-kee'-ton)*
Aromatic volatile compound perceivable in minute concentrations from yeast or from the metabolism of anaerobic bacteria (*Pediococcus*). Most significantly the butter flavor (also butterscotch or slippery sensation) of diacetyl, a vicinal diketone (VDK). The other significant compound of relevance to brewing is 2,3-pentanedione, a honeylike aroma and/or flavor.

dimethyl sulfide. *(day-meh'-thil suhl'-fayd)*
See: DMS.

dinner ale. *(di'-ner eiyl')*
Obsolete name for pale ale.

direct fired. *(day-rehkt' fay[e]rd)*
Flames used to heat the kettle.

disaccharide. *(day-sae'-kuh-rayd)*
A compound sugar composed of two monosaccharide molecules joined by the elimination of one water molecule.

disconnect. *(dis-kuh-nehkt')*
A fitting between the keg and the gas or liquid line for ball- or pin-lock kegs.

distilled water. *(di-stild' wa'-d:er)*
Water that has been purified by heating until the water vaporizes; large molecules like salts will remain behind while organic molecules either vaporize earlier than water or have a higher boiling point and stay behind.

distiller's beer. *(di-sti'-lerz beeyr')*
Fully fermented, nonhopped, all-malt beer that is distilled directly into whiskey. **Syn:** wash beer.

distinctive. *(di-sting[k]'-tiv)*
Displaying unique characteristics of flavor and aroma.

distingué. *(di-stae~-gei')*
1. In France, a beer glass with a capacity of 50 centiliters. **See also:** *botte*; *demi*; *lion*. **2.** In Belgium, the same word applies to an 80-centiliter-size glass.

dizythum. *(day-zay'-them)*
See: *zythum*.

dl.
Abbreviation for deciliter.

DMS.
Abbreviation for dimethyl sulfide, a major sulfur compound of lagers not normally found in ales because their malts are highly modified at very high temperatures. DMS is released during boiling as a gas that dissipates into the atmosphere. The precursor of DMS, S-methylmethionine, remains present in the wort and converts to DMS if the wort is not cooled rapidly.

Dog's Nose. *(dagz' noz')*
A mixed drink of hot beer that is laced with gin and flavored with sugar. **Syn:** Purl.

dolo. *(do'-lo)*
A type of millet beer made in Africa. It is brewed locally and varies considerably from one region to another and even within the same region. Neither hopped nor filtered, it is flavored with various bitter plants such as sisal, castor-oil bean, cassia, and sometimes pimento and tobacco leaves. Jimson was also an ingredient but was eventually outlawed because of its toxicity. The sugary pulp of cassia is added to increase the alcoholic strength.

domestic brewer. *(do-meh'-stik broo'-wer)*
Synonym for homebrewer.

door talker. *(dor' ta'-ker)*
Promotional signage, mounted on door of cooler or refrigerator, often used by retailers of beer, wine, and other alcoholic beverages.

doppelbock. *(doh'-pel-bohk)*

In Germany, a beer much stronger than simple *bock* but not necessarily doubly so, as the German adjective *doppel,* meaning double, implies. According to German law, *doppelbock* must be brewed from an original wort gravity of 18–28 °P (1.072–1.120), resulting in a strength of 7.5–13 percent alcohol by volume. The brand names of doppel bocks always end with the suffix *-ator* (Animator, Salvator, Optimator, Delicator, Maximator, Triumphator). The original of the style, named Salvator (after the Saviour) was brewed by the Italian monks of the order of St. Francis of Paula, in Bavaria, during the counter-revolution period. They were granted permission to sell their product by the court of Bavaria in 1780. The monastic brewery is now operated by the privately owned Paulaner-Thomas-Braü. Also spelled: *doppel bock.* **See also:** *bockbier; eisbock.*

dopskal. *(dup-skohl)*

In Sweden, a small drinking bowl with one or two handles, with or without a cover and used in the seventeenth century for serving hot brandy.

dormancy. *(dohr'-men[t]-see)*

The inability of barley grains to germinate immediately after harvesting. Dormancy varies in intensity between different varieties of barley; it may last up to a few weeks then ceases during storage, when the grains have matured and have acquired oxygen (which can be accelerated by steeping the grains in oxygenated solutions). Some types of barleys—especially those grown in cold or maritime climates or grown during a cool, wet season or harvested during a wet spell—retain a second type of dormancy called water sensitivity. These types of barley benefit from steeping to a low-moisture content level, with more water being added after an air rest period. **See also:** germinative energy.

dormant. *(dohr'-ment)*

Characteristic of newly harvested barley that exhibits a reluctancy to germinate. **Syn:** immature.

Dort. *(doght')*

Short for Dortmunder.

Dortmunder. *(doght'-mun-der)*

A blonde- or gold-colored, bottom-fermented beer from Dortmund (Westphalia), Germany's largest brewing city. Although the brewing rights of that city were granted by imperial decree in 1293, the Dortmund-style beer was not introduced until the 1840s. The original of this style is often symbolized by the acronym DAB, which stands for Dortmunder Aktien Brauerei and is better known locally as export because it was once brewed for exportation. Outside Germany, in

Belgium and Holland, for example, beers brewed in this style are often called Dort. In style it is intermediate between a Pilsener and a *helles*. Dortmunder is darker and less bitter than Pilsener (200–220 grams per hectoliter of hops as opposed to 400–500 grams per hectoliter), drier, less malty than helles (which has 180–200 grams per hectoliter of hops), paler than helles, and slightly stronger than both, containing 4.2 percent alcohol by weight or 5.2 percent by volume. **Syn:** Dort.

dosage. *(do'-sij)*
The addition of yeast and/or sugar to the cask or bottle in order to aid secondary fermentation.

double bock. *(duh'-bel bak)*
See: *doppelbock.*

double-gauge regulator. *(duh'-bel geyj rey'-gyuh-lei-d:er)*
A regulator that measures both in-line pressure and tank pressure (indicating remaining volume).

double mashing. *(duh'-bel mae'-shing)*
A procedure in which two separate mashes are mashed-in simultaneously. The first is all malt and constitutes about 90 percent of the recipe's total malt and is raised to 122 °F (50 °C). The second mash consists of the remainder of the recipe's malt and all of the adjuncts. This mash is brought up to 158 °F (70 °C) and is held for about fifteen minutes to allow alpha-amylase action to occur. The adjunct mash is then boiled for twenty minutes and added to the main mash so the resulting temperature is 158 °F (70 °C). Double mashing ensures the adjunct starch is gelatinized and completely converted.

double-stage fermentation. *(duh'-bel steij' fuhr-mehn-tei'-shen)*
Synonym for two-stage fermentation.

dough-in, to. *(do' in, too)*
Synonym for to mash.

doughing-in. *(do'-ing-in)*
Mixing ground malt with water, usually 2–4 hectoliters per 100 kilograms of malt. **Syn:** mashing-in.

downy mildew. *(daw'-nee mil'-doo)*
A fungal disease that attacks hops. The fungus, an obligate parasite for hops, overwinters as mycelium in the infected rootstock and manifests itself in spring

when the buds of the crown start to lengthen. Downy mildew (*Pseudoperonospora humuli*) was first observed in Japan in 1905, in the United States in 1909, and was unknown in Britain before 1920.

Dr. Butler's ale. *(dak'-ter buht'-lerz eiyl')*
A medicinal ale concocted by the physician of James I, consisting of ale flavored with spices and medicinal herbs.

draff. *(draef)*
The solid material, spent grains, remaining in the lauter tun after sparging.

draft beer. *(draeft' beeyr')*
Beer drawn from casks or kegs rather than cans or bottles. Draft beer is stored (usually under pressure) in metal kegs and is often nonpasteurized and minimally filtered, served from the tap, and preferably consumed within one week of brewing (thirty days at the limit). **Syn:** tap beer; draught beer; beer from the wood; beer on tap.

dragon's milk. *(drae'-genz milk')*
An old British name for strong ale.

draught. *(draeft)*
Orthographic variant of draft.

draw, to. *(droh', too)*
To transfer a liquid from one container to another.

drawing off. *(droh'-wing af')*
The action of transferring a liquid from one vessel to another or to bottles and casks.

dregs. *(drehgz)*
Sediments at the bottom of a vessel.

dried malt extract. *(drayd' mohlt' ehk'-straekt)*
Synonym for dry malt.

drinking horn. *(dringk'-ing hohrn')*
1. An ancient Greek horn-shaped ceremonial drinking vessel originally made from the horn of an ox or buffalo or from the ivory of an elephant and later made of earthenware or metal. **Syn:** rhyton.

drinking water. *(dringk'-ing wa'-d:er)*
    Water suitable for drinking which, by definition, is colorless, odorless, tasteless, devoid of pathogenic or parasitic matter, without any chemical pollutants, and not overmineralized. Ideally, potable water should contain, per liter, 125 milligrams of magnesium, 250 milligrams of chloride, 250 milligrams of sulfate, a maximum of 44 milligrams of nitrates, and 2 grams of mineral salts. City water is monitored with regard to bacteriological and chemical purity, but content of mineral salts varies considerably from one city or region to another. **Syn:** potable water; city water; tap water.

dropping. *(dra'-ping)*
    Using gravity to transfer a fluid to another vessel at a lower level.

dropping system. *(dra'-ping sis'-tem)*
    A brewing method whereby the fermenting wort is dropped into a secondary vessel about halfway through fermentation, leaving trub, hop debris, and surplus yeast behind.

drum malting. *(druhm' mohl'-ting)*
    A pneumatic malting method using perforated drums fitted with ventilation tubes and rotated along the long axis on supporting rollers.

drum washer. *(druhm' wae'-sher)*
    A spraying unit for washing bottles on a revolving drum. The bottles are first soaked in a washing tub after which they are sprayed and jetted while in an upside-down position.

drunk. *(druhngk)*
    Having physical and mental facilities impaired by alcohol.

dry. *(dray')*
    Characteristic of a low-sugar beer as opposed to sweet.

dry beer. *(dray' beeyr')*
    Refers to a beer brewed with more adjuncts (corn and rice), using a strain of yeast that ferments the wort more completely. This produces a beer with less residual sweetness and less aftertaste but also less flavor.

dry hop, to. *(dray' hap', too)*
    To add dry hops to fermenting or aging beer to increase its hop character or aroma.

dry hopping. *(dray' hap'-ing)*

    1. The addition of loose dry hops to the primary fermenter (when the wort has cooled down to 75 °F, 24 °C), the secondary fermenter, or to casked beer to increase the aroma and hop character of the finished beer without significantly affecting its bitterness. Homebrewers usually add 50–60 grams of aroma hops or hop pellets per 5-gallon batch during primary or, more often, secondary fermentation. Hop extracts are not recommended for dry hopping because they may contain traces of the organic solvents used for their extraction. **2.** In England, dry hopping more specifically refers to the addition of fresh hops to a cask of draft beer when it is racked from the primary fermenter. **See also:** fermentation hopping.

dry hops. *(dray' haps')*

    Aromatic (or finishing) hops to be used for dry hopping.

drying. *(dray'-ing)*

    Synonym for kilning.

dry kit. *(dray' kit')*

    A homebrewing kit consisting of malt, flour (or dry malt), hops, malt grains, and sometimes crystal malt.

dry malt. *(dray' mohlt')*

    Malt extract in dry, powdered form as opposed to liquid or syrup malt. Dry malt is never hopped. **Syn:** dried malt extract.

dry mead. *(dray' meed)*

    A mead free of sugar as opposed to sweet mead.

dry priming. *(dray' pray'-ming)*

    In homebrewing, the process of adding corn sugar to the beer before bottling to create carbonation.

dry stout. *(dray' stawt)*

    The Irish version of stout, slightly more bitter than the English sweet stout, with a coffeelike character from roasted barley. Dry stout is exemplified by Guinness Extra Stout. **See also:** stout.

dubbel. *(du'-bel)*

    A Belgian ale with a fruity, sweet character and dark amber to brown color.

dunder oppe. *(doon'-der oh'-pe*)*
A mild beer brewed in Brussels in the fifteenth century.

dunge(on). *(duhnj'-[en])*
In early malt kilns, a fire basket located in the lower part of the installation immediately below the kiln floor.

dunkelweizen. *(dung'-kel-vayt-sen)*
A beer style similar to a *weizen* but darker in color and with a pronounced malt sweetness.

Düsseldorfer alt(bier). *(du'-sel-dohgh-fer alt'-[beegh])*
Synonym for *altbier*.

dusty yeast. *(duh'-stee yeest')*
Yeast that does not quickly precipitate out of suspension at the end of fermentation. Also called: powdery yeast.

dwójniack. *(dvoy'-nee-ak*)*
A sweet mead produced in Poland by fermenting equal parts of honey and water with an osmophilic yeast. It averages 16 percent alcohol by volume and is aged for five to seven years in large 4,000-liter wooden vats. Also spelled: *dwójniak*.

Early Cluster. *(ehr'-lee kluh'-ster)*
A variety of hops grown in Washington containing 7.5–8 percent alpha acids.

Easter ale. *(ee'-ster eiyl')*
In Old England, a special ale prepared for Easter celebrations.

East Kent Goldings. *(eest' kehnt' gohl'-dingz)*
A variety of hops grown in England containing 9–10 percent alpha acids.

EBC.
Abbreviation for European Brewery Convention. **See also:** EBC test; nephelometer.

EBC test. *(ee bee see tehst)*
A test to measure the colloidal stability of beer by storing it at 32 °F (0 °C) for one night, followed by forty-eight hours at 140 °F (60 °C) and another night at 32 °F (0 °C). The turbidity is then measured with a nephelometer in Formazin Turbidity Units (FTU) or EBC units.

EBC units. *(ee bee see yoo'-nits)*
Units of measurement for various brewing chemical analyses such as color or bitterness. **See also:** European Brewery Convention.

ebulliometer. *(eh-bu-lee-a'-muh-d:er)*
A device that measures the alcohol content of a beverage.

ebulum. *(eh'-byuh-luhm)*
In Old England, an ale flavored with elder, juniper, ginger, and other herbs and spices. Also spelled: ebulam.

effervescence. *(eh-fer-veh'-sen[t]s)*
The bubbling up, or fizz, in beer caused by dissolved carbon dioxide gas.

égart. *(eh-gagh')*
See: *bierkieser.*

Eighteenth Amendment. *(ei'-teenth uh-mehnd'-ment)*
See: Prohibition.

eisbock. *(ays'-bohk)*
The strongest type of *bock* beers. These ice beers are produced by lagering beer in very cold cellars to the freezing point of water (32 °F, 0 °C, well above that of alcohol -173 °F, -115 °C) and removing some of the iced water (hence, the name) thereby increasing the alcoholic strength of the beer. Kulminator, the strongest *doppelbock* in the world (28 °P, 13.2 percent alcohol by volume) is produced by this method at the Erste Kulmbacher Brewery in Kulmbach near Bayreuth. **See also:** *bockbier;* congelation; *doppelbock;* ice beer.

EMP pathway. *(ee-em-pee paeth'-wei)*
The biochemical sequence of enzymatic reactions that produce the breakdown of glucose and other carbohydrates. It also is called glucolytic pathway because these reactions are common to both alcohol production and the anaerobic glycosis of muscle. Etym: Named after Embden, Meyerhof, and Parnas—the three men who conducted research on the mechanism of alcoholic fermentation.

endosperm. *(ehn'-do-sperm)*
The starch-containing sac of the barley grain. The endosperm constitutes 80–85 percent of the dry weight of the grain. Part of this starch serves as a food reserve for the growing embryo during the cytolysis process while the remainder constitutes the bulk of the extract during mashing. The sugars found in the endosperm include glucose, fructose, maltose, sucrose, and higher fructosans. Also called: starchy endosperm.

English degree. *(ing'-glish di'-gree)*
Synonym for Clark degree.

enteric bacteria. *(ehn-teh'-rik baek-ti'-ree-uh)*
Gram-negative bacteria known to produce in wort several sulfur compounds, carbonyls, and phenols. They are inhibited at very low alcohol levels but can still contribute significantly to the flavor of *lambic* beers.

entire. *(ehn-tay[e]r')*
The original name for porter.

enzyme. *(ehn'-zaym)*
An organic protein substance produced by living cells and that acts as a catalyst in biological and biochemical changes such as synthesis, hydrolysis, oxidative degradation, and isomerization. Enzymes are highly specific and act on only one substrate and affect only one type of chemical reaction. Alpha-amylase, for example, converts starch to maltotriose and dextrins whereas beta-amylase converts dextrins to maltose, maltotriose, and alpha-limit dextrins. Enzymes are sensitive to heat and undergo denaturation at high temperatures and have a low tolerance to a pH of 4 or less.

epsomite. *(ehp'-suh-mayt)*
Synonym for Epsom salts.

Epsom salts. *(ehp'-sem salts')*
Formula: $MgSO_4 7H_2O$. Hydrated magnesium sulfate found in solution in mineral waters. Epsom salts are added to brewing water to make it hard. **Syn:** epsomite.

equilibrium. *(ee-kwuh-li'-bree-[y]em)*
A state in which opposing processes are occurring at equal rates, resulting in no net change.

Eroica. *(eh-ro'-i-kuh)*
A variety of hops grown in Idaho and Washington and containing 10.5–11.5 percent alpha acids.

erythrodextrin. *(uh-ri-thruh-dehk'-strin)*
Tasteless intermediate dextrin. Large alpha-limit dextrins. Faint red reaction with iodine.

essential oil. *(i-sehn'-chel oyl')*
A volatile, odoriferous, oily compound found in plants including hops. **See also:** hop oils.

éstaminets. *(eh-sta-mee-ney[z]')*
Belgian cafes or bistros.

esters. (eh'-sterz)
Volatile flavor compounds that form through the interaction of organic acids with alcohols during fermentation and contribute to the fruity aroma and flavor of beer. **See also:** volatiles.

estery. (eh'-ster-ee)
Possessing odors and flavors reminiscent of flowers, fruits, or vegetables—banana, apple, pear, strawberry, and others. **Syn:** fruity.

eswart. (ehs'-vaght*)
See: *bierkieser*.

ethanol. (eh'-thuh-nol)
Synonym for ethyl alcohol.

ethyl alcohol. (eh'-thel ael'-kuh-hohl)
Formula: C_2H_5OH (or CH_3CH_2OH). A colorless, combustible, and potable liquid soluble in water, chloroform, and methyl alcohol. It is the second member of the chemical series of alcohols of the general formula $C_NH_{2n}OH$. It has a specific gravity of 0.739 at 60 °F (15.6 °C), a boiling point of 172.9 °F (78.3 °C), and a calorific energy value of 7 kilocalories per gram. The term *alcohol*, when not preceded by a qualification, invariably means ethyl alcohol. Ethanol is the intoxicating element in beer, wine, and spirits. **Syn:** alcohol; ethanol; grain alcohol.

ethylaldehyde. (eh-thel-ael'-duh-hayd)
Synonym for acetaldehyde.

EtOH.
Scientific abbreviation for ethyl alcohol.

European Brewery Convention. (yur-uh-pee'-en broo'-[e]-ree kuhn-vehn'-shen)
An association created in 1947 to encourage scientific and technical research in brewing. It organizes congresses, conducts collaborative research, and develops analytical methods. Abbrev: EBC.

excess gravity. (ehk'-sehs grae-vuh-d:ee)
A form of expressing specific gravity as a whole number; for example, a specific gravity of 1.046 is given as 46. Excess gravity was created for convenience and to be used in formulas.

exponential phase. *(ehk-spuh-nehn'-shel feiz')*
Synonym for reproduction phase.

export. *(ehk'-spohrt)*
1. Any beer produced for the express purpose of exportation. **2.** Generally, the word *export* printed on a label stands for superior quality, a product "suitable for exportation," or a higher than usual alcoholic content. **3.** In Germany, a local name for Dortmunder. **4.** In Britain, another name for India pale ale from the fact that it was once exported to British troops stationed in India. **5.** In Belgium, a legal classificaion for strong beers that are brewed from original wort gravities of 11–13.5 °P. Since 1974 this classification has been called Category I.

exportbier. *(ehk-spohght'-beer)*
Tax law subcategory of *vollbier*. An *exportbier* has a starting gravity of no less than 1.050 (12.5 °P) and no more than 1.056 (14 °P).

extract. *(ehk'-straekt)*
1. The total amount of dissolved materials in the sweet wort after mashing and lautering malted barley and sometimes malt adjuncts such as corn and rice. Typical composition: 80 percent carbohydrates (dextrins, fermentable sugars); 8 percent nitrogenous matter; 5 percent glycerin; 3–4 percent mineral substances, resins, and gums. These extracts in solution determine the starting gravity of the wort, which is expressed in many different ways. It is measured with a saccharometer and expressed in degrees Balling or Plato as the number of grams of extract per 100 grams of wort at 63.5 °F (17.5 °C). In the United Kingdom it is expressed in brewer's pounds per quarter (336 pounds) of malt. **See also:** hot-water extract. **2.** A concentrate of the essential elements of a substance in a dry or liquid form. **See also:** malt extract.

extract beer. *(ehk'-straekt beeyr')*
In homebrewer's parlance, beer made from malt extract syrup or powder as opposed to grain beer, which is made from malted barley.

extract efficiency. *(ehk'-straekt ee-fi'-shen[t]-see)*
The yield of fermentable sugar from the mash, which can be measured directly as degrees of specific gravity per gallon of wort (per pound of grist) or as an absolute percentage of the dry grain weight, which is extracted into a standard mash.

extraction. *(ehk'-straek-shen)*
The process of removing one element from a complex of others.

extra special bitter. *(ehk'-struh speh'-shil bi'-d:er)*
Bitter ale with a higher starting gravity and more assertive flavor than an ordinary bitter or special bitter. It is often referred to as ESB. **Syn:** extra strong bitter.

extra strong bitter. *(ehk'-struh strang bi'-d:er)*
Synonym for extra special bitter.

F.
Abbreviation for Fahrenheit (°F).

Fahrenheit. *(fae'-ren-hayt)*
A thermometer scale in which the freezing point of water is 32° and the boiling point is 212°. Abbrev: °F. To convert degrees Fahrenheit to degrees centigrade and vice versa:

°F = (°C × 9/5) + 32 or (°C × 1.8) + 32
°C = (°F × 32) × 5/9 or (°F × 32) / 1.8

falling heat. *(fa'-ling heet')*
The temperature of sweet wort run from the mash tun.

false bottom. *(fals ba'-d:em)*
A perforated plate or screen set between 1/8 and 2 inches above the bottom of the lauter tun to separate grain from the mash liquor during sparging.

FAN.
Acronym for free amino nitrogen; generally used to characterize the amount of amino acids in the wort. The FAN content is measured and expressed in parts per million. A wort of 10 °B (1.040) contains approximately 220 parts per million of FAN, which is ideal for yeast growth. Raw unmalted barley makes an insignificant contribution to the FAN content.

farinator. *(fae'-ruh-nei-d:er)*
Synonym for corn cutter.

farnescene. *(far'-ni-seen)*
   A secondary component of hop oil found in varying proportions in different varieties of hops.

faro. *(fa'-roh)*
   In Belgium, a blend of equal parts of two types of *lambic* beer, one of high density (5.5–6 °B) and one of lower density (March beer: lambic of 3–3.5 °B), sweetened with sugar and sometimes colored with caramel and diluted with water. It is now practically extinct and the Vander Linden brewery is one of the very last to perpetuate this tradition. Also called: *faro-lambic*. **See also:** *gueuze*; *kriek*; lambic.

faro-lambic. *(fa'-roh lam'-beek)*
   Synonym for *faro*.

fatty acids. *(fae'-d:ee ae'-sidz)*
   A group of saturated and unsaturated monobasic aliphatic carboxylic acids, all of which impart a rancid, soapy flavor to beer, contribute to its staling, and affect its head retention.

faucet. *(fa'-sit)*
   Another name for a tap, spigot, or stop cock.

fecal bacteria. *(fee'-kel baek-ti'-ree-uh)*
   Coliform bacteria associated with sewage.

fecula. *(feh'-kyuh-luh)*
   Trub.

ferment, to. *(fuhr'-mehnt, too)*
   To undergo fermentation.

ferment. *(fuhr'-mehnt)*
   An enzyme or any substance capable of producing fermentation.

fermentable. *(fuhr-mehn'-tuh-bel)*
   Capacity of a solution to undergo fermentation.

fermentation. *(fuhr-mehn-tei'-shen)*
   The chemical conversion of fermentable sugars in the wort into approximately equal parts of ethyl alcohol and carbon dioxide gas, through the action of yeast,

resulting in a drop in the specific gravity from an average of 1.045 to about 1.012, but rarely to 1.000, as unfermented carbohydrates and nitrogen compounds always remain in the beer. There are two basic systems of fermentation in brewing, top fermentation and bottom fermentation, each of which is divided into two basic phases, primary and secondary fermentation. Etym: From the Latin *fervere*, meaning to boil. **See also:** bottom fermentation; hybrid fermentation; spontaneous fermentation; top fermentation.

fermentation bin. *(fuhr-mehn-tei'-shen bin')*
    Synonym for fermenter.

fermentation cellar. *(fuhr-mehn-tei'-shen seh'-ler)*
    A thermostatically controlled storage area, originally a cellar, where fermentation takes place. **Syn:** fermenting cellar.

fermentation hopping. *(fuhr-mehn-tei'-shen hap'-ing)*
    In England, a distinction is made between dry hopping (adding hops to ale to be aged in casks) and fermentation hopping (adding dry hops or hop pellets during primary or secondary fermentation). **Syn:** dry hopping.

fermentation lock. *(fuhr-mehn-tei'-shen lak')*
    In homebrewing, a one-way valve, usually made of glass or plastic, fitted into a centrally pierced cork or rubber bung and attached to the mouth of the carboy or secondary fermenter to allow carbon dioxide gas to escape from the fermenter while excluding ambient wild yeasts, bacteria, and contaminants. A fermentation lock is particularly useful for lagers that require long, closed fermentation. It also serves as a guide to the fermentation progress. **Syn:** airlock; bubbler; fermentation valve; water lock; water seal.

fermentation valve. *(fuhr-mehn-tei'-shen vaelv')*
    Synonym for fermentation lock.

fermentation vessel. *(fuhr-mehn-tei'-shen veh'-sil)*
    Synonym for fermenter.

fermenter. *(fuhr-mehn'-ter)*
    A generic name for any open or closed vessel in which primary and secondary fermentation takes place. Also spelled: fermentor. **Syn:** fermentation bin; fermentation vessel. **See also:** primary fermenter; secondary fermenter; single-stage fermenter.

fermenting. *(fuhr-mehn'-ting)*
   In the process of fermentation.

fermentor. *(fuhr-mehn'-ter)*
   Orthographic variant for fermenter.

festbier. *(fehst'-beegh)*
   In Germany, a special beer brewed for festive occasions, such as Christmas or Easter, or for a local folkloric event or beer festival.

fiery fermentation. *(fay'-[e]-ree fuhr-mehn-tei'-shen)*
   Anomalous fermentation characterized by a reduction of froth and the appearance of oily bubbles that burst.

fill, to. *(fil, too)*
   The action of filling bottles, cans, casks, or kegs.

filler. *(fil'-er)*
   A machine that pours liquids into bottles and other packaging containers.

filtering. *(fil'-ter-ing)*
   Synonym for filtration.

filter press. *(fil'-ter prehs')*
   A type of filter consisting of cloth-covered frames through which liquids are pumped.

filter pulp. *(fil'-ter puhlp')*
   Asbestos or wood pulp pressed into cakes for use in filtration.

filtration. *(fil-trei'-shen)*
   1. The passage of a liquid through a permeable or porous substance to remove solid matter in suspension. **2.** Separating the wort from the spent grains.

final attenuation. *(fayn'-el uh-teh-nyuh-wei'-shen)*
   Synonym for final degree of attenuation.

final degree of attenuation. *(fayn'-el di-gree' uhv uh-teh-nyuh-wei'-shen)*
   The maximum apparent attenuation attainable by a particular wort as determined in a laboratory. The final attenuation depends above all on the proportion of fermentable sugars in the wort, most of which have been

transformed before bottling to avoid biological reactions that affect the flavor, head retention, and stability of the beer. **Syn:** limit attenuation; final attenuation; attenuation final.

Formula: A = (B − b) × 100
A = final degree of attenuation
B = original gravity in °B (or °P)
b = final gravity in °B (or °P)

final gravity. *(fayn'-el grae'-vuh-d:ee)*
Synonym for final specific gravity.

final SG. *(fayn'-el ehs jee)*
Synonym for final specific gravity.

final specific gravity. *(fayn'-el spi-si'-fik grae'-vuh-d:ee)*
The specific gravity of a beer as measured when fermentation is complete (when all fermentable sugars have been converted to alcohol and carbon dioxide gas). **Syn:** final gravity; final SG; finishing specific gravity; terminal gravity.

fine, to. *(fayn', too)*
To clarify.

fines. *(faynz)*
The finely crushed, flourlike portion of the draff.

fining. *(fay'-ning)*
A clarifying process that adds organic or mineral settling agents during secondary fermentation to precipitate colloidal matter through coagulation or adsorption. **See also:** finings.

fining agents. *(fay'-ning ei'-jents)*
Synonym for finings.

finings. *(fay'-ningz)*
Various organic or mineral substances used to ensure a clear beer by causing impurities, yeast cells, and other suspended matter to coagulate and precipitate to the bottom of the fermentation container. Isinglass, gelatin, Irish moss, bentonite, egg whites (or egg albumin), charcoal, wood chips, and casein are examples of colloidal agents used for this purpose. **Syn:** fining agents.

finished beer. *(fi'-nisht beeyr')*
Technically, fermented and aged beer ready to be racked as opposed to wort or fermenting beer.

finishing. *(fi'-ni-shing)*
Postfermentation process.

finishing hops. *(fi'-ni-shing haps')*
Hops added to the wort near the end of the boiling phase or in the fermentation vessel to impart hops' aroma and character to the beer as opposed to hops' flavoring, which also contributes to the beer's bitterness. Some brewers recommend adding finishing hops one or two minutes before cooling whereas others suggest ten or fifteen minutes. Because finishing hops are selected for their aroma rather than for their bittering power, their alpha acid content is usually low. **Syn:** aroma hops; aromatic hops. **See also:** flavoring hops.

finishing specific gravity. *(fi'-ni-shing spi-si'-fik grae'-vuh-d:ee)*
Synonym for final specific gravity.

fir(k). *(fuhrk)*
See: firkin.

fire brewing. *(fay[e]r' broo'-wing)*
A traditional brewing method using direct fire to heat the brew kettle rather than steam or hot water, thus producing a good rolling boil that apparently improves the fullness and smoothness of beer. In the United States, Stroh's is one of the few major breweries to still use this method.

fire copper. *(fay[e]r' ka'-per)*
A brew kettle heated by direct flame.

fire flavor. *(fay[e]r' flei'-ver)*
A roasted or burnt flavor in beer.

Firestone keg. *(fay[e]r'-ston kehg)*
Same as Cornelius keg but usually having pin-lock fittings.

firkin. *(fuhr'-kin)*
A cask for beer with a capacity of 1/4 of a barrel, or 9 imperial gallons (40.9 liters). Two firkins equal 1 kilderkin. Abbrev: fir or firk. **See also:** pin.

first running. *(fuhrst' ruhn'-ing)*
Synonym for first wort.

first wort. *(furhst' wuhrt')*
The first batch of wort to be filtered in the straining vat. It is richer in extract than following batches. **Syn:** original wort; first running. **See also:** second wort.

fish gelatin. *(fish' jeh'-luh-tin)*
Synonym for isinglass.

fish stuffing. *(fish' stuhf'-ing)*
In England, a common name for isinglass.

fizz. *(fiz)*
1. The effervescence in beer caused by dissolved carbon dioxide gas. **2.** A mix of gin and soda, with lemons or limes and ice, usually served in a tall glass.

flagon. *(flae'-gen)*
1. Originally, a cylindrical or slightly tapered vessel for sacramental use. It was later adapted to hold or serve wine, water, beer, cider, or other liquors and was then called a tankard. **2.** A measure of capacity equal to 2 wine quarts (1.8926 liters).

flaked. *(fleykt)*
Grains that have been moistened and pressed or rolled into flakes. Flaked grains are gelatinized during the manufacturing process and can be added directly to the mash without pre-cooking.

flaked maize. *(fleykt' meiz)*
Partly gelatinized maize, the grain of which has been cracked, moistened, cooked, and flaked between rollers.

flakes. *(fleyks)*
Unmalted adjunct grains in flake form added directly to the mash kettle with the ground malt. Some U.S. brewers use up to 50 percent flakes in their mash. **See also:** adjunct.

Flanders brown. *(flaen'-derz brawn')*
A brown ale originating in Flanders and notable for a sour or lactic character. Also known as *oud bruin*.

flash pasteurization. *(flaesh' paes-chuh-ray-zei'-shen)*
A pasteurization method in which the product is held at a higher temperature than in normal pasteurization but for a shorter period of time; draft beer, for example, is steamed to a maximum temperature of 160–175 °F (71–79 °C) for fifteen to sixty seconds. **See also:** pasteurization.

flat. *(flaet)*
Describes a beer lacking in taste because it has little or no effervescence.

flatten. *(flae'-d:en)*
Conditioning under atmospheric pressure, which releases carbon dioxide from the beer.

flavor. *(flei'-ver)*
Sensations as perceived by the tastebuds. Most of the flavors in beer come from volatiles, the composition and concentration of which depend on the raw materials, the type of process (heating, conditioning, maturation), the properties of the yeast strain, and the development of contaminating microorganisms. **See also:** esters; volatiles.

flavor hops. *(flei'-ver haps')*
Synonym for flavoring hops.

flavoring hops. *(flei'-ver-ing haps')*
Hops added to the boiling wort to impart bitterness to beer as opposed to finishing hops, which contribute to its aroma and hop character. Alpha acids are not soluble in water or wort and only become so when they isomerize during the boil. The quantity of hops to be added varies according to taste, variety of hops, degree of bitterness desired, and brewing method. **Syn:** boiling hops; bittering hops; flavor hops. **See also:** finishing hops.

flavor wheel. *(flei'-ver [h]weel')*
A flavor terminology developed by the American Society of Brewing Chemists, the European Brewery Convention, and the Master Brewers Association of America in an effort to normalize the description and identification of flavors in beer. A total of 122 terms are divided into 14 classes and represented graphically for easy reference. Copies are obtainable from: American Society of Brewing Chemists, Inc., 3340 Pilot Knob Street, St. Paul, MN 55121, USA.

floating ants. *(flo'-d:ing aents')*
See: *p'ei.*

flocculate, to. *(fla'-kyuh-leit, too)*
To aggregate into small masses.

flocculating yeast. *(fla'-kyuh-lei-d:ing yeest')*
A bottom-fermenting yeast of low attenuation that aggregates into small masses during the fermentation.

flocculation. *(fla-kyuh-lei'-shen)*
The phenomenon by which yeast cells aggregate into masses toward the end of the fermentation process and sink to the bottom, thus contributing to the clarification of the beer. The ability of a yeast (either top- or bottom-fermenting) to flocculate or settle varies with the strain of yeast. **Syn:** breakage. **See also:** flocculent yeast; nonflocculent yeast.

flocculent yeast. *(fla'-kyuh-lent yeest')*
A generic name for yeast strains that clump and flocculate during fermentation. **See also:** flocculation.

floor corker. *(flor' kohr'-ker)*
Floor-mounted or freestanding device used to insert a cork into a bottle neck.

flooring. *(flo'-ring)*
Synonym for floor malting.

floor malting. *(flor' mohl'-ting)*
A traditional germination method that spreads the steeped barley over a flat surface in layers of 10–15 centimeters, where it germinates at relatively low temperatures of about 52.5–59 °F (12–15 °C), sometimes higher, for up to thirteen days. Originally, malting was carried out in winter, autumn, or spring to take advantage of cool weather. Slightly higher temperatures of 58–62 °F (14–16 °C) are preferred today. With the introduction of mechanical devices in the 1880s, floor malting was gradually superseded by pneumatic malting. **Syn:** flooring. **See also:** couch; piece; pneumatic malting.

floral. *(flo'-rel)*
The aroma of flower blossoms or perfume.

flotation. *(flo-tey'-shen)*
See cold trub flotation.

flour. *(flaw[e]r)*
Finely ground grain meal. The intentional use of flour is rare in large-scale brewing. Flour is used to a limited extent in the production of some Belgian specialty beers.

flour mill. *(flaw[e]r mill)*
A type of grain mill employing one rotating and one fixed plate to grind grain, which is forced between the plates by a rotating screw auger. The degree of grinding can be adjusted from a fine flour to a coarse grist by adjusting the distance between the plates. These mills grind rather than crush and do not leave husks entirely intact.

flowering cone. *(flaw'-[e]-ring kon')*
Synonym for strobile.

fluid ounce. *(floo'-wid awn[t]s')*
A unit of liquid capacity equal, in the United States, to 1/16 of a pint, or 1.804 cubic inches (29.573 milliliters) and, in Britain, to 1/20 of a pint, or 1.7339 cubic inches (28.412 milliliters). Abbrev: fl oz.

fl oz.
Abbreviation for fluid ounce.

foam. *(fom)*
The mass of bubbles on a glass of beer. **Syn:** cream; head; froth; collar; suds.

foaming agent. *(fo'-ming ei'-jent)*
Synonym for heading liquid.

foam retention. *(fom' ri-tehn'-shen)*
Synonym for head retention.

foam stability. *(fom' stuh-bi'-le-d:ee)*
Synonym for head retention.

foamy. *(fo'-mee)*
1. Covered with foam. **2.** Tasting of foam. **3.** Describes a beer that generates a good head of foam.

fob. *(fab)*
An English brewer's word for froth.

food additive. *(food' ae'-d:uh-d:iv)*
Synonym for additive.

food-grade. *(food' greid')*
Grade of plastic suitable for containing food. In homebrewing, high-density polythene and polypropylene make excellent fermenters. Containers made of lower grade plastic, such as wastebaskets, are inadequate because, for the most part, they impart a plastic flavor to the brew.

foot bath. *(fut' baeth)*
Slang for a large glass of beer.

Formazin Turbidity Unit. *(fohr'-muh-zin tuhr-bi'-d:uh-d:ee yoo'-nit)*
See: EBC test; nephelometer.

formidable. *(Eng: fohr-mi'-duh-bel; French: fogh-mee-da'-ble)*
1. In France, a beer glass with a capacity of 3 liters. **See also:** *baron.* **2.** In Belgium, a beer glass capable of holding 1 liter.

formula weight. *(fohr'-myuh-luh weyt')*
The sum of the atomic weights of each atom in a compound; the number of grams in 1 mole.

Forum Hordeum. *(fohr'-em hohr-dei'-em*)*
A famous hops market in Hamburg in the 1100s.

fountain. *(fawn'-tin)*
A sort of tap in bars for drawing beer from the cellar to the glass.

four ale. *(fo[e]r' eiyl)*
An obsolete synonym for mild ale.

four-rowed barley. *(fo[e]r'-rod' bar'-lee)*
A variety of barley considered as a form for six-rowed barley in which two opposing groups of two rows of grains have been compressed together, giving the impression of four rows. This variety is not used in the brewing industry.

four-vessel brewing. *(fo[e]r' veh'-sel broo'-[w]ing)*
Traditional decoction brewing method requiring a mash cooker, a mash tun, a lauter tun, and a kettle. Mashing is carried out in the mash tun and starts at a low temperature while portions of the mash are taken out and boiled in the cooker and later returned to the mash tun, thus gradually raising the temperature of the entire mash. The mash is then filtered in the lauter tun, and the resulting wort is boiled in the copper kettle.

4-vinyl-guaiacol. *(fo[e]r' vay'-nel g[w]ay'-uh-kohl)*
Phenolic compound usually present in levels above threshold in southern German–style wheat beer. It has a clovelike aroma.

fox lambic. *(faks lam'-beek)*
Young *lambic*.

framboise. *(fgha~-bwaz')*
A type of fruit *lambic* produced by adding raspberries to a young lambic or *gueuze* to induce a secondary fermentation. **Syn:** *frambozenbier*. **See also:** *gueuze; kriek*; lambic.

frambozenbier. *(fgham-bo'-zen-beegh)*
Synonym for *framboise*.

free amino nitrogen. *(free' uh-mee'-no nay'-tri-jen)*
See: FAN.

free house. *(free' haws)*
A pub (public house) that is not owned by a brewery. A free house is free to purchase any beer from any brewery that will sell it; consequently, many free houses have a wider selection.

French degree. *(frehnch' di-gree')*
A French unit of water hardness equal to 1 milligram of calcium carbonate ($CaCO_3$) per 1,000 liters of water.

1 °French = 10 ppm
= 0.583 gr per U.S. gal
= 0.7 Clark degrees
= 0.56 German degrees

freshness dating. *(frehshsh'-nis dey'-d:ing)*
The visible coding of beer bottles with a freshness date so that consumers know whether or not they are receiving fresh beer.

froth. *(frath)*
See: foam; fob; head.

fructose. *(frook'-tos)*
Formula: $C_6H_{12}O_6$. The sweetest of sugars (173% as sweet as sucrose) found in a natural state in some fruits and in honey, or combined with glucose (dextrose) as sucrose.

Frühjahrsbierfest. *(fghue'-yaghz-beegh-fehst)*
An annual springtime beer festival held in Munich starting on March 19, St. Joseph's Day.

fruit extract. *(froot ehk'-straekt)*
A concentrate or syrup made from various fruits that is sometimes used instead of whole fruit in making fruit-flavored beers.

fruit mead. *(froot' meed')*
Synonym for melomel.

fruity. *(froo'-d:ee)*
Synonym for estery.

FTU.
Abbreviation for Formazin Turbidity Unit.

Fuggles. *(fuh'-gelz)*
A variety of hops grown in England containing 4–5.5 percent and sometimes 6 percent alpha acids and 2.5–4 percent beta acids. It is also grown in Oregon with an alpha acid content of 4–6 percent.

full-bodied. *(ful' ba'-d:eed)*
A beer rich and mouth-filling as opposed to thin-bodied and watery.

fullness. *(ful'-nis)*
Synonym for body.

fully modified malt. *(ful'-ee ma-d:uh-fayd' mohlt')*
Malt in which most of the protein materials have been converted by the proteinase enzyme. **See also:** undermodified malt.

fusel alcohols. *(fyoo'-zel ael'-kuh-hohlz)*
Synonym for higher alcohols.

gail. *(geiy[e]l)*
Orthographic variant for gyle.

gal.
Abbreviation for gallon.

Galena. *(guh-lee'-nuh)*
A variety of very bitter hops grown in Washington and Idaho and containing 12.5–13.5 percent alpha acids.

gallon. *(gal'-en)*
1. In the United States, a liquid measure with a capacity of 231 cubic inches (3.7854 liters) equal to 126 fluid ounces. One U.S. gallon equals 5/6 of an imperial gallon. Abbrev: U.S. gal. **2.** In the United Kingdom and the Commonwealth, the imperial gallon (or U.K. gallon) is a liquid measure of 277.42 cubic inches (4.5459 liters) (10 pounds avoirdupois of water at 17 °C), equal to 160 fluid ounces. It is the fundamental unit of capacity in the United Kingdom and is defined in the Weights and Measures Act 11 & 12 Eliz. II, 1963. The gallon is mentioned in *Piers Plowman* (1342) and was given legal status as a unit in 1602. The imperial gallon is somewhat larger than the U.S. gallon: 1 imperial gallon equals 1.20094 (6/5) U.S. gallons. Abbrev: imp. gal; U.K. gal.

galopin. *(ga-loh-pae~')*
In France, a beer glass of a capacity of 15 centiliters. Because it is so small it is very rare and almost obsolete.

Gambrinus. (*gaem-bray'-nuhs*)

A corruption or contraction of the name Jean Primus, Duke Jean I of Brabant, Louvain, and Antwerp, born 1251 in Bourguignon and killed 1295 in a duel or in a tournament in Bar. He is the second patron (not a saint) of brewers and the first patron of beer lovers. He was not a brewer but a popular ruler well liked by his subjects and particularly by the brewers of Brussels, who placed his effigy in the meeting hall of their association in Brussels. According to legend Gambrinus could drink 144 pints of beer during a single feast. His name is synonymous with a joyful and exuberant way of life. Among the other etymological interpretations of the name Gambrinus there is one claiming that it was derived from the founder of Cambray, a brewing city where a brewer was once known as a *gambarius*. Another sees the origin of the word in the medieval German word *gambra*, meaning germination of grain, or from *cambier*, the name given to brewers in the north of France in the Middle Ages. Gambrinus is also the name of a Czech brewery established in Plzen in 1869, a famous cafe in San Polo di Piave in northern Italy, and that of an opera composed by Maurice Frank in 1961.

gas line. (*gaes' layn*)

Thick-walled, high-pressure tubing for carbon dioxide or nitrogen.

gassy. (*gae'-see*)

Containing excessive carbon dioxide gas.

Gay-Lussac. (*gay lue-saek'*)

An alcoholometer devised by Louis Joseph Gay-Lussac (1778–1850) in 1824 to determine the percentage of alcohol in a solution. In France, the alcoholometric strength of a beverage is expressed in terms of its volumetric alcohol content at 59 °F (15 °C). Pure alcohol has a strength of 100°, and the alcohol content is equal to the number of liters of alcohol per 100 liters of wine (or beer). Abbrev: °G.L.; °GL.

gel. (*jehl*)

A colloidal dispersion that does not flow. **See also:** SOL.

gelaeger. (*guh-la'-ger*)

Sediment left in the bottom of fermentation vessels.

gelatin. (*jeh'-luh-tin*)

A colorless, tasteless, and odorless water-soluble protein of little nutritive value prepared from albuminous substances and added to maturing beer to help clarify it.

gelatinization. *(jeh-laet-[e]-ni-zei'-shen)*
1. The intake of water and the resulting swelling of starch granules when moist heat is applied to starch. It is the first stage in the enzymatic breakdown of starch followed by liquefaction and saccharification. 2. The act of cooking malt adjuncts to a gelatinized form prior to adding them to the mash.

germ. *(jerm)*
The embryo of a cereal grain.

German degree. *(juhr'-men di-gree')*
A German unit of water hardness equal to 1 milligram of calcium oxide (CaO) per 1,000 liters of water.

$1°$ German = 17.9 ppm of calcium carbonate
= 1.4285 Clark degrees
= 1.044 gr per U.S. gal
= 1.78 French degrees

German beer purity law. *(juhr'-min beeyr' pyoo'-ruh-d:ee la)*
See: Reinheitsgebot.

germinal brush. *(juhr'-men-el bruhsh')*
Synonym for grain brush.

germinating. *(juhr'-muh-nei-d:ing)*
Synonym for germination.

germination. *(juhr-muh-nei'-shen)*
The second stage of the beermaking process that drains the steeped barley grains and allows them to sprout for seven to nine days. The process may be accelerated by the use of such products as gibberellic acid or may be prolonged up to eleven or thirteen days for a more thorough disintegration of the malt. While germinating, the embryo produces the enzyme amylase (sometimes called diastase), which will later convert some of the starch of the endosperm into maltose and dextrins. This treatment of the barley grains follows cleaning, sorting, grading, and steeping and takes place at 50–68 °F (10–20 °C). **See also:** floor malting; germination box; malting.

germination box. *(juhr-muh-nei'-shen baks')*
A large, rectangular, open-topped container with a capacity of about 200 quarts, often made of cement, fitted with a removable slotted bottom plate located

about 20 centimeters from the bottom and through which air of appropriate temperature and humidity is allowed to circulate. The barley grains, in layers of 60–100 centimeters, are constantly turned by a five-bladed propeller fitted on a vertical shaft. The process takes about six days. Also called: Saladin box.

germinative capacity. *(juhr'-muh-nei-d:iv kuh-pae'-si-d:ee)*
The percentage number of barley grains to have germinated in laboratory tests after six days in moist sand or damp filter pads. **See also:** germinative energy; Thunaeus test.

germinative energy. *(juhr'-muh-nei-d:iv eh'-ner-jee)*
The percentage of barley grains to germinate under specific conditions. In laboratory tests, at least three sets of one hundred or several hundred barley grains are germinated in moist sand or between damp filter pads on 9-millimeter petri dishes at 50–68 °F (15–20 °C). After three days the number of corns that have chitted are counted; that value constitutes the germinative energy, which should be more than 95 percent and preferably closer to 98 percent. A second count, taken after six days, constitutes the germinative capacity. The difference between the germinative capacity and the germinative energy is a measure of the dormancy of the barley grain.

germinative power. *(juhr'-muh-nei-d:iv paw'-er)*
The capacity of barley grains to germinate, and which must be more than 98 percent to be acceptable for malting.

gibberellic acid. *(ji-buh-reh'-lik ae'-sid)*
Formula: essentially Ga_3. A microbiological product having plant growth hormones extracted from a parasite mushroom (the fungus *Gibberella fujikuroi*) from Japanese rice fields and identical to a material secreted by the barley embryo. It is added to steeping water at a rate of 0.5 milligram per kilogram of barley to break dormancy and to accelerate plant growth. Also, it is sprayed on germinating barley at about 0.25 milligram per kilogram to trigger or accelerate germination, hasten the secretion and action of proteolytic enzymes, the respiration rate, the modification rate, the heat production rate, and the growth of the embryo, thus reducing germination time. However it has very little effect on amylase.

gildenbier. *(gil'-den-beegh)*
A Belgian word meaning corporation beer, synonymous with *bière de Diest*.

gill. *(gil)*
1. A capacity measure for liquids equal to 1/4 of a pint. It first came into use in the thirteenth century as a wine measure. 2. Ground ivy (*Glechoma hederacea*) or beer flavored with it instead of hops.

ginger. *(jin'-jer)*
A spice especially popular in holiday-style beers.

ginger ale. *(jin'-jer eiyl')*
A nonalcoholic, carbonated beverage that is flavored with ginger. **See also:** ginger beer.

ginger beer. *(jin'-jer beeyr')*
A beverage similar to ginger ale but flavored with fermented ginger.

Ginger Beer. *(jin'-jer beeyr')*
A cocktail consisting of 1 part champagne, 1 part *framboise*, 1 part ginger ale, 3 parts beer, and a touch of powdered ginger.

GL.
Abbreviation for Gay-Lussac. Also: G.L.

glass. *(glaes)*
1. A drinking vessel made of glass. 2. Refers to the quality of the contents of such a vessel. 3. Synonym for ginger ale.

glucoamylase. *(gloo-ko-ae'-muh-leis)*
Synonym for amyloglucosidase.

glucophilic. *(gloo-ko-fi'-lik)*
Describes an organism that thrives on glucose.

glucose. *(gloo'-kos)*
A simple fermentable sugar formed in the wort by the enzymatic action of yeast on maltose and maltotriose. In industry it is obtained by the hydrolysis of starch with dilute acids. Pure, commercial glucose, sometimes called dextrose, always contains a certain amount of dextrins which, being unfermentable, remain in the beer and give it a sweet, mellow flavor. **Syn:** dextrose; corn sugar.

glume. *(gloom)*
Either of the empty sterile bracts at the base of a grass spikelet, or a similar structure on the spikelets of sedges.

glycolysis. *(glay-ka'-luh-sis)*
Sugar being broken down into its component parts during fermentation.

glycoprotein. *(glay-ko-pro'-teen)*
Protein with carbohydrate links, derived from the barley. Unmalted grains are rich in glycoprotein. Assists head retention.

goblet. *(gab'-lit)*
1. A drinking vessel similar to a chalice, with a deep bowl on a proportionately short stem, without a handle, and which has a capacity, in English glassware, of 1 gill or more. **2.** In modern stemware classification, the goblet is the tallest glass and holds 9–12 fluid ounces.

godisgood. *(gad:-iz-gud'*)*
An early name given to yeast by English brewers who did not understand its chemistry and workings but guessed that it was responsible for fermentation. Also spelled: godesgood; goddisgood.

Goldings. *(gohl'-dingz)*
A variety of hops grown in England and containing 4.6–5.2 percent alpha acids.

gondale. *(goh~-dal'-[e]*)*
The name given in medieval France to a type of beer brewed in the city of Lille. The term is derived from *goodale* and *goodall*.

goods. *(gudz)*
A brewer's term for the total content of the mash tun at the end of the mashing process.

goudalier. *(goo-da-lyei'*)*
The name given in medieval times to a beer merchant in the north of France.

goût de jeune. *(goo de zhoen'-[e])*
The French name given to the unpleasant smell associated with green beer. In German: *jungbukett*. **See also:** green beer.

grading. *(grei'-d:ing)*
  The process of sorting barley grains according to size.

graetzer. *(greht'-ser)*
  A low-gravity, strongly hopped beer made with a high percentage of smoked, roasted wheat malt.

grain. *(greyn')*
  A unit of weight based on the weight of a grain of wheat taken as an average of the weight of grains from the middle of the ear. **See:** appendix C.

grain alcohol. *(greyn' ael'-kuh-hohl)*
  Synonym for ethyl alcohol.

grain bag. *(greyn' baeg)*
  Bags with an open weave made from cloth or synthetic fabrics used to contain grains during mashing, sparging, or steeping. The open weave allows liquid to penetrate to the grain and acts as a colander to strain the grain.

grain bed. *(greyn' behd)*
  The collection of solid particles and grain husks on top of the false bottom of the lauter tun. Once established, the grain bed allows for the separation of the clear sweet wort from the spent grains during sparging. The typical grain bed ranges from 12–18 inches deep.

grain beer. *(greyn' beeyr')*
  Beer that is made from malted barley rather than from malt extract. **Syn:** all-grain beer.

grain bill. *(greyn' bil')*
  The list of grains and their amounts used for a particular recipe.

grain brush. *(greyn' bruhsh')*
  In malting, a machine used mainly at the end of the cleaning process to remove impurities adhering to the surface of barley grains. **Syn:** germinal brush.

grain mill. *(greyn' mil')*
  A device used to crush grain into small pieces and to separate the grain from the husk. Grain mills use hammers and rotating plates or rollers to pulverize the interior of the grain while leaving the husk largely intact.

grains. *(greynz')*
Spent goods.

grains of paradise. *(greynz' uhv pae'-ruh-days)*
The pungent seeds of a tropical African plant (*Aframomum melegueta*) once used to flavor ale and later gin and cordials.

grain weevil. *(greyn' weev'-el)*
A parasitic insect (*Calandra granaria*) that feeds on and infects the malt. **Syn:** malt worm.

grainy. *(grey'-nee)*
Tastes like cereal or raw grain.

gram. *(graem)*
A metric unit of mass. Abbrev: g.

Granny. *(grae'-nee)*
In Britain, a mix of old and mild ale.

grant. *(graent)*
A small cylindrical vessel, usually made of copper, fitted with one or more drain cocks for draining and inspecting the mash when it is transferred from the mash tun to the lauter tun.

grave ale. *(greiv' eiyl')*
A beer served at a Danish feast or after a funeral to keep away the spirit of the departed.

gravity (SG). *(grae'-vuh-d:ee)*
Specific gravity as expressed by brewers. For example, specific gravity 1.046 is expressed as 1046 (ten forty-six). Density of a solution as compared to water; expressed in grams per milliliter (1 milliliter of water weighs 1 gram, hence specific gravity equals 1.000).

gravity units (GU). *(grae'-vuh-d:ee yoo'-nits)*
A form of expressing specific gravity in formulas as a whole number. It is equal to the significant digits to the right of the decimal point. For example, specific gravity 1.046 becomes 46 gravity units.

green beer. *(green' beeyr')*
Newly fermented beer before maturing or lagering. At this stage one of two products can be obtained: scotch or beer. Scotch is produced by distilling unhopped green beer. **See also:** *goût de jeune.*

green malt. *(green' mohlt')*
Newly germinated barley not yet dried or kilned.

grinder. *(grayn'-der)*
A machine generally consisting of one or more pairs of cylinders (or rollers) that crushes malted barley. **Syn:** malt mill; malt crusher; mill; roller mill.

grinding. *(grayn'-ding)*
Synonym for milling.

gripperhead. *(gri'-per-hehd)*
Part of an automatic filling machine that grips the head (or neck) of the bottle.

grist. *(grist)*
1. Grains to be ground. 2. Sieved and ground malt ready for mashing. 3. A quantity of ground malt sufficient for one mashing.

grist cage. *(grist keij')*
A large conical-shaped vessel into which grist is collected after milling.

grit. *(grit)*
Adjuncts such as cereal grains used as substitutes to barley. **Syn:** raw grain.

Grodzisk. *(grad'-zisk)*
A specialty beer of Grodzisk, Poland, made with a high proportion of oak-smoked malted wheat.

grouchevoï. *(groo'-sheh-voy*)*
Kvas in which pears have macerated.

growler. *(graw'-ler)*
A jug- or pail-like container once used to carry draft beer bought by the measure at the local tavern.

gruit. *(groyt')*

A mixture of herbs and spices—principally sweet gale (bog-myrtle), marsh (wild rosemary), coriander, yarrow, and milfoil, as well as other ingredients such as juniper berries, caraway seed, aniseed, ginger, nutmeg, and cinnamon—once used to flavor English and European ales before the introduction of hops. Hops and sometimes resin also entered into the composition of gruit in some countries. After the organization of brewers' guilds, the preparation of gruit became the work of specialists who operated in gruthouses, or gruit houses. Once spelled: grut; gruyt; grug; gruz.

gruitbier. *(groyt'-beegh)*

From the Middle Ages to the fifteenth century, a beer flavored with gruit. **See also:** gruit.

Grundy tanks. *(gruhn'-dee taengks)*

British-manufactured brewing vessels with a capacity of 3.5 or 7 barrels.

gueuze. *(guez'-e)*

In Belgium, a beer prepared by blending two *lambic* beers of different age, a young lambic with an old one, usually in a ratio of 2:1. This blending causes a new fermentation to occur, and the brew is bottled and aged for one more year producing a dry, fruity beer with champagnelike effervescence. It contains about 4.4 percent alcohol by weight or 5.5 percent by volume (5.2 °Belgian). Etym: From the name of a street in Belgium, Guezenstraet (rue des Gueux), where this type of beer was once sold. *Gueux* means beggar or vagabond. Also, it is claimed to have been introduced in 1870 by the brewer and burgomaster of Lembecq who hired the engineer Cayerts to apply the technique of bottle conditioning used in making champagne to the production of lambic. The product was first called *lambic de chez le gueux* and later *lambic du gueux*. **Syn:** *gueuze-lambic*. **See also:** cherry beer; *faro; framboise; kriek; lambic;* Mort Subite.

gueuze-lambic. *(guez'-e lam'-beek)*

Synonym for *gueuze*.

gumming. *(guhm'-ing)*

The action of spraying a coat of glue on beer labels.

gushing beer. *(guh'-shing beeyr')*

A beer that foams out vigorously when uncapped. **Syn:** wild beer.

gyle. *(gay[e]l)*
   1. The portion of unfermented wort added to finished beer to condition it and raise its alcohol content. **2.** The quantity of beer produced by a single brewing. Sometimes spelled: gail. **3.** A fermentation vessel.

gyle vat. *(gay[e]l vaet')*
   In Old English, a fermentation vessel.

gyngleboy. *(jing'-gel-boy)*
   A leather bottle or black jack used in sixteenth-century England and lined with silver or gilt metal and ornamented with silver bells that, according to Thomas Dekker (*The Seven Deadly Sins of London*, 1606), rang "pearles of drunkeness."

gypsum. *(jip'-suhm)*
   Formula: $CaSO_4 2H_2O$. Hydrated calcium sulfate used in the treatment of soft or neutral water to harden it. **Syn:** plaster of Paris.

hag. *(haq)*
A type of beer produced in ancient Egypt (circa 2000 BC) from what was called "red barley of the Nile." Also spelled: *hak; hek; hequ(p)*.

haircloth. *(hehr'-clath)*
A horsehair blanket placed on the floor of traditional hop-drying kilns. **Syn:** horse-hair cloth.

halbe. *(hal'-be)*
In Germany, a beer mug with a capacity of 1/2 a liter. **See also:** *masskrug*.

Half-and-Half. *(haef' end haef')*
A blend of equal parts of drinks of the same nature such as mild and bitter, ale and stout, or ale and porter.

half en half. *(haef' en haef')*
An old-style *lambic* made from a blend of equal parts of lambic and *Mars* (a French-style beer similar to *bière de garde)*.

Hallertau. *(hal'-egh-taw)*
A variety of hops cultivated in Bavarian Germany containing 7–8 percent alpha acids. Because of disease, it is being replaced by Brewers Gold, Northern Brewer, and Hersbrucker. The same variety, grown in Washington and Idaho, yields 5–6.5 percent alpha acids and 4–6 percent beta acids.

hammer capper. *(hae'-mer kae'-per)*
A manual bottle capper used with a hammer.

hand pump. *(haend' puhmp)*
A device for dispensing draft beer using a pump operated by hand. The use of a hand pump allows the cask-conditioned beer to be served without the use of pressurized carbon dioxide.

hang. *(haeng)*
Lingering bitterness or harshness.

Hansen, Emil Christian. *(haen'-sin eh-meel' krisch'-[ee]-en)*
The first laboratory to isolate a strain of beer yeast and prove beyond a doubt that this organism was responsible for alcoholic fermentation (circa 1850 at Carlsberg Laboratories).

harbor beer. *(har'-ber beeyr')*
Slang expression for very weak beer.

hard cider. *(hard' say'-d:er)*
A fermented beverage made from apples.

hardness of water. *(hard'-nis uhv wa'-d:er)*
Synonym for water hardness; the quality of water in relation to the amount of calcium and magnesium salts it contains.

hard resins. *(hard' reh'-zinz)*
Amorphous substances formed from the oxidation and polymerization of alpha and beta acids during hop storage. The alpha acids gradually lose their crystalline structure, aroma, and their bittering and preservative powers. In the later stages of this conversion, resinification occurs whereby hard resins are formed that are useless in the brewing process. **See also:** soft resins.

hard water. *(hard' wa'-d:er)*
Water containing significant quantities of calcium and magnesium salts.

harsh. *(harsh)*
Synonym for astringent.

haze. *(heiz)*
Abbreviated form of chill haze.

hazy. *(hei'-zee)*
Synonym for cloudy.

HBU.
1. Abbreviation for hop bitterness unit. **2.** Abbreviation for homebrew bittering unit.

head. *(hehd')*
1. The foam at the top of a glass of beer. **Syn:** cream; collar; foam; suds. **2.** The froth that forms on top of the wort during primary fermentation. **3.** The flat end of a cask or barrel.

head brewer. *(hehd' broo'-wer)*
Synonym for master brewer.

heading liquid. *(heh'-d:ing li'-kwid)*
An additive used to ensure a firm, long-lasting head or to increase its thickness. **Syn:** foaming agent; heading compound.

head retention. *(hehd' ri-tehn'-shen)*
The foam stability of a beer as measured, in seconds, by the time required for a 3-centimeter foam collar to collapse. **Syn:** foam stability; foam retention.

headspace. *(hehd'-speis)*
Synonym for ullage.

heat chamber. *(heet' cheim'-ber)*
The part of the kiln where heat is stored and distributed evenly under the floor of the kiln.

Heater and Cooler. *(hee'-d:er end koo'-ler)*
A short glass of liquor followed by a tall glass of beer.

heat exchanger. *(heet' ehks-chein'-jer)*
Process equipment for heating or cooling the wort or beer rapidly.

heavy beer. *(heh'-vee beeyr')*
Synonym for high-gravity beer.

heavy wet. *(heh'-vee weht')*
An old name for strong ale.

hectoliter. *(hehk'-tuh-lee-d:er)*
One hundred liters. About 22 (21.9976) imperial gallons, or 26.4 U.S. gallons. Abbrev: hl.

hefe. *(heh'-fe)*
Yeast in German.

hek. *(haq)*
Note: the ancient Egyptian word for beer was *hnqt*. Conventionally written with vowels by Egyptologists as *henqet*, which phonetically would be "hehn'-qeht." The Coptic version is "hen-keh'." Orthographic variant for *hag*.

hequ(p).
Orthographic variant for *hag*. **See:** *hnqt* or *hnk* for the pronunciation.

herb beer. *(uhrb' beeyr')*
1. A beer, usually an ale, that has been flavored with herbs. **2.** Misnomer for fermented sugar flavored with herbs, sometimes referred to as an herb wine.

Hersbrucker. *(hehrs'-bruk-er)*
A variety of hops grown in Washington and containing 5–6.5% alpha acids, sometimes less.

hexose. *(hehk'-sos)*
Any monosaccharide containing six carbon atoms; includes glucose, fructose, lactose, mannose, and galactose.

Het Pint. *(heht' paynt')*
A traditional Scottish drink consisting of ale, whiskey, and eggs.

high-alpha hops. *(hay' ael'-fuh haps)*
See: bittering hops.

higher alcohols. *(hay'-er ael'-kuh-holz)*
Alcohols that have a higher boiling point than ethanol and are derived from keto acids during the yeast protein synthesis. The formation of higher alcohols varies with yeast strain and yeast growth, fermentation temperature

(an increase in temperature promotes the formation of alcohols), and fermentation method (in some cases a stirred fermentation produces more alcohols). There are two classes of higher (fusel) alcohols: (1) volatile alcohols, most often called aliphatic alcohols (examples: propyl alcohols, butyl alcohol, amyl alcohols); and (2) nonvolatile alcohols (examples: phenol alcohols like tyrosal). **Syn:** alcohols; fusel alcohols. **See also:** volatiles.

high fermentation. *(hay' fuhr-mehn-tei'-shen)*
Synonym for top fermentation.

highly modified malt. *(hay'-lee ma-d:uh-fayd' mohlt')*
Malt containing few complex proteins, many free amino acids, and having a large amount of soluble starch available for conversion. Highly modified malt typically exhibits an acrospire growth between three-quarters and the full length of the barley kernel. This type of malt provides several advantages to the brewer. The presence of free amino acids aids yeast growth in the final wort. The absence of complex proteins also reduces the likelihood of haze problems in the finished product; because of this, there is no need for a protein rest, which simplifies the mashing schedule and allows the use of a single-step infusion mash. Highly modified malt, however, gives a lower yield to the maltster because the malted barley kernel loses more of its weight to the growth of the acrospire than less modified malt.

hhd.
Abbreviation for hogshead.

hiya. *(hee-ya)*
In Japan, cold *saké*.

high-gravity beer. *(hay' gra'-vuh-d:ee beeyr')*
Any beer that is brewed from an original wort gravity of 1.050 or more. **Syn:** heavy beer.

high kraeusen. *(hay' kroy'-zen)*
See: *kraeusen.*

hl.
Abbreviation for hectoliter.

hippocras. *(hip'-uh-kras)*

A combination of melomel and metheglin—a mead of honey, raisin juice, herbs, and spices—once prepared for medicinal purposes. Etym: Named after Hippocrates (460–377 BC), Greek writer and father of medicine.

hnke. *(hen-keh)*

Coptic for beer.

hnqt. *(hehn-qeht)*

Middle Egytian for beer.

hoan tsie'u. *(ho-an tsee-oo*)*

A type of Chinese *saké*. The term means yellow rice wine.

Hoegaardse wit. *(hoe-gar'-tse vit'*)*

Synonym for *blanche de* Hoegaarden.

Hoff-Stevens tap. *(haf' stee'-vinz taep)*

Two-pronged tap head for commercial-style kegs.

hogs. *(hagz')*

Abbreviation for hogshead.

hogshead. *(hagz'-hehd)*

1. A large barrel-shaped cask for holding liquids, the capacity of which ranges from 54–140 gallons. **2.** A precise capacity measure that once varied according to the liquid or commodity it contained, originally equal to 63 old wine gallons (52.5 imperial gallons). The London hogshead for beer had a volume of 54 gallons while that for ale had a volume of 48 gallons. Today, it has a volume of 63 gallons (238.5 liters) in the United States and 54 imperial gallons (245 liters) in the United Kingdom. Abbrev: hhd or hogs.

homebrew. *(hom'-broo)*

Beer brewed at home. **Syn:** homemade beer.

homebrew bittering units. *(hom'-broo bi'-d:er-ing yoo'-nits)*

A formula devised by Dave Line and adopted by the American Homebrewers Association to estimate the bitterness value of hopped malt extract by multiplying the equivalent number of ounces of hops by the alpha acid percent of the hops employed.

(Example: If 2 ounces of 5 percent alpha acid hops are present in a 3.3-pound can of hopped malt extract this would yield 7.5 home bittering units.) Abbrev: HBU. **See also:** alpha acid units; bittering units; bitterness units; hop bittering coefficient; hop bitterness units.

homebrewed beer. *(hom'-brood beeyr')*
Synonym for homebrew.

homebrewer. *(hom-broo'-wer)*
One who brews beer for personal consumption. **Syn:** amateur brewer; domestic brewer.

homebrewing. *(hom-broo'-wing)*
The art of making beer at home. In the United States, homebrewing was legalized by President Carter on February 1, 1979, through a bill introduced by Senator Alan Cranston. The Cranston Bill allows a single person to brew up to 100 gallons of beer annually for personal enjoyment and up to 200 gallons in a household of two persons or more aged eighteen and older. In England, homebrewing was again legalized in 1963 by Chancellor Reginald Maudling, who lifted all restrictions on homebrewing, provided the beer was not sold.

homemade beer. *(hom-meyd' beeyr')*
Synonym for homebrew.

homofermentive. *(ho-mo-fuhr-mehn'-tiv)*
Characterizes organisms that metabolize only one specific carbon source.

Honeybeer. *(huh'-nee-beeyr)*
A cocktail prepared by heating a pint of ale and adding 1 soupspoon of honey.

honey wine. *(huh'-nee wayn')*
Synonym for mead. The term is rejected by many wine purists and legislators (including those of France) who maintain that the term *wine* can only apply to a product of the vine. **Syn:** pyment.

hoop. *(hoop)*
The circular band of metal surrounding the staves of a wooden cask or barrel and holding them together.

hoop binding. *(hoop' baynd'-ing)*
   1. The action of binding together the staves of a wooden barrel or cask.
2. The circular piece of metal used for that purpose.

hop, to. *(hap', too)*
   To add hops to the wort or the fermenting beer.

hop. *(hap')*
   Orthographic variant of hops.

hop back. *(hap' baek')*
   A large sieving vessel fitted with a perforated false bottom to separate the spent hops from the bitter wort after boiling. **Syn:** strainer; hop jack; hop strainer. **See also:** hop separator; Moor's head.

hop bine. *(hap' bayn')*
   The growing stem of the hop plant. **Syn:** bine.

hop bitterness coefficient. *(hap' bi'-d:er-nis ko-ee-fi'-shent)*
   The coefficient obtained when multiplying the alpha-acid percentage of a variety of hops by the number of ounces to be boiled in the wort. This coefficient is useful to homebrewers when the hop variety mentioned in a recipe is not available and another must be substituted. For example, 2 ounces of hops at 5.25 percent alpha acids can be substituted in a recipe calling for 1.5 ounces of hops at 7 percent alpha acids. **See also:** alpha acid units; bittering units; bitterness units; homebrew bittering units; hop bitterness units.

hop bitterness units. *(hap' bi'-d:er-nis yoo'-nits)*
   A formula devised by Fred Eckhardt to calculate the bitterness of a homebrewed beer or the amount of hops required to produce a beer of a predetermined bitterness level.

   Formula: $HBU = (a \times w) / K$
   a = alpha acid percentage of hops: whole, pellets, or extract
   w = a constant based on weight of hops: whole, pellets, or extract
        ounces per gallons: oz/U.S. gal or oz/U.K. gal
        grams per gallon: g/U.S. gal or g/U.K. gal
        grams per liter: g/l
        Example: 1.5 oz of hops per 5 U.S. gal batch = 0.3 oz/U.S. gal
   K = a constant based on figures obtained from technical sources. It varies

according to the system of units used for "w":
= 0.093 for oz/U.S. gal
= 0.078 for oz/U.K gal
= 2.7 for g/U.S. gal
= 3.2 for g/U.K. gal
= 0.7 for g/l

Conversely, the amount of hops to be used to obtain a determined bitterness unit can be calculated by rearranging the formula:

$$w = K / (a / HBU)$$

Abbrev: HBU. **See also:** alpha acid units; bittering units; bitterness units; homebrew bittering units; hop bittering coefficient.

hop break. *(hap' breik')*
The precipitation of protein and tannic material when hops are added to the boiling wort. A new hop or hot break occurs with each addition of hops.

hop cone. *(hap' kon')*
Synonym for strobile.

hop essential oils. *(hap' i-sehn'-shel oylz)*
Synonym for hop oils.

hop extract. *(hap' ehk'-straekt)*
Bitter resins and hop oils extracted from hops by organic solvents, usually methylene chloride or hexane, whereas tannins, sugars, and proteins are extracted with hot water. The solvents and water are later removed by evaporation. The use of such extracts is increasing in the brewing industry because they store well, they are less bulky, they require no refrigeration, boiling time is shorter, and straining spent hops is not required. Hop extracts are sometimes isomerized by alkalis or by magnesium salts at neutrality, or by exposure to light of a specific wavelength. Iso-alpha-acid hop extract (or isomerized hop extract) is added as late as possible, usually during secondary fermentation.

hop field. *(hap' feeyld')*
Synonym for hop garden.

hop flea beetle. *(hap′ flee bee′-d:el)*
An insect (*Psylloides attenuata*) that eats holes in young hop leaves.

hop flour. *(hap′ flaw[e]r′)*
Obsolete synonym for lupulin.

hop flower. *(hap′ flaw[e]r′)*
Synonym for strobile.

hop fly. *(hap′ flay′)*
Synonym for Damson hop aphid.

hop garden. *(hap′ gard′-en)*
A field where hops are cultivated. **Syn:** hop field.

hop grower. *(hap′ gro[e]r′)*
One who grows hops.

hop jack. *(hap′ jaek′)*
Synonym for hop back.

hop kiln. *(hap′ kil[n])*
A oast house in which hops are dried twenty-four hours after picking at 167–176 °F (75–80 °C) to 8–10 percent moisture.

hop mill. *(hap′ mil′)*
Synonym for hop tearing machine.

hop mold. *(hap′ mold′)*
A disease produced by the fungus *Sphaerotheca macularis* that attacks hops. **Syn:** white mold; red mold; powdery mildew.

hop oils. *(hap′ oylz′)*
1. One of the two active ingredients in hops (the other being the soft resins). Hop oils belong to the terpene group of hydrocarbons and contain several hundred different compounds of which terpene hydrocarbons account for about 70 percent, alcohols (mainly geraniol and linalool) constitute the remaining 30 percent. Other constituents include aldehyde and esters. Hop oils are responsible for the hop aroma or character of beer. Like all essential oils, they are very volatile and are largely lost by steam evaporation during

the boil. **Syn:** hop essential oils. **See also:** soft resins. **2.** A concentrated oil extracted from hops.

hop pellets. *(hap'peh'-lits)*
Highly processed hops consisting of finely powdered hop cones compressed into pea-size tablets used in both home and commercial brewing. Regular hop pellets are, by weight, 20–30 percent stronger than the same variety in loose form; 1 pound of hop cones yields about 10–12 ounces of pellets. Concentrated pellets, as used in the brewing industry, are first processed to remove the non-resinous material, thus reducing the weight and volume. Standardized pellets are made from blends of hops to obtain a specific alpha acid level. Hop pellets keep better when stored in a sealed container around 54 °F (12 °C). **Syn:** pelletized hops.

hopping. *(hap'-ing)*
The addition of hops to the boiling wort or fermenting beer. **See also:** dry hopping; fermentation hopping; boiler hopping; late hopping; alpha acid; beta acid; hop oils.

hopping beer. *(hap'-ing beeyr')*
An early name given in England to hopped beer as opposed to unhopped "spiced ale."

hoppy. *(ha'-pee)*
Characteristic odor of the essential oil of hops. Does not include hop bitterness.

hop rate. *(hap'reit')*
The quantity of hops to be added to a given volume of sweet wort during boiling. In commercial brewing, hop rates are quoted in pounds per barrel or grams per hectoliter whereas homebrewers refer to ounces per five gallons.

hop resin. *(hap'reh'-zin)*
Highly processed hops consisting of hop resins and oils extracted by a solvent.

hop(s). *(hap[s])*
A perennial climbing vine, also known by the Latin botanical name *Humulus lupulus*, a member of the Cannabinaceae family. The female plant yields flowers of soft-leaved pinelike cones (called strobile) measuring about an inch in length. Only the female ripened flower is used for flavoring beer. Because hops reproduce through cuttings, the male plants are not cultivated and are even routed out to prevent them from fertilizing the female plants, the cones of which

would then become weighed-down with seeds. Seedless hops have a much higher bittering power than seeded ones. There are presently over one hundred varieties of hops cultivated around the world. The best known are: Brewer's Gold, Bullion, Cascade, Cluster, Comet, Eroica, Fuggles, Galena, Goldings, Hallertau, Nugget, Northern Brewer, Perle, Saaz, Styrian Goldings, Tettnang, Willamettes, and Wye Target. Hops are grown in Czechoslovakia, Bavaria (Germany), Kent (England), Tasmania (Australia), Willamette Valley (Oregon), and Yakima Valley (Washington). Apart from contributing bitterness, hops impart aroma and flavor, reduce the surface tension during the boiling stage, assist in forming a yeast head during ale fermentation, and inhibit the growth of bacteria in wort and beer. Hops are added at the beginning of the boiling stage (called flavoring, boiling, or bittering hops) to give the brew its bitter flavor, and at the end of the boil (called finishing or aromatic hops) to give it aroma and hop character. In commercial brewing, about 200–700 grams of hops are required for every hectoliter of wort. The addition of hops to beer dates from 7000–1000 BC; however, hops were used to flavor beer in pharaonic Egypt around 600 BC. They were cultivated in Germany as early as the AD 300 and were used extensively in French and German monasteries in medieval times and gradually superseded other herbs and spices around the fourteenth and fifteenth centuries. Pépin le Bref, ruler of the Franks, gave hop gardens (*humlonaria*) to the Abbaye de St. Denis, near Paris, in 768. Hop fields also were cultivated at the Abbaye de St. Germain des Prés in 800 and at the Abbaye de Corvey sur le Wesser in 822. In Flanders, Jean Sans Peur founded the Ordre du Houblon in 1409 to encourage the use of hops in beermaking. Prior to the use of hops, beer was flavored with herbs and spices such as juniper, coriander, romarin, cumin, nutmeg, oak leaves, lime blossoms, cloves, rosemary, gentian, guassia, chamomile, and others. **See also:** alpha acid; beta acid; hop oils; *Humulus lupulus;* kiln-dried hops; lupulin; preservative value; soft resins.

hop separator. *(hap'seh'-puh-rei-d:er)*
A chestlike vessel containing a sieve and a screw conveyor for removing spent hops and for squeezing the wort out of them. It is used in some breweries instead of the hop back.

hop strainer. *(hap'strei'-ner)*
Synonym for hop back.

hop tannin. *(hap'tae'-nin)*
Tannins derived from hops as opposed to malt tannins. **See also:** tannin.

hop tearing machine. *(hap' tehr'-ing muh-sheen')*
An apparatus that separates the various parts of the hops: lupulin, bracts, stems. **Syn:** hop mill.

hop tonic. *(hap' ta'-nik)*
A nonalcoholic beer once brewed at home as a temperance beverage but suspected of often containing various amounts of alcohol.

hordein. *(hohr'-dee-in)*
A protein (prolamine) found in barley.

Hordeum distichum. *(hohr'-dee-em di'-sti-kem* [can also be: di'-stee-kem])*
The botanical name for two-rowed barley.

Hordeum hexastichum. *(hohr'-dee-em hehk-sae'-sti-kem)*
The botanical name for six-rowed barley.

Hordeum spontaneum. *(hohr'-dee-em span-tey'-nee-em)*
A wild grass believed to be the principal ancestor of barley.

horse-hair cloth. *(hohrs' hehr clath')*
Synonym for haircloth.

hose, to. *(hoz, too)*
To draw beer from the fermentation vessel to the storage cellar.

hosing. *(ho'-zing)*
Drawing beer from the fermentation vessel to the storage cellar.

hospitality room. *(has-puh-tal'-uh-d:ee room)*
A special room in a brewery where visiting guests are invited to taste the products of the brewery.

hot break. *(hat' breik')*
1. The coagulation and precipitation of protein and polyphenol matter during the boiling stage. In homebrewing, hot-break trub can be improved by the addition of Irish moss during the last fifteen minutes of the boil or it can be removed with a hop-back filtration of the wort or by allowing the hot wort to settle out before drawing it to the wort chiller. **Syn:** hot-break trub; hot trub. **See also:** cold break; hop break. **2.** Haziness caused by protein sediments.

hot-break trub. *(hat'-breik troob)*

Synonym for hot break.

hot-side aeration. *(hat'-sayd eiy-[e]-rei'-shen)*

Exposing hot wort to oxygen. Some believe this can have an adverse effect on beer quality, resulting in decreased shelf life and other problems.

hot trub. *(hat' troob')*

Synonym for hot break.

hot-water extract. *(hat-wa'-d:er ehk'-straekt)*

In laboratory tests, the quantity of dissolved solids present in a sweet wort solution prepared from malt and/or other materials. Abbrev: HWE.

household sugar. *(haw'-sold shu'-ger)*

A common name for cane sugar or sucrose.

Huckle My Buff. *(huhk'-el may buhf')*

In England, a mix of hot beer, brandy, and eggs.

hukster. *(huhk'-ster)*

In medieval England, a woman who retailed beer and ale, which she bought from the brewster or ale wife.

humlonaria. *(hyoom-lo-na'-ree-uh*)*

The name given to hop yards or gardens given to the Abbey of St. Denis by King Pépin le Bref in 768. Hop yards are also mentioned as *humularium* in the records of the bishopric of Freising in Upper Bavaria between 855 and 875.

humulene. *(hyoo'-myuh-leen)*

A primary component of the essential oil of the hop cone. Although rarely found in beer in this native form, it is processed into a number of flavor-active compounds that are significant in beer. The quantity of humulene found in a hop varies by hop variety, year, and growing region.

humulone. *(hyoo'-myuh-lon)*

Synonym for alpha acid, one of the two soft resins found in hops, composed of humulone, co-humulone, and ad-humulone.

Humulus lupulus. *(hyoo'-myuh-luhs loo'-pyuh-luhs)*
The botanical name for hops. The Romans called it *Lupus salictarius* because the plant grew wild among the willows like a wolf.

husar(d). *(hoo-sar[d]'*)*
Synonym for husky grain.

husk. *(huhsk)*
The dry outer layer of certain cereal seeds. The husk of barley consists of two closely adherent strawlike bracts (the lemma and the palea) that partially overlap. The barley husk provides protection for the grain, endosperm, and growing acrospire during the various stages of the malting process. It also plays an important role as a filter bed during lautering.

husky. *(huh'-skee)*
See: astringent.

husky grain. *(huh'-skee greyn')*
Overgrown malt with the acrospire reaching beyond the end of the grain. **Syn:** *husar(d)*; overgrown malt.

HWE.
Abbreviation for hot-water extract.

hydrocarbon. *(hay-dro-kar'-ben)*
Any compound made up entirely of carbon and hydrogen atoms.

hydrogen-ion concentration. *(hay'-druh-jen ay'-en kan[t]-sen-trei'-shen)*
The concentration of hydrogen ions in a solution, usually expressed in pH units, and used as a measure of the normality of the solution. **See also:** pH.

hydrolysis. *(hay-dro'-luh-sis)*
The degradation or alteration of an organic substance by water. The molecular composition of both the substance and the water are split, and the ions of water, OH (hydroxyl) and H (hydrogen), each react with a fraction of the cleaved substance. The presence of an acid or alkali is usually needed to act as a catalyst. For example, proteins are hydrolyzed to amino acids; alcohols and acids form esters; and disaccharides yield monosaccharides.

Example: Sucrose hydrolyzes into glucose and fructose
Formula: $C_{12}H_{22}O_{11} = C_6H_{12}O_5 + C_6H_{12}O_6$

hydromel. *(hay'-dro-mehl)*
Mead in French.

hydrometer. *(hay-dra'-muh-d:er)*
A glass instrument for measuring the specific gravity of liquids as compared to that of water, consisting of a graduated stem resting on a weighted float. Most hydrometers are calibrated for use at 60 °F (15.6 °C), and tables or charts are provided listing corrections for variations to that temperature. The accuracy of a hydrometer is tested in water at 60 °F (15.6 °C), where it should read zero. **See also:** hydrometer jar.

hydrometer float. *(hay-dra'-muh-d:er flot')*
The bulb- or spindle-shaped float of a hydrometer weighted with lead, mercury, or pitch.

hydrometer jar. *(hay-dra'-muh-d:er jar')*
A tall, cylindrical, transparent glass or plastic jar in which the liquid to be measured is poured. The hydrometer is then floated in the liquid and spinned to dislodge adhering bubbles. The reading is taken at the waterline. **Syn:** testing jar; test tube.

hydroxide. *(hay-drak'-sayd)*
A compound, usually alkaline, containing the OH (hydroxyl) group.

iablochny. *(ya-bloch'-nee*)*
Kvas in which apples have been macerated.

I.B.U.
Abbreviation for International Bitterness Units. Also written: IBU.

ice beer. *(eis' beeyr')*
A North American lager that has been conditioned at temperatures cold enough for a portion of the water to freeze into ice crystals. The beer is separated from the ice, but U.S. laws require the brewery to replace the lost water prior to bottling. **See also:** *eisbock.*

idromele. *(ee-dro-meh'-leh)*
Mead in Italian.

imiak. *(ee'-mee-ak)*
Name given in Greenland to a homebrewed malt beer.

immature. *(i-muh-tyoo[e]r')*
Synonym for dormant.

immersion heater. *(i-muhr'-zhen hee'-d:er)*
A thermostatically controlled heating device, usually 50 watts strong, used by homebrewers for maintaining a constant temperature in the mash tun.

imperial gallon. *(im-pi'-ree-el gal'-en)*
A capacity measure in the United Kingdom and the Commonwealth equivalent to 1.2 U.S. gallons, or 4 liters. **Syn:** U.K. gallon. **See also:** gallon.

imperial gill. *(im-pi'-ree-el gil')*
   See: gill.

imperial pint. *(im-pi'-ree-el paynt')*
   See: pint.

imperial quart. *(im-pi'-ree-el kwohrt)*
   A liquid measure of the United Kingdom and the Commonwealth with a capacity of 1/4 of a gallon, 40 fluid ounces, or 69.318 cubic inches (1.135 liters).

imperial Russian stout. *(im-pi'-ree-el ruh'-shen stawt)*
   Synonym for Russian stout.

imperial stout. *(im-pi'-ree-el stawt)*
   Synonym for Russian stout.

Independent Tied House chains *(in-duh-pehn'-dent tayd' haws' cheyn)*
   A company that owns a chain of pubs but is not a brewery. The individual pubs are tied to the chain, which controls what brand of beer is served. But because the pubs are not owned by a brewery company, they are technically independent under the licensing laws "independent."

Indian corn. *(in'-dee-en kohrn')*
   A popular name for maize.

India pale ale. *(in'-dee-uh peiyl eiyl')*
   1. An ale brewed in England for British troops stationed in India in the eighteenth century. It was brewed very strong with a high hop bitterness to survive a voyage that could take as much as six months. **2.** The term now refers to bottled pale ales, specially those intended for exportation.

Indicator Time Test. *(in'-di-kei-d:er taym' tehst')*
   A method for measuring the degree of oxidation of a beer. The test measures the time, in seconds, for a solution of dichloro indophenol (dichloro-2,6 phenol-indophenol-sodium) to become discolored when beer is added. In the case of beers treated with antioxidants, the indicator may be close to zero; nontreated beers of average density rate about 500 Indicator Time Test (or seconds); some oxidized beers may reach many thousands of seconds. Abbrev: I.T.T.

indirect fire kiln. *(in-di-rehkt' fay[e]r' kil[n])*
A type of kiln that has a heat chamber into which the air is first warmed and then ventilated through the layers of malt.

infection. *(in-fehk'-shen)*
Spoilage of beer by wild yeast or bacteria. The bacteria are principally members of the genera *Pediococcus, Achromobacter, Lactobacillus,* and *Acetobacter.*

infusion brewing method. *(in-fyoo'-zhen broo'-wing meh'-thed)*
Synonym for infusion mashing.

infusion mashing. *(in-fyoo'-zhen mae'-shing)*
One of the three mashing methods and the traditional method for top-fermenting beer. The process is carried out at a constant temperature and in a single vessel, a mash tun fitted with a perforated false bottom. The mash, which is not boiled, is sprayed with hot water to raise the mashing temperature gradually to 149–154 °F (65–68 °C) for one to two hours. After mashing is complete, the wort is drawn through the slotted base, which can be opened to filter the liquid while straining the spent grains. **Syn:** infusion brewing method. Sometimes referred to as single-temperature mashing. **See also:** decoction mashing; mashing.

initial fermentation. *(i-ni'-shel fuhr-mehn-tei'-shen)*
Synonym for primary fermentation.

initial heat. *(i-ni'-shel heet')*
The temperature at which mashing begins.

inoculate. *(i-na'-kyuh-leyt)*
To introduce a microbe into surroundings capable of supporting its growth.

International Bitterness Units. *(in'-ter-naesh'-[e]-nel bi'-d:er-nis yoo'-nits)*
Synonym for bitterness units. Abbrev: I.B.U. or IBU.

inversion. *(in-vuhr'-zhen)*
The breakdown of sucrose into its composite monosaccharides, namely, glucose and fructose.

invertase. *(in-vuhr'-teis)*
An enzyme that hydrolyzes disaccharides to monosaccharides, especially sucrose into the invert sugars glucose and fructose. **Syn:** sucrase; saccharase.

invert sugar. *(in-vuhrt' shu'-ger)*
Processed common sugar (sucrose) separated into two sugars, fructose and glucose, by a modification of the molecular structure. It is obtained industrially by the inversion of sucrose with diluted acid, usually sulfuric acid, into equal parts of glucose and fructose. It does not contain dextrins and can be used as an adjunct or for priming.

iodine (starch) test. *(ay'-uh-dayn [starch] tehst')*
Synonym for starch test.

ion. *(ay'-en)*
An atom or molecule that, by loss or addition of one or more electrons, has acquired an electric charge: **See also:** anion; cation.

IPA.
Abbreviation for India pale ale.

Irish moss. *(ay'-rish mas')*
A red seaweed, *Chondrus crispus*, added during the last minutes of the boiling process to help clear the beer by causing haze-forming substances to coagulate and settle out. **Syn:** carrageen.

Irish Picon. *(ay'-rish pay'-kan*)*
A cocktail prepared by pouring Amer Picon and Guinness stout over ice in a large glass. Add a zest of lemon and serve cold.

isinglass. *(ay'-zing-glaes)*
A gelatinous substance processed from the swimming bladder of sturgeon from U.S. and Soviet rivers (containing 70–77 percent gelatin) and other fishes such as cod, ling, and carp, and added to beer for fining purposes. **Syn:** fish stuffing; fish gelatin.

Island Grog. *(ay'-lend grag')*
A cocktail prepared by heating 12 ounces of Pilsener with 4 coffeespoons of powdered sugar and 1 soupspoon of white rum. Remove from heat just before boiling and serve hot.

iso. *(ay'-so)*
Abbreviation for isomer.

isoamyl acetate. *(ay'-so-ae'-mil ae'-suh-d:eit)*

Formula: $CH_3COOC_5H_{11}$. An amylic ester derived from acetic acid and responsible for the fruity or bananalike odor in beer. Syn: banana oil; banana ester. See also: butyl acetate.

iso-humulones. *(ay'-so-hyoo'-myuh-lonz)*

See: alpha acid.

iso-alpha-acids. *(ay'-so ael'-fuh ae'-sidz)*

See: alpha acid.

isomer (iso). *(ay'-suh-mer)*

Organic compounds of identical composition and molecular weight, but having a different molecular structure.

isomerized hop extract. *(ay'-so-mer-ayzd hap ehk'-straekt)*

See: hop extract.

I.T.T.

Abbreviation for Indicator Time Test.

Jacob's ladder. *(jei'-kuhbz lae'-d:er)*
A ladderlike conveyor for transporting ale casks from the cellar to the brewery or pub.

Jacob's ladderman. *(jei'-kuhbz lae'-d:er-men)*
The person responsible for operating a Jacob's ladder.

Japanese rice wine. *(jae-puh-neez' reis wayn')*
Another name for *saké*. Also called: Japanese rice beer.

Jenlain. *(zhe~-lae~'*)*
A deep bronze-colored, fruity, apéritif beer brewed by top fermentation at the Brasserie Duyck in the northern French town of Jenlain, south of Valenciennes. It is full-bodied, of 20 °B, filtered but not pasteurized, and is sold in 75-centiliter champagnelike corked bottles.

jetting machine. *(jeh'-d:ing muh-sheen')*
An automatic machine for washing bottles.

Jingle. *(jing'-gel)*
A mix of ale sweetened and flavored with nutmeg and apples.

Joao Weisse. *(zhwaw~'vay'-se)*
A cocktail prepared by adding 1 soupspoon of red port and 1 coffeespoon of powdered sugar to a pint of *weissbier* and crushed ice. Mix slowly; sprinkle a pinch of grated nutmeg and serve cold.

jockey box. *(ja'-kee baks)*

A beverage-dispensing system, often used to serve beer, consisting of a picnic cooler with an internal cooling coil and one or more externally mounted taps. The cooler is filled with ice, and the beverage is chilled as it passes through the coil to the tap. This device is useful because of its portability, and it allows beverages to be served cold without refrigeration.

jug. *(juhg)*

A vessel for holding and pouring liquids, usually deep, often pear shaped with a bottle-type mouth closed with a cork.

Julifest Maubergeoise. *(yoo'-li-fehst mo-behrgh-zhwaz'*)*

Alternative name for the beer festival Kermesse de la Bière de Mauberge.

jungbukett. *(yung'-bu-keht')*

German for *goût de jeune,* or unpleasant-smelling green beer.

jungfrauenbecher. *(yung'-fghaw-en-beh'-cegh)*

A German festive drinking cup manufactured in the sixteenth and seventeenth centuries depicting a young lady in a long bell-shaped skirt holding a pivoting basket over her head. When the basket figure is inverted, the woman's skirt forms a first bowl and the pivoting basket forms a second, smaller one. Such cups were used at wedding feasts where the groom was expected to drink from the larger bowl, without spilling the contents of the smaller one, which he passed to the bride.

juniper berries. *(joo'-ni-per beh'-reez)*

Fruit of the juniper often used to flavor gin and sometimes used to flavor beer.

kachasu. *(kuh-sha'-suh*)*
Orthographic variant of *kuchasu.*

kafir beer. *(kae'-fer beeyr')*
The traditional beverage of the Bantu-speaking people of Africa. It was traditionally prepared from millet (*Panicum milaiceum*) steeped for twenty-four hours, packed in cloth bags to germinate for another forty-eight hours, and then sundried. The malted grains were mashed with raw grains, brought to a boil, cooled in open air, and fermented by wild yeasts. It was first brewed commercially in Salisbury in 1908 (then Rhodesia, later Zimbabwe). It is presently made in South Africa from fermented malted sorghum, which is known locally as *kafir* corn. Elsewhere it is prepared from a mixture of malted sorghum and malted barley or, as in Nigeria, with the addition of *gari*, a starchy cassava preparation. This beer is neither hopped nor filtered and, hence, contains large amounts of particulate matter. After initial fermentation it is pasteurized, and a secondary fermentation is induced by priming and re-yeasting. It is sold in an active state of fermentation and officially holds 3 percent alcohol, but because the beer is still fermenting, the alcohol content may vary considerably. **Syn:** Bantu beer; sorghum beer.

kaoliang. *(kaw-lee-ang'* [can also be: /kaw'/])*
A form of beer made from sorghum in China during the Sung dynasty (AD 960–1279). Sorghum is also called *kaoliang* and was cultivated in the Sechouan province.

kaulms. *(kohlmz*)*
Synonym for culms.

kava. *(ka'-vuh)*
A sort of beer once brewed in Polynesia from the roots of a giant tree called *Piper methysticum*, the dried roots of which were chewed, spat, and brewed.

keg. *(kehg)*
A small cask usually with a capacity of 10 gallons or less. In Britain, aluminum or stainless steel kegs have a 9-, 10-, or 11-gallon capacity (41, 45.5, or 50 liters, respectively).

keg beer. *(kehg beeyr')*
In England, draft beer that is filtered and cooled before kegging and that will be forced out of the keg by pressurized carbon dioxide gas. It is served chilled whereas real ale is served at an ambient temperature (55.94 °F, 13.3 °C). **See also:** real ale.

kegging. *(keh'-ging)*
Drawing beer from a fermenter to kegs.

Kent Goldings. *(kehnt' gohl'-dingz)*
A variety of hops that is grown in England and contains about 5 percent alpha acids.

Kermesse de la Bière de Mauberge. *(kehr-mehs'-[e] de la byergh' de mo-beghzh')*
A beer festival started in 1961 in the town of Mauberge, France, with the encouragement of the Porter 39 Brewery. It is held yearly in July from noon to midnight for twelve to sixteen days, usually starting around the thirteenth. It also is known as Julifest Maubergeoise.

kettle. *(keh'-d:el)*
Synonym for brew kettle.

kg.
Abbreviation for kilogram.

khadi. *(ka'-dee*)*
A meadlike alcoholic beverage, or melomel, brewed in Botswana from a mixture of honey and wild berries.

kick. *(kik)*
Synonym for punt.

kiesel. *(kee'-zel)*
A form of beer once made from rye and oats in the former Soviet Union and in Central Europe. **Syn:** *zur.*

kieselguhr. *(kee'-zel-goor)*
Finely powdered sedimentary silica composed of the skeletons of diatoms and used for clarification or fining.

kieselguhr filter. *(kee'-zel-goor fil'-ter)*
A type of filter consisting of a thick layer of kieselguhr through which the beer is pumped.

kil(d). *(kil')*
Abbreviation for kilderkin.

kilderkin. *(kil'-der-kin)*
In England, a cask for beer with a capacity of 2 firkins, or 18 imperial gallons (81.8 liters). Abbrev: kil; kild. **See also:** firkin; pin.

kiln. *(kil[n])*
A large furnace with a perforated floor, formerly heated by open fire but now mostly from oil-fired heaters, through which controlled drafts of hot air dry and roast the malt. **Syn:** malt kiln.

kiln-dried hops. *(kil[n]' drayd' haps')*
Hops dried in a special kiln shortly after harvesting. Freshly picked hop cones contain 75–80 percent moisture that must be reduced rapidly to 12 or 13 percent to prevent the soft resins and essential oils from oxidizing and polymerizing. The drying temperature should not exceed 122 °F (50 °C), otherwise the quality will be impaired by a loss of lupulin.

kiln fan. *(kil[n]' faen')*
The rotating apparatus inside a kiln.

kiln floor. *(kil[n]' flor')*
Name given to each of the platforms inside a kiln.

kilning. *(kil[n]'-ing)*
The process of heat-drying malted barley in a kiln to stop germination and to produce a dry, easily milled malt from which the brittle rootlets are easily

removed. Kilning also removes the raw flavor (or green-malt flavor) associated with germinating barley, and new aromas, flavors, and colors develop according to the intensity and duration of the kilning process. Kilning results in a loss of about 30–60 percent of the enzymatic activity of the green malt as well as arresting further enzyme activity in the malt itself. Kilning is carried out in stages: a drying phase to about 10 percent moisture (called hand-dry malt) at 113–122 °F (45–50 °C) or less followed by a curing phase at 176– 230 °F (80–110 °C) or higher when the moisture content is reduced to about 6 percent or, as in ale brewing, to about 2 percent. The temperature also affects the color of the malt husks and, consequently, the color of the beer. Pale-hued mild-tasting beers are produced by removing the malted barley immediately after drying whereas darker, stronger beers require a longer drying period at higher temperatures. **Syn:** drying. **See also:** melanoidins.

kilocalorie. *(kee'-lo-kal'-[e]-ree)*
See: calorie.

kilogram. *(kee'-lo-graem)*
One thousand grams (2.2046 pounds). Abbrev: kg.

Kindl Berliner weisse. *(kin'-del behgh-lee'-ner vay'-se)*
See: Berliner *weisse*.

kiu. *(kee'-oo*)*
Orthographic variant for *chiu*.

Kjeldahl method. *(kehl'-dal meh'-thuhd)*
An analytical method of determining the nitrogen content of an organic compound. Named after Johan Kjeldahl.

Kloeckera. *(klo-eh'-ke-ruh)*
A yeast species appearing in the early phase of *lambic* fermentation.

Klosterbräu. *(klo'-ster-broy)*
See: abbey beer.

koji. *(ko'-jee)*
Rice inoculated with *Aspergillus oryzae*, a mold similar to those of the genus *Penicillium*.

kölsch. *(koelsh)*

A very pale, golden-hued, top-fermented beer produced in the metropolitan area of Bonn-Cologne. Under German law, when *kölsch* is brewed elsewhere in Germany, the name of the locality must precede the word *kölsch*. It is highly hopped, mildly alcoholic (± 3.7 percent alcohol by weight, 4.6 percent alcohol by volume), and slightly winy in taste. Etym: From Köln, the German name for the city of Cologne, and *kölschbier*, beer from that city.

korma. *(kohr'-muh*)*

1. In ancient Egypt, sweet barley wine (beer) that is flavored with ginger. **2.** A millet beer brewed by the Celts. Also spelled: *corma*. Also called: *kurmi*. Compare: courni.

kraeusen. *(kroy'-zen)*

The "rocky" or "cauliflower" heads of foam that appear on the surface of the wort during the first days of fermentation. When they reach their peak, between the fourth and the seventh day, they are called high *kraeusen*.

kraeusen beer. *(kroy'-zen beeyr')*

Beer that is in the *kraeusen* stage of fermentation. May be used to kraeusen another batch of beer in a later stage of fermentation in order to carbonate and condition the latter.

kraeusening. *(kroyz'-[e]-ning)*

A method of conditioning that adds a small quantity of young fermenting wort (about 15–20 percent) to a fully fermented lagering one to create a secondary fermentation and natural carbonation.

Krebs cycle. *(krehbz' say'-kel)*

Synonym for citric acid cycle. Etym: Named after Sir Hans Krebs, British scientist who first studied this sequence of enzyme-catalyzed reactions.

kriek. *(kgheek)*

A beer produced in Belgium by steeping Shaarbeek cherries in young *lambic* or *gueuze* to induce a new fermentation. The red cherries (called *kersen*) and the black cherries (called *krieken*), harvested in late July and early August, are added at a rate of 100 kilos per 500 liters of lambic and macerated for four to eight months. The beer is then filtered, clarified, and bottled and is aged for another year. When *kriek* is kept over five years it gains in alcoholic strength but loses in cherry flavor. It is cherry red, has a fine creamy foam, a bittersweet flavor, and a strength of about 4.8 percent alcohol by weight (6 percent by volume). Most of the cherries now come from the Senne River valley or from the north of France (Morello cherries). **Syn:** *kriek(en)-lambic; kriekenlambic;* cherry beer. **See also:** *framboise;* gueuze; *kriekenbier;* lambic.

kriekenbier. *(kghee'-ken-beegh)*
A type of beer, not to be confused with *kriek,* produced in Belgium by macerating cherries in top-fermented barley beer.

Krupnik. *(kroop'-neek*)*
An alcoholic drink made in Poland from a mix of local whiskey and honey.

Ku-Baba. *(koo-ba-buh)*
A breweress and tavern-keeper who lived in Sumer in the year 2400 BC. A remarkable woman and successful brewer, she founded the city of Kish (about 20 kilometers northeast of Babylonia), eventually becoming sovereign of that city, and founded the Third Dynasty of Kish.

kuchasu. *(kuh-sha'-suh)*
A spirit made in Zimbabwe by distillation of a native beer. Also spelled: *kachasu.* Sometimes called: *tileque.*

Kulminator. *(kul'-mi-na-d:er*)*
One of the strongest beers in the world, a double *bock* of 13.2 percent alcohol by volume, brewed in Kulmbach in northern Bavaria, Germany.

kupferstube. *(kup'-fer-shtoo-be)*
A copper-colored, bottom-fermented beer of 12.8 °B that is brewed in Nürnberg, Franconia, in Germany, the color of which is caused by the use of smoky, roasted malts.

kurunnu. *(koo-roo-noo*)*
A type of beer made from spelt (an early form of wheat) in ancient Babylonia.

kvas(s). *(ke-vas')*
A Russian beery drink, mildly alcoholic (0.2–2 percent), traditionally made by fermenting rye bread, one that does not include any other grain besides rye. The fermenting liquid will be turned bitter by oats or other grains. *Kvas* was brewed by the proto-Slavs as early as 2,000 years ago. The basic recipe consisted of mixing dried breadcrumbs with hot water, then adding a sugar solution and

yeast for fermentation. The brew was flavored with raisins, mint, absinth, juniper, honey, sugar, or (rarely) hops during fermentation. Wealthy people flavored their kvas with bilberries, Morello cherries, currants, apples, lemons, pears, raspberries, and lingonberries. The importation of English ales in the eighteenth century marked the decline of this beverage. Kvas is still produced in the northern Republic of Soviet States. Rye bread is covered with boiling water, churned, and left standing for twenty-four hours after which time more water and yeasts are added and the brew is fermented in casks for two to three days. It is later delivered in cistern trucks, and people buy it directly from the cistern on street corners and market places. **Also spelled:** *kwas(s); quas(s).* **See also:** *grouchevoï; iablochny; malinovoï.*

kwas(s). *(kvas')*
    Orthographic variant for *kvas(s).*

l.
Abbreviation for liter.

label. *(lei'-bel)*
A piece of paper or foil glued to a bottle on which is printed various information—brand name, alcohol content, brewery name, and others.

labeler. *(lei'-b[e]-ler)*
A machine for sticking labels to bottles. **Syn:** labeling machine.

labeling machine. *(lei'-b[e]-ling muh-sheen')*
Synonym for labeler.

lace. *(leis)*
The lacelike pattern of bubbles sticking to a glass of beer once it has been partly or totally emptied.

lack of body. *(laek' uhv ba'-d:ee)*
Descriptive of a thin, watery beer as opposed to a light-, medium-, or full-bodied one.

lactic acid. *(laek'-tik ae'-sid)*
Formula: CH_3-CHOH-COOH. A mild-flavored carboxylic acid found in milk (hence its name) and known in three forms of which the Dl-form (also known as Dl-lactic acid or ordinary lactic acid) may develop as bacteria in the mash during brewing and acidify the mash at temperatures of 113–116.6 °F (40–47 °C); however, lactic acid formation is more likely to occur in fermentation and aging (via infection).

Lactobacillus. *(laek-to-buh-si'-lis)*

Genus of bacteria that ferments wort sugars to produce lactic acid. Although considered undesirable in most breweries and beer styles, it plays a significant role in the production of some beers, such as Berliner *weisse* and *lambics.*

Lactobacillus delbruckii. *(laek-to-buh-si'-lis dehl-bru'-kee-[ee])*

Homofermentive strain (species) of *Lactobacillus* isolated by Professor Max Delbruck. Used in the production of Berliner *weisse.*

lactophilic. *(laek-to-fi'-lik)*

A description of an organism that metabolizes lactose more readily than glucose.

lactose. *(laek'-tos)*

A nonfermentable sugar used to add body and sweetness to stouts and brown beers.

lady's waist. *(lei'-d:eez weist')*

In Ireland and Australia, a beer glass with a capacity of about 3.5 ounces (± 1 deciliter).

lagales. *(lag'-eiylz)*

A term coined by beer author Howard Hillman, a contraction of the words *lager* and *ale,* to describe hybrid brews produced by blending bottom-fermented lagers with top-fermented ales.

lager. *(la'-ger)*

A generic term for any beer produced by bottom fermentation, usually by decoction mashing, as opposed to top-fermented ales, usually produced by infusion mashing. Lager brewing was introduced in the 1840s and is now the predominant brewing method worldwide except in Britain where top fermentation is dominant. Lagers constitute a category including Münchener, Vienna, Pilsener, Dortmunder, *bock,* and *doppelbock.* Most lagers are of the Pilsener style; they tend to be paler, crisper, drier, and less alcoholic than ales. True lagers are matured (lagered) in cold storage rooms for one to three months and sometimes longer, but modern methods complete aging much more rapidly. Etym: From the German verb and noun *lagern,* meaning to store or storage area. **Syn:** bottom-fermented beer. **See also:** ale; bottom fermentation; bottom-fermenting yeast.

lagered beer. *(la'-gerd beeyr')*

A bottom-fermented beer that has matured in cold cellars for many weeks or even months at near-freezing temperatures.

lagering. *(la'-ge-ring)*
Storing bottom-fermented beer in cold cellars at near-freezing temperatures for periods of time ranging from a few weeks to several months and occasionally up to a year, during which time the yeast cells and proteins settle out and the beer improves in taste. This technique originated in the Bavarian Alps in the fifteenth century and was later practiced on a larger scale in Munich, Vienna, and Plzen. **Syn:** cold lagering.

lager weisse. *(la'-gegh vay'-se)*
In Germany, a bottom-fermented wheat beer.

lager yeast. *(la'-ger yeest')*
Synonym for bottom-fermenting yeast.

lag period. *(laeg' pi'-ree-uhd)*
Synonym for lag phase.

lag phase. *(laeg' feiz')*
Associated with yeast viability, the time between yeast pitching and the start of activity as signaled by the appearance of foam at the surface of the wort. During this time the yeast cells use oxygen for sterol synthesis and become larger but do not produce any buds. The time ranges from about two hours for worts of 1.010 original gravity to four hours for those of a gravity of 1.100. **Syn:** lag period. **See also:** reproduction phase.

lamb ale. *(laem' eiyl')*
In medieval England, an ale prepared for the sheep-shearing season.

lambic. *(lam'-beek)*
A unique Belgian wheat beer produced only in a 15-kilometer radius southwest of Brussels in the area called Pajottenland. *Lambic* is traditionally brewed and spontaneously fermented in winter (October 15 to May 15) because the microflora of the Senne Valley are too unpredictable during the summer. The mash, consisting of 60–70 percent barley and 30–40 percent wheat, is spontaneously fermented by these airborne wild yeasts (*Brettanomyces bruxellensis* and *Brettanomyces lambicus*) and bacteria (thermo bacteria and lactic bacteria). The fermentation vessels consist of large oak or chestnut tuns of 252 gallons each. Fermentation starts after three days, and an attenuation of 80 percent is reached after the first summer and is almost complete after the second. It is flavored with old hops (600 grams per hectoliter), which provide preservative properties but very little bitterness. Lambic

may be served young (three months to one year) or old (at least two years old, usually three to four). Young lambic is very sour, slightly cloudy, and produces little or no froth. Old lambic has lost some of its sourness, acquired a vinous bittersweet flavor, and produces a fine froth. When young and old lambics are blended, bottled and aged one more year, the end product is called *gueuze*. In 1965 the terms *lambic*, *gueuze*, and *gueuze-lambic* were defined by royal decree: Such beers must be made by spontaneous fermentation of a wort of at least 5 °Belgian (with a maximum tolerance of 5 percent) containing at least 30 percent wheat, and the packaging must bear the name of the producer and that of the place of origin. Etym: Possibly from the French *alambic,* meaning still, or from the Latin *lamper.* Sometimes spelled locally: *lambick.* **See also:** *faro;* gueuze; *kriek;* Mort Subite; wheat beer.

lambic doux. *(lam'-beek doo)*
Sweetened young *lambic.*

Lamb's Wool. *(lambz' wul')*
A popular drink in seventeenth-century England prepared by adding the pulp of roasted apples (five or six) together with sugar, grated nutmeg, and a pinch of ginger to 1–3 quarts of warm strong ale. Also spelled: Lambswool.

last running. *(laest' ruh'-ning)*
The last of the wort to be filtered from the straining vat.

Late Cluster. *(leit' kluh'-ster)*
A variety of hops grown in Idaho and Washington containing 5.5–7.5 percent alpha acids.

late hopping. *(leit' ha'-ping)*
In homebrewing, the addition of aroma hops ten to twenty minutes before the end of the boil.

latent heat. *(lei'-tent heet')*
The amount of heat required for a liquid to vaporize.

lauter, to. *(law'-d:er too)*
To run the wort from the mash tun. Etym: From the German word to clarify.

lauter. *(law'-d:er)*
Name given to the mash once saccharification is complete.

lautering. *(law'-d:er-ing)*

The process of separating the sweet wort from the spent grains with a straining apparatus. Etym: From the German word *lauter,* meaning clarifying.

lauter tun. *(law'-d:er tuhn')*

A large vessel fitted with a false slotted bottom and a drain spigot in which the mash is allowed to settle and the sweet wort is removed from the grains through a straining process. In smaller breweries and in the infusion system the mash tun is used for both mashing and lautering. **Syn:** lauter tub.

leaven. *(lehv'-en)*

The name given to yeast in the Old and New Testaments and later applied to any substance that could cause fermentation such as barm, yeast, baking powder, or sour milk.

lees. *(leez)*

The sediments of yeast, bacteria, and other solid matter that accumulates on the bottom of fermentation vessels or storage containers.

Lemon Shandy. *(leh'-men shaen'-dee)*

See: Shandy (Gaff).

length. *(lehng[k]th)*

The amount of wort brewed each time the brew house is in operation.

Leuven Bier Festival. *(loe'-ven beer feh'-stuh-vel*)*

A beer festival held annually at Whitsuntide (May 12–15) in the town of Louvain in Belgium.

Leuvense wit. *(loe'-ven-ze vit')*

Synonym for *blanche de* Louvain.

lever capper. *(leh'-ver kae'-per)*

A hand-held, hand-operated bottle-crimping device.

lever corker. *(leh'-ver kohr'-ker)*

Hand-held, single- or double-handled device used to insert a cork into a bottle neck.

li. *(lee*)*
A type of rice beer made in China during the Han dynasty (200 BC) at the beginning of the Chinese Empire. **See also:** *chiu; shu; t'ien tsiou.*

Liberty. *(li'-ber-tee)*
A variety of hops cultivated in the United States containing 3–5.5 percent alpha acids.

lickspigot. *(lik-spi'-get)*
Obsolete British slang for an ale-house keeper.

licorice root. *(lik'-[e]-reesh root')*
A dried root sometimes used to flavor holiday-style or other beers.

life expectancy. *(layf' ehk-spehk'-ten-see)*
Synonym for shelf life.

light ale. *(layt' eiyl')*
1. In Britain, a beer of lighter color than mild ale or one slightly less alcoholic than pale ale. **2.** A bottled version of bitter, thus, a synonym for pale ale.

Light and Mild. *(layt' end may[e]ld')*
A mix of equal parts of pale ale and mild ale.

light beer. *(layt' beeyr')*
1. In the United States, a low-calorie beer containing no dextrins. Such beers are often advertised as less filling or less fattening. Light beers contain about 90–160 calories per bottle. **See also:** diet beer. **2.** In the United States, a low-alcohol beer ranging from 2.3–3.2 percent alcohol by weight (2.8–4 percent by volume). **3.** In Europe and the United States, a pale beer, usually a lager, as opposed to a dark one.

lightstruck. *(layt'-struhk)*
An unpleasant flavor in beer caused by exposure to light, causing undesirable chemical reactions of hydrogen sulfide and other sulfur compounds with a side chain of the iso-humulones and the formation of phenyl mercaptan (3-methyl-2-butene-1-thiol), which imparts a skunklike flavor. **Syn:** sunstruck.

limewood. *(laym'-wud)*
Wood of the linden tree (*Tilia* sp.) known in England as lime tree and in Scotland as *lorit*.

limit attenuation. *(li'-mit uh-teh-nyuh-wei'-shen)*
Synonym for final degree of attenuation.

lintner. *(lint'-ner)*
A unit of measure of the diastatic power of a malt.

lion. *(lee-o~')*
In France, a beer glass with a capacity of 40 centiliters. **See also:** *botte; demi; distingué.*

lipid. *(li'-pid)*
Any of a class of compounds that contains long-chain aliphatic hydrocarbons and their derivatives; includes fats and waxes. In the brewing process, lipids inhibit foam stability and, upon decomposition, contribute stale flavors. Also spelled: lipoid.

lipoid. *(li'-poyd)*
See: lipid.

liquefaction. *(li'-kwuh-faek'-shen)*
See: dextrinization.

liquefying enzyme. *(li'-kwi-fay-ing ehn'-zaym)*
Synonym for alpha-amylase.

liquid line. *(li'-kwid layn')*
Thick-walled, low-pressure tubing that carries a beverage from serving tank or keg to dispensing tap.

liquid pint. *(li'-kwid paynt')*
See: pint.

liquor. *(li'-ker)*
The name given, in the brewing industry, to water used for mashing and brewing, especially natural or treated water containing large amounts of calcium and magnesium salts. **Syn:** brewing water; mashing liquor; brewing liquor. **See also:** brewing water.

lite beer. *(layt' beeyr')*
An American spelling for light beer.

liter. *(lee'-d:er)*
A metric unit of volume defined as the volume of 1 kilogram of pure water at 39 °F (4 °C). It is equal to about 1.76 imperial pints, or 2.113 U.S. pints. Abbrev: l.

logarithmic phase. *(loh-guh-ridh'-mik feiz')*
Synonym for reproduction phase.

long glass. *(lohng' glaes)*
Synonym for yard of ale.

loose hops. *(loos' haps')*
Hops picked from the vine and packaged without further processing other than separating the leaves from the cones after drying. **Syn:** whole hops.
See also: pocket.

loss in yield. *(lohs' in yee[e]ld')*
The loss in weight and yield during the various stages of the beermaking process. The scientific study of these phenomena (beer loss, malting loss) is intended to increase efficiency and maximize the yield.

Lovibond. *(luh'-vi-band)*
The scale on which malt, wort, and beer color are usually measured.

low-alcohol(ic) beer. *(lo'-ael'-kuh-ha'-[lik] beeyr')*
Synonym for near beer.

low-cal beer. *(lo-kal' beeyr')*
An abbreviated form for low-calorie beer.

low-calorie beer. *(lo-kal'-uh-ree beeyr')*
A beer of low caloric content in which the dextrins have been converted by amyloglucosidase. Abbrev: low-cal beer. **See also:** diet beer; light beer.

low fermentation. *(lo' fuhr-mehn-tei'-shen)*
A synonym for bottom fermentation.

Lublin. *(loo'-blin)*
A variety of hops that is cultivated in Poland and containing 3–4 percent alpha acids.

luda. (loo'-duh*)

The name given to beer by the Ossets (or Ossetians), a Caucasian tribe of Aryan tongue and Iranian descent. Spring barley was called *kheri,* and hops were called *suah.* The Ossets are credited for having built a 600-liter beer reservoir, the largest in antiquity. It was discovered in Tappakallah and dates back to 600 BC. The Ossets' toast was "Dazaranbon danasa," which translates into "I drink to your health." Also spelled: *ludi.*

lug. (luhg)

A kind of protruding handle on a vase or vessel.

lunatic broth. (loo'-nuh-tik brohth')

See: old ale.

lupomaniac. (loo-pyuh-mei'-nee-aek)

A term coined by beer author Terry Foster for a "hop fanatic," one who appreciates a well-hopped beer and does not believe in the expression "too hoppy."

lupulin. (loo'-pyuh-lin)

What appears as finely granular yellow powder at the base of each flower petal of the hop cone. It contains essential oils and bitter resins that impart bitterness and aromatic flavor to beer along with a sterilizing quality. Once called: hop flour. **See also:** alpha acid; beta acid; hop oils; hops; soft resins.

lupulin gland. (loo'-pyuh-lin glaend')

The gland (approximately 0.1 millimeter in diameter) at the base of the bracteole of the female flower in which the bitter resins and essential oils of the hop plant develop.

lupulon(e). (loo'-pyuh-lan [-lon])

Synonym for beta acid, one of the two resins found in hops, composed of lupulone, co-lupulone, and ad-lupulone.

Lupus salictarius. (loo'-puhs sa-lik-ta'-ree-uhs*)

The name given by Pliny the Elder (AD 23) and his contemporaries to hops, meaning "wolf among scrubs" because hops then grew wild among willows like a wolf in the forest. The botanical name for hops, *Humulus lupulus,* is derived from this expression.

Lüttje Lage. *(luet'-ye la'-ge)*

A German term meaning small one, referring to a "small beer" brewed especially for the Schutzenfest (Sharpshooter's Festival). It is usually accompanied by a Korn (schnapps) not in the beer chaser style but to be drunk simultaneously, the smaller glass held above the larger one, both liquids blending in the pouring and drinking process.

L-xyloascorbic acid. *(ehl' zay-lo-uh-scohr'-bik ae'-sid)*

Synonym for ascorbic acid.

maas. *(mas*)*
An Old Alsatian capacity measure estimated at 1.63 liters.

macerate. *(mae'-suh-reyt)*
The process of softening and separating the parts of a substance by steeping it in liquid.

Madagascar gum. *(mae-duh-gaes'-ker guhm')*
Synonym for agar-agar.

Madureira. *(ma-doo-rei'-ruh)*
A cocktail consisting of Pilsener and Madeira wine served chilled in a tall glass.

maibock. *(may'-bohk)*
A light-colored *bock* beer produced for consumption in the spring. **Syn:** pale bock; *helles* bock.

Maillard reactions. *(may-yard' ree-aek'-shenz)*
A complex series of chemical reactions beginning with the reaction of carbohydrates and amino acids that occur during the processing of many foods and result in the production of dark pigments, called melanoidins, and many different flavors.

maize. *(meiz)*
A grain used as an adjunct. Flaked maize does not need to be pre-boiled but whole maize first must be degermed to remove the oily embryo. Maize flour contains 12–13 percent moisture, 63 percent starch, and 9 percent protein. **Syn:** Indian corn. **See also:** flaked maize.

maize meal. *(meiz' meeyl)*
Ground maize, not to be confused with maize flour, which is better known as corn flour.

malic acid. *(mae'-lik ae'-sid)*
A component of acid blend used frequently in wine- or meadmaking.

malinovoï. *(ma-lee-no-voy*)*
Kvas in which raspberries have been macerated.

malt, to. *(mohlt', too)*
To convert barley into malt.

malt. *(mohlt')*
Processed barley that has been steeped in water, germinated on malting floors or in germination boxes or drums, and later dried in kilns for the purpose of converting the insoluble starch in barley to the soluble substances and sugars in malt. Three factors determine the value of good malt: (1) its protein content must be as low as possible (preferably below 12.8 percent); (2) its starch content must be as high as possible; and (3) its germinative power must be superior to 98 percent. **Syn:** malted barley. **See also:** black malt; caramel malt; crystal malt; dextrin malt; malting; Munich malt; pale malt; toasted malt.

Composition of Barley and Malt
(percentage dry weight)

	Barley	Malt
Amino acids and peptides	0.5	1–2
Cellulose	4–5	5
Hemicelluloses	8–10	6–8
Lipids (fats)	2–3	2–3
Mineral salts	2	2.2
Nucleic acids	0.2–0.3	0.2–0.3
Other substances	5–6	6–7
Other sugars	1.0–1.2	2–4
Protein (nitrogen × 6.25)	8–11	8–11
Reducing sugars	0.1–0.2	3–4
Soluble gums	1.0–1.5	2–4
Starch	63–65	58–60
Sucrose	1–2	3–5

Source: G. Harris, *Barley and Malt.* Edited by A. H. Cook. London; Academic Press, 1962, p. 435.

malt adjunct. *(mohlt' ae'-juhngkt)*
Synonym for adjunct.

maltase. *(mohlt'-eiz)*
An enzyme responsible for the transformation of maltose to dextrose.

malt beer. *(mohlt' beeyr')*
Usually refers to nutritious malt beverages of very low alcohol content brewed originally for nursing mothers and children and now enjoyed by sportsmen and health-conscious people. In France it is called *bière de malt* and in Germany *malzbier*.

malt beverage. *(mohlt' beh'-vrij)*
Any alcoholic or nonalcoholic beverage made from malted barley.

malt cleaning machine. *(mohlt' klee'-ning muh-sheen')*
An apparatus consisting of a perforated metal drum used to degerminate (remove the rootlets) malted barley.

malt comes. *(mohlt' coomz' [can also be: /cumz/])*
Synonym for malt tails.

malt crusher. *(mohlt' kruh'-sher)*
Synonym for grinder.

malted. *(mohl'-tid)*
1. Converted into malt. **2.** Treated with or made from malt.

malted barley. *(mohl'-tid bar'-lee)*
Synonym for malt.

malt extract. *(mohlt' ehk'-straekt)*
1. A thick, sugary syrup or dry powder prepared from malt. Basically it is sweet wort reduced to a syrup or powder form by removing most or all of the water by low-vacuum evaporation and packaged in cans of 2, 2.2, 2.5, 3, 3.3, or 3.5 pounds. **See also:** dry kit; wet kit. **2.** A dark and thick beerlike malt drink of low alcohol content.

malt floor. *(mohlt' flor')*
In traditional-style maltings, a flat horizontal surface area where steeped barley grains are spread in layers of 10–15 centimeters to germinate. Because

they require considerable space, malting floors have been replaced by mechanical devices such as the germination box. **Syn:** malting floor.

malt heap. *(mohlt' heep')*
The uniform layer of malt on the malt floor. **Syn:** couches.

malt hopper. *(mohlt' ha'-per)*
A funnel-like apparatus for channeling the dried malt to the mill.

malthouse. *(mohlt'-haws)*
A building where barley is converted into malt.

malting. *(mohl'-ting)*
The process of converting barley into malt. It is divided into three stages: (1) steeping—the barley is immersed in water until a chosen moisture level has been reached; (2) germination—the wet barley is allowed to germinate under controlled conditions; and (3) kilning—the germinated barley (green malt) is heat dried and roasted to different grades.

malting floor. *(mohl'-ting flor')*
Synonym for malt floor.

maltings. *(mohl'-tingz)*
The buildings in which malt is processed.

malt kiln. *(mohlt' kil[n])*
Synonym for kiln.

malt liquor. *(mohlt' li'-ker)*
1. Generally speaking, a beer of higher alcohol content than regular beer. **2.** In the United States, an alternative name given to beers that exceed the alcohol level defined by law and that are therefore too alcoholic to be labeled lager or beer. On the average they contain 4.5–6 percent alcohol by weight (5.6–7.5 percent alcohol by volume), in contrast to the 3.2–4 percent (4–5 percent alcohol by volume) in standard lager beers.

maltman. *(mohlt'-men)*
Synonym for maltster.

maltmaster. *(mohlt'-mae-ster)*
Synonym for maltster.

malt mill. *(mohlt' mil')*
Synonym for grinder.

malt oar. *(mohlt' o[e]r')*
Synonym for turner.

maltobiose. *(mohl-to-bay'-os)*
Synonym for maltose.

maltodextrin. *(mohl-to-dehk'-strin)*
A general name for compounds of maltose and dextrins formed by the diastatic hydrolysis of starch during saccharification.

maltogenic amylase. *(mohl-to-jeh'-nik ae'-muh-leis)*
Synonym for beta-amylase.

maltose. *(mohl'-tos)*
Formula: $C_{12}H_{22}O_{11}$. A fermentable sugar consisting of two molecules (disaccharide) of glucose obtained by the enzymatic hydrolysis of starch. It is water soluble and 33 percent as sweet as sucrose. **Syn:** malt sugar; maltobiose.

maltotetraose. *(mohl-to-teh'-truh-os)*
An unfermentable polysaccharide or dextrin derived during mashing.

maltotriose. *(mohl-to-tree'-os)*
A slowly fermentable trisaccharide.

malt plow. *(mohlt' plaw)*
An instrument or apparatus for turning the germinating barley on the malt floor.

malt polisher. *(mohlt' pa'-lish-er)*
An apparatus consisting of two revolving brushes used for polishing the malt.

malt screen. *(mohlt' skreen)*
A sieve with the double purpose of removing dust, sand, and stones while grading the grains.

malt sprouts. *(mohlt' sprawts)*
Synonym for rootlets.

maltster. *(mohlt'-ster)*
A person who makes malt. **Syn:** maltman; maltmaster.

malt sugar. *(mohlt' shu'-ger)*
Synonym for maltose.

malt tails. *(mohlt' teilz)*
The bearded chaff removed from the drying or dried malt and used as fodder or fertilizer. **Syn:** malt comes; beard.

malt tannins. *(mohlt' tae'-ninz)*
Tannins that are derived from the malt husks as opposed to hop tannins. **See also:** tannin.

malt-to-sugar ratio. *(mohlt'-tuh-shu'-ger rei'-sh[e]o)*
In homebrewing, the maximum amount of sugar that can be added to the boiling wort or malt extract without affecting taste. This ratio preferably should be greater than 2:1.

malt worm. *(mohlt' wuhrm)*
Synonym for grain weevil. Scientific name: *Calandra granaria*.

malty. *(mohl'-tee)*
1. Displaying the characteristic flavor of malt. **2.** Related to malt.

malzbier. *(malts'-beegh)*
In Germany, a dark, sweet, aromatic malt beverage containing only 0.5–1.5 percent alcohol by weight. Not a true beer but rather a tonic once brewed for children and nursing mothers, yet now enjoyed by sportsmen and health-conscious people. Examples include: Mumme, Karamalz, Vitamalz. **See also:** *bière de malt;* near beer; malt beer.

manioc. *(mae'-nee-ak)*
See: tapioca.

manioc beer. *(mae'-nee-ak beeyr')*
An alcoholic drink made from the manihot plant. The first description of such a beer produced by the Tupi cannibal tribes of the coastal regions of Brazil dates back to Hans Staden, *Véritable histoire et description d'un pays habité . . .,* written in 1557. The Tupinamba tribes were decimated in the seventeenth and

eighteenth centuries, but manioc beer is still the daily and sacred beverage in the Amazon and the favorite drink of the Jivaros. **Syn:** cassava beer.

manway. *(maen'-wey)*
Entry port to the interior of the brewing vessel.

marl. *(mar[e]l)*
Soil consisting of clay and lime, sometimes placed on covers of wooden conditioning tanks, intended to filter out wild yeasts or other microflora in the air before the wood can breathe them into the beer.

mars. *(marz)*
An old-style *lambic* produced from late, low-gravity worts.

Märzen(bier). *(mehr'-tsen[-beegh])*
1. In Germany, before the advent of artificial refrigeration, beer was brewed in winter and the last batch was brewed in March. Märzen was made especially strong to survive the many months of maturation before it was drunk at the end of summer. **2.** The name given by Josef Sedlmayr, owner of the Zum Franziskanerkeller, to a Vienna-style bottom-fermented blonde beer he invented in 1871 in contrast to the brown beers then popular in Bavaria. The first batch was brewed in March 1872, hence the name March beer, and was served for the first time at the Oktoberfest of the same year. Today's Märzenbiers, still a favorite of the Oktoberfest, contain about 4.5 percent alcohol by weight (as opposed to 3.5–3.9 percent for ordinary pale beers called *helles*) and are fermented at an original wort gravity of 12.5–13 °B. **3.** Because of the similarities, the Vienna and Märzen beer styles are sometimes synonymous.

mash, to. *(maesh', too)*
To mix ground malt with hot water. **Syn:** to dough-in.

mash. *(maesh')*
A mixture of ground barley malt and hot water that forms the sweet wort after straining. **Syn:** mash goods.

mash copper. *(maesh' ka'-per)*
Synonym for mash kettle.

masher. *(mae'-sher)*
A container into which grist and water are mixed.

mash filter. *(maesh' fil'-ter)*
A filter press fitted with either cloth or plates for filtering the mash.

mash goods. *(maesh' gudz)*
1. The portion of wort boiled separately in the decocting brewing method.
2. The total amount of barley required for a single brew. **Syn:** mash.

mashing. *(mae'-shing)*
The process of mixing ground malt with water in the mash tun to extract the malt, degrade haze-forming proteins, and further convert grain starches to fermentable sugars and nonfermentable carbohydrates (dextrins) that will add body, head retention, and other characteristics to the beer. This conversion is operated by the hydrolytic action of endogenous enzymes, mainly alpha- and beta-amylases. Alpha-amylases convert insoluble and solubilized starch into maltotriose and dextrins; beta-amylases then convert dextrins into glucose, maltose, maltotriose, and alpha-limit dextrins. The whole process is carried out in one of three ways: (1) infusion mashing, in a single vessel, at 149–154 °F (65–68 °C) as for ales; (2) decoction mashing, by boiling portions of the mash in a separate vessel to raise the temperature from 113–168 °F (45–76 °C) as for lagers; and (3) mixed mashing, a combination of the infusion and decoction methods. Mashing requires several hours (one to seven) and produces a sugar-rich liquid called sweet wort. **See also:** decoction mashing; infusion mashing.

mashing-in. *(mae'-shing in')*
Synonym for doughing-in.

mashing liquor. *(mae'-shing li'-ker)*
Synonym for liquor.

mashing time. *(mae'-shing taym')*
The period of time required for infusion or decoction mashing.

mashing tun. *(mae'-shing tuhn')*
Synonym for mash tun.

mash kettle. *(maesh' keh'-d:el)*
The metal vat into which part of the mash is boiled for the decoction brewing method. **Syn:** mash copper.

mash out. *(maesh' awt)*

The final stage of decoction and step mashing. During the mash out, the temperature is raised to 168 °F (76 °C), and the mash is allowed to rest for five minutes. This procedure is used to terminate enzymatic activity and to improve the flow of the sugar solution during lautering.

mash rest. *(maesh' rehst)*

Maintaining the mashing temperature at a specific level ideal for certain desired enzymatic reactions. **See also:** strike temperature.

mash tub. *(maesh' tuhb)*

Synonym for mash tun.

mash tun. *(maesh' tuhn)*

A large vessel for holding the mash, usually made of copper, brass, or stainless steel. The mash tuns used for infusion mashing are fitted with a perforated false bottom and a system of pipes for drawing off the wort and sparging machinery for washing the spent grains. Mash tuns used for decoction mashing are fitted with a propeller or stirrer at the rounded bottom and have a dome with a sliding door and a chimney for the evaporation of steam at the top. **Syn:** mashing tun; mash tub.

mash-tun rake. *(maesh' tuhn reik')*

A rake with claws to cut and remove dregs.

maskin' loom. *(maes'-ken loom)*

Mash tun.

mass filter. *(maes' fil'-ter)*

A type of filter consisting of layers of pressed pulp fitted into perforated frames through which beer is pumped under pressure. **Syn:** pulp filter.

masskrug. *(mas'-kghook)*

In Germany, a beer mug with a capacity of 1 liter. **See also:** *halbe.*

master brewer. *(maes'-ter broo'-wer)*

1. An expert brewer. **2.** One who supervises the brewing operations in a brewery. **Syn:** head brewer; brewmaster.

matted couche. *(mae'-d:id kawch'*)*
Malting barley that has not been turned at the proper time, resulting in long intermixed radicles. **See also:** couch; radicle; turner.

maturation. *(mae-chuh-rei'-shen)*
The improvement of the quality of beer by aging in a storage container at near freezing temperatures for lagers and at around 40–45 °F (4.4–7.2 °C) for ales during which time the yeast cells precipitate and the finished beer acquires a smooth, mellow flavor. **Syn:** maturing; aging.

maturing. *(muh-tyoo'-ring)*
Describes a beer in the process of aging.

mead. *(meed)*
An alcoholic beverage produced by fermenting honey and water. Mead can be dry, sweet, or sparkling. Etym: From the Indo-European word *medhu*, later evolving into *met, med, meda,* and *meath.* **Syn:** honey wine. **Obselete syn:** bees wine. **See also:** black mead; cyser; hippocras; melomel; metheglin; pyment; red mead.

meadery. *(mee'-d:uh-ree)*
An establishment where mead is made.

mealie beer. *(mee'-lee beeyr')*
A beer brewed in South Africa from maize or millet and other plants.

meadmaker. *(meed'-mei-ker)*
A person who makes mead.

measure. *(meh'-zher)*
Capacity vessel of standard size used for measuring liquids. The British Imperial System of measures was introduced in 1824. **See also:** appendix C and D.

medicinal. *(mi-dis'-[e]-nel)*
Synonym for phenolic.

medicinal beer. *(mi-dis'-[e]-nel beeyr')*
See: *brutolé.*

medovina. *(meh-doh-vee-nuh)*
Mead in Czech.

medu. *(meh-doo)*
Mead in German.

medus. *(mey-doos)*
Honey in Lithuanian.

melanoidins. *(meh-luh-noy'-d:enz)*
Dark-colored (brown or black) organic compounds that form during kilning and kettle boiling through a complex series of chemical reactions (called Maillard reactions) involving amino acids and sugars. Dark malts are colored by melanoidins. **See:** Maillard reactions.

melibiose. *(meh-luh-bay'-os)*
Formula: $C_{12}H_{22}O_{11}$. A naturally occurring disaccharide based on 6 (alpha-D galactoside)-D-glucose; a reducing sugar.

mellow. *(meh'-lo)*
Describes a beer that is sweet and soft in taste, not irritating.

melomel. *(meh'-lo-mehl)*
Any mead in which part of the honey has been replaced by crushed fruits or fruit juices. **Syn:** fruit mead; mulsum. **See also:** black mead; cyser; pyment; red mead.

meniscus. *(mi-nis'-kuhs)*
The slight curvature of liquid adhering to glass objects caused by surface tension. Also called: meniscus effect.

meodu. *(mey-o-doo)*
Mead in Old English.

merissa. *(muh-ri'-suh*)*
See: *bilbil.*

mertzbier. *(mehghts'-beegh)*
A type of beer brewed in 1763 in Strasbourg, Alsace. It was so named because it was brewed in wintertime in the best of conditions and served in March after several months of maturation in cold cellars.

metallic. *(muh-tae'-lik)*
Possessing an undesirable taste of metal.

methanol. *(meh'-thuh-nol)*
Synonym for methyl alcohol.

metheglin. *(meh-theh'-glin)*
Any mead flavored with herbs and spices. Etym: From the Welsh words *medclydlin* and *meddyglyn,* meaning medicine. **See also:** sack metheglin.

méthode champenoise. *(me-tod' sha~-pe-nwaz'-[e])*
In France and Belgium a secondary fermentation that takes place in the bottle when making champagne and, occasionally, beer.

methyl alcohol. *(meh'-thil ael'-kuh-hohl)*
Formula: CH_3OH. A highly toxic alcohol; the first member of the alcohol series. **Syn:** methanol; wood alcohol.

methylated alcohol. *(meh'-thi-lei'-d:id ael'-kuh-hohl)*
Ethyl alcohol denatured with methyl alcohol.

methylene blue. *(meh'-thuh-leen bloo')*
A blue dye used in laboratory tests to determine the number of dead yeast cells (which are stained blue) in a yeast sample. Living cells do not stain because their plasma membrane is impermeable to the dye. The test solution usually contains 0.01 percent methylene blue and 2 percent sodium citrate.

mg.
Abbreviation for milligram.

microaerophile. *(may-kro-ae'-ruh-fayl)*
An organism that is inhibited in a well-oxygenated environment and yet requires some oxygen for its metabolic functions.

microbrewery. *(may-kro-broo'-e-ree)*
Small brewery generally producing less than 15,000 barrels per year. Sales are primarily off-premise.

micromalting. *(may'-kro-mohl-ting)*
Small-scale malting in a laboratory to determine the germinative power, dormancy, and best suitable steeping and germination procedure to apply to a particular type or batch of barley.

middy. *(mi'-d:ee)*
In Australia, a beer glass with a capacity of 10 ounces in New South Wales and 7 ounces in Western Australia.

midus. *(mee-doos)*
Mead in Lithuanian.

mild. *(may[e]ld')*
Describes a smooth, well-balanced beer that is lacking harshness or excessive bitterness.

mild ale. *(may[e]ld' eiyl')*
In Britain, a dark brown top-fermented beer, light- to medium-bodied, malty, sweet, and lightly hopped, more or less contrasted by bitter ale. It is prepared from an original wort gravity of 1.030–1.036 (8–9 °B) and may be bottled or casked but is best appreciated as a draft beer. It is served mainly in the East and West Midlands and northwest of England.

Mild and Bitter. *(may[e]ld' end bi'-d:er)*
A mix of equal parts of mild and bitter ales.

Milk Ale. *(milk' eiyl')*
A cocktail prepared as follows: One liter of ale is heated in a pan with 1 coffeespoon of sugar, a pinch of powdered ginger, and a pinch of grated nutmeg. One liter of milk is then heated to boiling point in a separate vessel and is added to the ale.

milk of amnesia. *(milk' uhv aem-nee'-zhuh)*
See: old ale.

milk stout. *(milk' stawt)*
Synonym for sweet stout.

mill, to. *(mil, too)*
To grind malt into grist. **Syn:** to grind.

mill. *(mil)*
Synonym for grinder.

millet. *(mi'-lit)*
General name for the cereal from various species of Gramineae, all of which have a fibrous root system and rather small grains (smaller than wheat or rice).

millet beer. *(mi'-lit beeyr')*
A type of beer once brewed in Africa. The germinated millet grains were dried and ground, boiled for twelve hours, then filtered and boiled again several times before fermentation.

milligram. *(mi'-luh-graem)*
One-thousandth of a gram. Abbrev: mg.

milliliter. *(mi'-luh-lee-d:er)*
One-thousandth of a liter. Abbrev: ml.

milling. *(mi'-ling)*
The grinding of malt into grist (or meal) to facilitate the extraction of sugars and other soluble substances during the mashing process. The endosperm must be crushed to medium-size grits rather than to flour consistency. It is important that the husks remain intact when the grain is milled or cracked because they will later act as a filter aid during lautering. **Syn:** grinding.

millipore filtration. *(mi'-luh-por fil-trei'-shen)*
A type of filtration process sometimes used instead of pasteurization.

millivals. *(mi'-luh-vuhlz)*
Equivalent weight is milligrams per liter.

miòd. *(myod)*
Mead in Polish.

misérable. *(mee-seh'-ghuh-ble*)*
An Old French capacity measure equal to half a *posson,* or 1/16 of a pint.

mitaca. *(mee-ta'-kuh)*
See: *chicha.*

Mittelfrueh. *(mi-tel-fghue'-e)*
"Noble-type" Bavarian lager hops grown in Germany. Bavaria's Hallertau region has only 400 acres of hop-growing land with the perfect soil and climate

for growing Mittelfrueh hops. Currently, the entire strain is close to extinction due to the verticillium wilt disease.

mixed brewing method. *(mikst' broo'-wing meh'-thuhd)*
Synonym for mixed mashing.

mixed mashing. *(mikst' mae'-shing)*
A cross between the infusion and the decoction brewing methods. It is used, for example, in Belgium for the preparation of *lambic* and other wheat beers, where the wheat is boiled in a separate vessel while the malt is mashed by the infusion process. **Syn:** mixed brewing method.

mjød. *(myoed)*
Mead in Danish and Norwegian.

mjöd. *(myoed)*
Mead in Swedish.

ml.
Abbreviation for milliliter.

modification. *(ma-d:uh-fi-kei'-shen)*
1. The physical and chemical changes occurring in barley during malting. Physically, the grain is rendered millable. Chemically, complex molecules are broken down to simpler, soluble ones by the formation of hydrolytic enzymes that later begin to catalyze the hydrolytic degradation of the starchy endosperm and its cell walls. **2.** The degree to which malt has been converted during the malting process as determined by the extent of the growth of the acrospire.

modified. *(ma-d:uh-fayd')*
Is said of malt in describing the extent of the modification process. U.S. malts are usually undermodified whereas European, especially English, malts are fully modified. **See also:** fully modified malt; undermodified malt.

mõdu. *(mo-doo)*
Mead in Estonian and is mentioned in their national anthem.

Moenen. *(moe'-nen)*
In Belgium, especially in the hop-growing region of Asse, a mythical hop demon (*diable du houblon*) blamed for bad crops, bugs, diseases, and all other evils victimizing

the poor hop farmer. In winter he chases drunk farmers out of the pole storage shed; in spring he plagues young plants with bad spells; in summer he causes hop plants to fall to the ground; and in autumn, just before harvest, he is captured.

mole. *(mol)*
A unit of measure for chemical compounds that is equal to 6.02×10^{23} molecules. The weight, in grams, of a mole of any compound is the atomic weight of the substance.

monastery beer. *(ma'-nuh-steh-ree beeyr')*
Synonym for abbey beer.

monosaccharide. *(ma-no-sae'-kuh-rayd)*
A carbohydrate consisting of a single chain of carbon atoms with a hydroxyl group of all carbons (except the aldehic or ketonic carbons). Monosaccharides cannot be reduced to simpler forms by hydrolysis. Their name ends with the suffix *-ose* (for example, maltose, sucrose, dextrose, glucose, and galactose) and are classified according to the number of carbon atoms as triose (3), tetrose (4), pentose (5), hexose (6), and heptose (7).

Moor's head. *(moo[e]rz' hehd')*
A type of hop strainer used in small breweries consisting of a cone pierced with numerous holes.

morath. *(mo'-raet)*
Mead made with mulberries. Also spelled: morat.

Moreau Index. *(moh-gho' in'-dehks)*
A method used to identify pure varieties of hops. The index is calculated by counting the number of nodes (n) in 100 stigs (or rachis) and measuring the length (l) in centimeters. The ratio 10 n/l gives the value of the Moreau Index. The results are plotted on a graph and compared with curves of existing hop varieties.

Morellenbier. *(mo-gheh'-len-beegh)*
A type of beer once brewed in the Belgian province of Limbourg by adding Morello cherries to fermenting wort.

Mort Subite. *(mohgh' soo-beet')*
1. The name of a famous Belgian cafe located, in 1910, at the corner of Assaut and Montagne streets in Brussels. The cafe, owned by Théophile Vossen, was then

called La Cour Royale. Its clientele—brokers, civil servants, and bank clerks—played a game of dice called "421" in a *pitjesbak* (an octagonal wooden box 40 centimeters wide and 10 centimeters high). The loser was said to be dead, but if he had to leave suddenly, he was "suddenly dead"; hence, the expression sudden death (*mort subite*). In 1927, the cafe moved to a new location (7 rue Montagne-aux-Herbes) and was renamed Mort Subite. **2.** The name of a famous *gueuze* produced by the Kobbegem brewery De Keersmaeker and served at that cafe. **See also:** *gueuze.*

Mother-in-Law. *(muh'-dher in loh')*
A mix of equal parts of stout and bitter ale.

mouthfeel. *(mawth'-feeyl)*
Synonym for body.

Mt. Hood. *(mawnt hud')*
A variety of hops cultivated in the United States containing 5–8 percent alpha acids.

mug. *(muhg)*
A drinking vessel or cup, made of various materials, usually cylindrical or baluster shaped, with a base rim and a plain or scroll-like handle.

mughouse. *(muhg'-haws)*
In England, an early form of the Victorian and Edwardian music hall where only men were admitted and only stout and ale were served. In it was a large room presided over by a chairman, with a harpist at one end, in which members sang in turn or made speeches or toasts. **Syn:** mugroom.

mugroom. *(muhg'-room)*
Synonym for mughouse.

Mull. *(muhl)*
In England, a mix of hot ale with sugar and spices (often ginger) and sometimes other ingredients such as eggs. Mull is traditionally heated with a red-hot poker.

muller. *(muh'-ler)*
A vessel for preparing mull.

mulsum. *(muhl'-sem)*
Synonym for melomel.

multum. *(mool'-toom*)*
A preparation of quassia and licorice once used to adulterate beer.

mum. *(muhm)*
A strong, nonhopped ale brewed in Braunschweig (Germany) in the eighteenth century and apparently first brewed by Christian Mumme in the late fifteenth century (circa 1487). Not to be confused with *mumme,* a *malzbier* brewed in Germany. Also spelled: *mumm.*

Münchener. *(muench'-ner)*
A bottom-fermented beer produced in the Bavarian city of Munich since the mid-nineteenth century. The original Münchener was dark. In 1928, the Paulaner Brewery introduced a paler version, called *helles,* that has almost entirely overtaken the darker brew. Both versions, *helles bier* (or Munich pale lager) and *dunkel bier* (or Munich dark lager), are lightly hopped (180–200 grams per hectoliter), distinctively malty because of the use of Munich malt, and have an alcohol content of about 3.5–4 percent by weight (4.4–5 percent alcohol by volume). Munich-style beers brewed outside Germany are usually dark. **Syn:** Munich (beer); Münchner.

Munich (beer). *(myoo'-nik beeyr')*
Munich-style beer (Münchener, in German).

Munich malt. *(myoo'-nik mohlt')*
Malted barley kilned at slightly higher temperatures than pale malt but for a shorter period of time. It imparts sweetness, roundness of flavor, and a reddish hue to such beer styles as Oktoberfest and *bock.*

murbimeter. *(muhr-bi'-muh-d:er*)*
An apparatus for measuring the hardness of barley and malt grains.

mutchkin. *(muhch'-kin)*
A Scottish capacity measure for liquids equal to half a Scottish chopin (0.425 liter, 3/4 of an English pint, or 0.9 of a U.S. pint).

muscat. *(muh'-skaet)*
A fruit derivative of *lambic,* which is made by macerating grapes in a blend of young lambics.

must. *(muhst)*

1. In winemaking, the unfermented juice of grapes or other fruit. 2. In meadmaking, the unfermented mixture of honey and water.

musty. *(muh'-stee)*

Moldy, mildewy character that can be the result of cork or a bacterial infection.

myddyglyn. *(muh-dhu-glen)*

Mead in Welsh.

myrcene. *(mer'-seen)*

A primary component of the essential oil of the hop cone. Although rarely found in beer in this native form, it is processed into a number of flavor-active compounds that are significant in beer. The quantity of myrcene found in a hop varies by variety, year, and growing region.

natural conditioning. *(nach'-[e]-rel kuhn-di'-shen-ing)*
A secondary fermentation occurring in the maturing vat when the brew still contains live yeast cells.

near beer. *(neeyr' beeyr')*
A malt beverage having a very low alcoholic content, usually around 0.5–2 percent by volume. During Prohibition, these beers were produced by distilling or cooking the alcohol out of the beer. In the United States, near beers must contain less than 0.5 percent alcohol by weight. In Germany the alcohol limit is 0.6 percent. Examples include: Moussy, Panther, St. Christopher, Metbrew, Vita-Stout, Near Beer, Malta, and Birrell. In Czechoslovakia, a nonalcoholic beer is called *promo,* a near bear is called *pito* (0.5 percent alcohol by volume), and true beer is called *pivo.* **Syn:** low-alcohol(ic) beer.

neck. *(nehk)*
The upper, narrow part of a bottle immediately below the mouth.

nephelometer. *(neh'-fuh-la'-muh-d:er)*
An apparatus for measuring the turbidity (haze) in liquids. The test is carried out at 158 °F (70 °C) because the wort invariably throws a haze upon cooling. Some instruments are graduated in Formazin Turbidity Units (or Formazin Haze Units) whereas others have their own standards such as degrees Nephelos (°N) on the Coleman Nephelometer. **See also:** EBC test.

neutralize, to. *(noo'-truh-layz, too)*
To render a solution neutral, that is, neither acid nor alkaline. The pH of a neutral solution is 7.

ngarlu. *(ng[g]ar'-loo)*
Honey in the aborigine's dialect from Australia.

Nidaba. *(nee-da-buh)*
The goddess of beer in ancient Babylonia.

Nin-Bi. *(neen-bee)*
The goddess of beer in ancient Sumer. **See also:** *sikaru.*

Ninkasi. *(neen-ka-zi)*
The Sumerian goddess of beer; the lady who fills the cup. In Sumer (3600 BC) eight types of beer were produced from barley and another eight from an early type of wheat. Also spelled: Nin.KA.SI.

Ninurta. *(nee-noor-tuh)*
The Babylonian goddess of wheat and barley.

nip. *(nip)*
In England, a small bottle for beer and other drinks with a capacity of 1/2 a reputed pint (28.4 centiliters). Also spelled: nyp. **Syn:** split.

nitrogen content. *(nay'-tri-jehn can'-tehnt)*
The percentage of the weight of barley or malt that is nitrogen. Protein content of the grain is about 6.25 times the nitrogen content.

"noble-type" hops. *(no'-bel haps')*
Hop varieties prized for their quality flavor and aroma. Grown only in four small areas in Europe: three in Germany and one in Belgium.

nog. *(nag)*
A strong beer produced in East Anglia.

noggin. *(na'-gin)*
A small drinking vessel of about 1/4 of a pint (0.118 liter). **See also:** pony.

nonalcoholic beer. *(nan'-ael-kuh-ha'-lik beeyr')*
Any malt beverage similiar in taste to beer. Not to be confused with near beer (or low-alcohol beer), which may contain up to 2 percent alcohol by volume.

nondeposit beer. *(nan-di-pa'-zit beeyr')*
Synonym for chillproof beer.

nonflocculating yeast. *(nan-fla'-kyuh-lei-d:ing yeest')*
1. A generic name for yeast strains that do not form clumps and flocculate during fermentation. **Syn:** nonflocculent yeast. **2.** A bottom-fermenting yeast of high attenuation that appears powdery or dusty during the fermentation.

nonflocculent yeast. *(nan-fla'-kyuh-lent yeest')*
Synonym for nonflocculating yeast.

nonhopped. *(nan-hapd')*
Describes a beer or malt extract not flavored with hops. **Syn:** unhopped.

nonreturnable packaging. *(nan-ri-tuhr'-nuh-bel pae'-kuh-jing)*
Packaging material to be disposed of after use.

Northdown. *(north'-dawn)*
A variety of hops cultivated in the United Kingdom and containing 6–7 percent alpha acids.

Northern Brewer. *(nohr'-dhern broo'-wer)*
1. A variety of hops grown in Kent, England, containing 8.5–11 percent alpha acids. It also is grown in Washington and Oregon with an alpha acid content of 9.5–10.5 percent and a beta acid content of 4.5–5.5 percent. **2.** The title of a periodical published by the Canadian Amateur Brewers Association.

nose. *(noz)*
A taster's descriptive for the total fragrance, aroma, and bouquet of a beer.

Nugget. *(nuh'-git)*
A variety of hops that are grown in Oregon and contain 9.6–13 percent alpha acids.

nutrients. *(noo'-tree-ents)*
1. The necessary elements, mainly nitrogen and phosphorous, required for the health and growth of yeast during fermentation. **2.** An additive containing these elements added to the wort after pitching the yeast to assist fermentation and keep yeasts healthy.

Nuts and Bolts. *(nuhts' end bolts')*
In England, especially in East Anglia, a mix of mild and bitter.

nyp. *(nip)*
Orthographic variant for nip.

oafka. *(of'-ka*)*
A synonym for *tiswin*.

oats. *(ots)*
A cereal grain from any plant of the genus *Avena* in the Gramineae family.

oatmeal. *(ot'-meeyl)*
Ground oats.

off-dry. *(af'-dray')*
A wine evaluation term that refers to wine that has 0.5–1 percent residual sugar, not sweet but not bone dry.

off-flavor. *(af'-flei'-ver)*
An unpleasant flavor that develops in bottled or canned beer during storage. Carbonyls for the most part are responsible for off-flavors. **Syn:** stale flavor; aged flavor; oxidized flavor.

off-scent. *(af'-sehnt')*
A sour, grassy, stale, or musty smell in beer.

OG.
Abbreviation for original gravity.

oils. *(oylz)*
See: essential oils; hop oils.

oil of barley. *(oyl uhv bar'-lee)*
  Slang expression for beer.

okole. *(o'-kuh-lei)*
  A mildly alcoholic fermented beverage brewed by ancient Hawaiians, the root of the sacred *ti* plant is baked in an underground oven, transforming the root into a molasseslike sugar used as a fermentable. Also called: *oke.*

Oktoberfest. *(ohk-to'-ber-fehst)*
  1. A beer festival held annually in Munich's Theresienwiese (Theresa's meadow) for sixteen days and nights in late September and early October. The festival originated with the wedding festivities of the Bavarian heir prince Ludwig to the princess Theresa in 1810. **2.** A bottom-fermented Vienna- or Märzen-style beer originally brewed especially for the Oktoberfest but now available year-round. Oktoberfest beer, brewed from an original wort gravity of 1.050–1.060 (12.5–15 °B), is copper-colored, malty, and sweet.

ol. *(il)*
  Scandinavian for beer.

old ale. *(old' eiyl')*
  In Britain, a strong, dark-colored draft beer usually prepared from an original wort gravity of at least 1.055 to 1.065 and often higher. Such ales are sometimes described as lunatic broth, milk of amnesia, or chateau collapse-o.

old boy. *(old' boy')*
  A name given in eighteenth-century England to a strong ale.

oligosaccharides. *(a-li-go-sae'-kuh-raydz)*
  Polysaccharides composed of four or more molecules. These sugars are not fermentable by *Saccharomyces* yeast and include maltotetraose. These are intermediate fractions that occur during the reduction of starch during mashing.

omalofo. *(o-muh-lo'-fo*)*
  A type of beer once brewed in southwest Africa from *kafir* corn (millet of the *Panicum miliaceum* type). Possibly a synonym for *kafir.*

omm bilbil. *(oom bil-bil)*
  Synonym for *bilbil.*

omphacomel. *(am[p]-fa'-kuh-mehl)*
Mead made with verjuice, the juice of unripe grapes.

open fire kiln. *(o'-pen fay[e]r' kil[n])*
A type of kiln in which cool air mixed with combusting gas is fanned into the layers of malt.

ordinary bitter. *(ohrd-[e]-neh'-ree bi'-d:er)*
Bitter ale prepared from an original wort gravity of 1.033–1.038. **See also:** bitter.

Ordre du Houblon. *(ohgh'-dghe due oo-blo~')*
An order founded in 1409 by Jean Sans Peur, duke of Burgundy, to honor those brewers who brewed hopped beer. The insignia of the order carried the arms of Flanders with (in the center) a gold lion surrounded by a crown of hop leaves and flowers. The listel carried the Flemish motto "Ich zuighe," meaning "I savor."

original extract. *(uh-rij'-[e]-nel ehk'-straekt)*
This is the concentration of extract, fermentable and nonfermentable, that is present in wort at the start of the fermentation. It is measured both in gravity units, the ratio of the weight of wort to an equivalent volume of wort, or as percent Balling or Plato. The latter is the grams of extract per 100 grams of wort.

original gravity. *(uh-rij'-[e]-nel grae'-vuh-d:ee)*
The specific gravity of the wort prior to fermentation at the temperature under consideration as compared to the density of water at 39 °F (4 °C), which is conventionally given the value 1.000. It is a measure of the total amount of solids that are dissolved in the wort. Abbrev: OG. **Syn:** starting gravity; starting specific gravity; original wort gravity. **See also:** terminal gravity.

original wort. *(uh-rij'-[e]-nel wuhrt')*
Synonym for first wort.

original wort gravity. *(uh-rij'-[e]-nel wuhrt' grae'-vuh-d:ee)*
Synonym for original gravity.

oscura. *(o-skoo'-ruh)*
A name used in Latin American beers that have an amber hue. Beers that fall into the deep gold / light amber classification are sometimes called *semi-oscura.*

outcrop. *(awt'-crap)*
Synonym for crop.

overgrown malt. *(o'-ver-gron mohlt')*
Synonym for husky grain.

overcarbonation. *(o'-ver-kar-buh-nei'-shen)*
Excessive effervescence. In homebrewing, overpriming may cause bottles to explode or the foam to overflow when the bottle is uncapped.

overhopped. *(o'-ver hapd')*
A very bitter beer produced by adding too much hops. **See also:** underhopped.

overpriming. *(o'-ver pray'-ming)*
In homebrewing, adding too much sugar to the beer before putting it into bottles or kegs, causing the formation of excessive carbon dioxide that, in turn, may be responsible for bottle explosions and gushing.

oversteeping. *(o-ver-stee'-ping)*
A prolonged steeping period causing excessive absorption of water. Oversteeping delays the onset of germination and encourages the formation and growth of mold and bacteria.

ox-horn cup. *(aks' hohrn kuhp')*
A rare synonym for drinking horn.

oxidation. *(ak-suh-dei'-shen)*
1. A chemical reaction in which one of the reactants (beer, food) undergoes the addition of oxygen. **2.** Exposure to oxygen.

oxidized. *(ak'-si-dayzd)*
Stale, winy flavor of wet cardboard, paper, rotten pineapple, or sherry, as a result of oxygen as the beer ages or is exposed to high temperatures.

oxidized flavor. *(ak'-suh-dayzd flei'-ver)*
Synonym for off-flavor.

oxymel. *(ak'-si-mehl)*
Mead mixed with wine vinegar.

P.
Abbreviation for Plato (°P).

pachwaï. *(pach-way'*)*
In northern India the name given to a type of *saké* to which *Cannabis sativa* is added.

package. *(pae'-kij)*
A general term for containers used to market beverages. Beer is packaged in three forms: bottles, cans, and kegs (barrels or casks). **Syn:** packaging.

packaging. *(pae'-kuh-jing)*
Synonym for package.

pa-e-bi. *(pa-ei-bee)*
In pre-dynastic Mesopotamia (3000 BC), the official brewer who prepared beer for the royal family and the court.

palate fullness. *(pae'-lit ful'-nis)*
See: body.

pale. *(peiyl)*
A light-colored beer. The term is less confusing than *light,* which also may refer to alcoholic or caloric content.

pale ale. *(peiyl eiyl')*
In England, an amber- or copper-colored, top-fermented beer brewed with very hard water and pale malts; the bottled equivalent of a bitter but drier,

hoppier, and lighter. Distinct from darker brews such as brown ale, stout, and porter, pale ales are brewed from original wort gravities of 1.044–1.056 (11–14 °B) and contain about 3.4 percent alcohol by volume. Classics of this style include Bass Pale and Worthington's White Shield. Pale ales are sometimes called Burton ales because the popularity of this style of beer originated from the versions brewed in Burton-on-Trent in the 1780s. **Syn:** light ale. Rarely called: dinner ale. **See also:** India pale ale.

pale crystal malt. *(peiyl' kri'-stel mohlt')*
A form of crystal malt used with pale beers; it is prepared by drying green malt at high temperature after saccharification but without curing. Larger amounts than 10 percent impart a disagreeable flavor to the beer. **Syn:** CaraPils.

pale malt. *(peiyl' mohlt')*
The most common form of malt used in brewing; pale-colored malts are dried at about 176 °F (80 °C).

pallet. *(pae'-lit)*
A wood frame on which crates of bottles or casks are stacked for ease of handling with a forklift.

Panaché. *(pa-na-shei')*
In France, a mix of equal parts of beer and lemonade. **See also:** Shandy (Gaff).

papain. *(puh-pay'-in)*
Papaya enzyme used in Burton water salts.

parachute. *(pae'-ruh-shoot)*
A conical device fitted at the side or in the middle of the fermentation vessel to recover top yeast froth. The yeast, overflowing from the edge of the parachute, falls down a tube and into a receiving vessel called a yeast back. This device is now largely superseded by suction tubes that pull the yeast froth from the surface to the yeast back. **See also:** skimming oar.

paradise seeds. *(peh'-ruh-days seedz)*
A peppery herb with an aroma of citrus and pine. Also called: grains of paradise.

Paraflow. *(pae'-ruh-flo)*
A brewery plate heat exchanger–type of wort cooler.

parfait. *(pagh-fei')*
In France, a 1-liter glass for beer.

particulate matter. *(par-ti'-kyuh-lit mae'-d:er)*
Particles of a various nature—protein, yeast cells, and others—suspended in a liquid.

parts per million. *(parts' per mil'-yen)*
See: ppm.

party barrel. *(par'-d:ee bae'-rel)*
In England, a small ale barrel of 5- or 10-liter capacity used for parties, celebrations, and festivities.

Party Pig. *(par'-d:ee pig)*
A dispensing device of approximately 2.5 gallons that is pressurized by a chemically inflated bladder.

Pasteur effect. *(pas-toegh' i-fehkt')*
The conversion of an anaerobic pathway into an aerobic one, as when beer is racked before the completion of fermentation, thus introducing air into the anaerobic phase.

pasteurization. *(paes[h]-chuh-ri-zei'-shen)*
The application of intense heat to bottled, canned, or kegged beer for a specific period of time for the purpose of stabilizing it biologically by killing microorganisms, germs, and bacteria, stopping fermentation, and prolonging shelf life. Pasteurization can be accomplished by one of two methods: in bulk, prior to bottling, by plates of tube pasteurizers activated by hot water or steam, or individually by gradually heating packaged beer up to 140–167 °F (60–75 °C) for twenty to thirty minutes. Draft beer is pasteurized by flash heating for twenty to thirty seconds. In Germany, export beers only are pasteurized. In England, cask-conditioned ales are, by definition, not pasteurized. Etym: After Louis Pasteur. **See also:** flash pasteurization; tunnel pasteurization.

Pasteurization Unit. *(paes[h]-chuh-ri-zei'-shen yoo'-nit)*
A unit measuring the lethal effect (biological destruction) produced by pasteurization. It is defined as a one-minute exposure at 140 °F (60 °C). Bottled beer is usually pasteurized at 15–30 PU. Abbrev: PU or P.U.

pasteurizer. *(paes[h]'-chuh-rei-zer)*
An apparatus for pasteurizing liquids.

PBW.
Powder brewery wash; a commercial, noncaustic cleaning agent commonly used in breweries.

peat malt. *(peet mohlt')*
Malt that has been dried over burning peat. It imparts a unique smoked flavor to beers and is sometimes used in Scotch ales.

pâche. *(pehsh)*
A fruit derivative of *lambic* that is made by macerating peaches in a blend of young lambics.

pectin. *(pehk'-tin)*
A vegetable substance (a chain of galacturonic acid) that becomes gelatinous in the presence of sugars and acids.

Pediococcus. *(peh-dee-uh-ka'-kuhs)*
A strain of lactic acid bacteria vital to the production of *lambic* beers because it produces lactic acid and causes a pH drop in the wort.

peg tankard. *(pehg' taeng'-kerd)*
A type of communal tankard popular in the late seventeenth century fitted with a row of pegs, usually eight, inside the drum on the handle side, each peg marking an individual share. The number of pegs varies according to the size of the tankard. A 2-quart tankard had eight pegs each, indicating 1 gill of liquid. This practice may have originated from a royal decree issued by King Edward and suggested by Archbishop Dunstan of Canterbury from 959–975 in an effort to restrain heavy drinking. It was then ordered that pins or nails would be fastened inside drinking vessels and that whoever drank beyond such a mark in a single draft would be severely punished. This gave rise to the expressions "pin-drinking," "to drink to pins," and "nick the pin." **Syn:** pin tankard.

p'ei. *(bei*)*
A type of beer made in ancient China during the Tang dynasty (618–907). It was a popular nonfiltered beer also called "floating ants" because of the refuse of grains floating at its surface. **See also:** *chiu; li; sang-lo; shu; t'ien tsiou.*

pelletized hops. *(peh'-luh-d:ayzd haps')*
Synonym for hop pellets.

penny pot. *(peh'-nee pat')*
In seventeenth-century England, a quart of best ale cost one penny, while that of small ale was fixed at one halfpence.

peptidase. *(pehp'-ti-deys)*
The proteolytic enzyme that works to break large- and medium-sized protein molecules into amino acids. It is more thermolabile than protease so it is denatured quickly at higher temperatures.

peptides. *(pehp-taydz)*
A class of proteins consisting of between two and thirty amino acid molecules bound by peptide links. Peptides enhance the viscosity, or fullness, of beer.

pentosan. *(pehn'-tuh-saen)*
A hemicellulose present in cereals and other plant tissues. It yields sugars with five carbon atoms (pentoses).

pentose. *(pehn'-tos)*
Any carbohydrate containing five atoms of carbon.

peptization. *(pehp-ti-zei'-shen)*
The stabilization of colloidal solutions (also called SOL) by the addition of electrolytes, which is a peptizing agent, that are adsorbed on the particle surface.

peptonization temperature. *(pehp-tuh-ni-zei'-shen tehmp'-[e]-ruh-chur)*
The optimum temperature for the degradation of nitrogenous matter during mashing: 113–122 °F (45–50 °C).

peptonizing. *(pehp'-tuh-nay-zing)*
The action of proteolytic enzymes upon protein, successively yielding albumin / proteoses, peptides, and amino acids.

percent alcohol. *(per-sehnt' ael'-kuh-hohl)*
See: alcohol by volume; alcohol by weight.

Perle. *(English: per'-el; German: pehgh'-le)*
A variety of hops grown in Germany and Oregon containing 7–8.5 percent alpha acids.

permanent hardness. *(puhr'-muh-nent haerd'-nis)*
The hardness of water after boiling. **See also:** water hardness.

PET.
In England, a plastic container for beer with a capacity of 1.5 liters. Abbreviation for polyethylene, the plastic from which these containers are made.

pH.
Abbreviation for potential hydrogen, used to express the degree of acidity and alkalinity in an aqueous solution, usually on a scale of 1–14, where H^+ is the hydrogen-ion concentration. Technically, pH is defined as the negative logarithm of the effective hydrogen-ion concentration in gram equivalents per liter of solution: pH equals $\log_{10}(1/H^+)$. A pH value of 7 (pure water at 77 °F, 25 °C) indicates neutrality, lower numbers indicate acidity, and higher numbers indicate alkalinity. The pH can be measured by specially prepared pH test papers. **Syn:** pH value.

pH measurement. *(pee eich' meh'-zher-ment)*
The determination of the hydrogen-ion concentration in an ionized solution.

pH meter. *(pee eich' mee'-d:er)*
An instrument with a digital display that measures, calculates, and displays the pH of a solution. This device must be calibrated with a solution of known pH. A properly calibrated pH meter is more accurate than pH paper because visual comparison of color is not required.

pH paper. *(pee eich' pey'-per)*
Chemically treated strips used to measure the pH of a solution. The strips change color in response to the acidity or alkalinity of a solution. The degree of color on the strip is compared to a standard scale to determine the level of acidity or alkalinity.

pH value. *(pee eich' vael'-yoo)*
Synonym for pH.

phenolic. *(fee-no'-lik)*
Describes an unpleasant solvent-, medicinal-, or chemical-like flavor.
Syn: medicinal.

phenols. *(fee'-nolz)*
Volatiles found in small quantities in beer. Higher concentrations, due to the brewing water, infection of the wort by bacteria or wild yeasts, cleaning agents, or crown and can linings, impart off-flavors characterized as phenolic, medicinal, or pharmaceutical. Sixty volatile phenolic compounds are present in beer, and their concentration is greater in dark beers than in pale beers.

Phoenix. *(fee'-niks)*
A variety of hops cultivated in the United Kingdom and containing approximately 7.8 percent alpha acids.

Phorodon humuli. *(foh'-ruh-dan hyoo'-myuh-lay)*
Scientific name of the Damson hop aphid.

phosphates. *(fas'-feyts)*
Molecules that are the source of phytic acid created during malting and during decoction mashes. They contribute to the acidulation of the mash.

phytase. *(fay'-teys)*
An enzyme that reduces the mash pH by creating phytic acid from the phytin of the malt. Phytase aids saccharification, wort clarification, and fermentation.

pickle. *(pi'-kel)*
The kernel of barley or malt.

piece. *(pees)*
In traditional floor malting, a couch, or layer, of germinating barley usually about 4 inches (10 centimeters) thick. In pneumatic malting each piece, or bed, of barley in the germination box is about 3-feet deep. **See also:** couching; matted couche; thinning the piece; turner.

pigtail. *(pig'-teyl)*
Thin, tank-mounted coil used to dispense a small sample of beer.

Pils. *(pilz)*
Synonym for Pilsener.

Pilsen. *(pil'-zen)*
Synonym in Germany for Pilsener.

Pilsener. *(pilz'-[e]-ner)*
A general name for pale, golden-hued, highly hopped bottom-fermented beers. The original Pilsener was first brewed at the Bürgerlisches Brauhaus in the Bohemian town of Plzen (meaning green meadow) in Czechoslovakia in 1842. It was then the palest beer available, and the style was soon copied worldwide. The archetypal Pilsener is presently known as Plzensky Prazdroj or Pilsner Urquell (Urquell meaning original source), and the name was patented in 1898. It is brewed from an original wort gravity of 12 °B for an alcohol content of 4 percent by weight (5 percent by volume), with very soft, almost mineral-free water. It is highly hopped with local Saaz hops at a rate of 400–500 grams per hectoliter (as opposed to 200–220 grams per hectoliter for a Dortmunder and 300–400 grams for a German Pilsener). **Syn:** Pils; Pilsner; Pilsen.

Pilsener malt. *(pilz'-[e]-ne[r] mohlt')*
A light-colored base malt used in many beers, especially lagers.

Pilsner. *(pilz'-ner)*
Synonym in Czechoslovakia for Pilsener.

pin. *(pin)*
A liquid measure of 4.5 imperial gallons (20.45 liters), that is, half a firkin or 1/4 of a kilderkin.

pint. *(paynt)*
1. In the United States, a liquid measure equal to 1/8 of a U.S. gallon, or 29.875 cubic inches (0.473 liter). Also known as a liquid pint, distinguished from a dry unit of volume of 33.6 cubic inches called a pint or dry pint. **2.** In England, a dry and liquid measure, also called imperial pint, equivalent to 1/8 of an imperial gallon, or 34.678 cubic inches (0.567 liter). **3.** In New South Wales, a beer glass with a capacity of 20 ounces. **See also:** reputed pint.

pin tankard. *(pin taeng'-kerd)*
Synonym for peg tankard.

pinte. *(pae~t'-[e])*
An Old French capacity measure for liquids equal to half a *quarte,* or 0.931 liter.

pipe. *(payp)*
A wooden cask with a capacity of 5.5 barrels.

pitch, to. *(pich, too)*
1. To spray the inside walls of a cask or barrel with pitch to protect the beer from infection. **2.** To pitch with yeast, which is the action of adding yeast to the cooled wort.

pitch. *(pich)*
A black sticky substance derived from coal tar. It is sprayed into casks and barrels as a protective layer against moisture and infections.

pitcher. *(pi'-cher)*
A large jug made of metal but more often of earthenware, usually with a handle and spout or lip.

pitching. *(pi'-ching)*
1. The addition of yeast to the wort once it has cooled down to a minimum of 75–80 °F (24–27 °C). The ideal pitching temperature for top-fermenting yeasts is usually 57–59 °F (14–15 °C) whereas that for bottom-fermenting yeasts is 43–47 °F (6–8 °C). **Syn:** yeasting. **2.** Coating the inside walls of wooden barrels and casks with pitch or tar to prevent the beer from coming in contact with the wood.

pitching machine. *(pi'-ching muh-sheen')*
A spraying unit for coating the insides of casks and barrels with pitch.

pitching rate. *(pi'-ching reit')*
The amount of yeast required to ferment a single batch of beer, usually 200–600 grams of pressed yeast per hectoliter of wort.

pitchy taste. *(pi'-chee teist')*
An off-taste caused by improper pitching of the casks or their having been filled before proper cooling of the pitch.

pito. *(pee'-to*)*
In Nigeria, a type of beer made from malted sorghum.

piva. *(pee'-va*)*
An alcoholic beverage prepared in the Aleutian Islands by fermenting potatoes, raisins, and other sugar-containing products.

pivo. *(pee'-vo)*
Beer in Czechoslovakian.

piwo. *(Russ: pee'-vuh)*
Beer in Russian and Polish.

piwowar. *(pee'-voh-var*)*
Brewer in Polish.

piwowarstwo. *(pee-voh-var'-stvo*)*
Brewery in Polish.

piwsko. *(peev'-sko*)*
Bad beer in Polish.

placbier. *(plas'-byehgh')*
The name given to first quality, or the strongest, beer (also called *bière de luxe*) in Belgium in the fifteenth century.

plasma. *(plaez'-muh)*
The substance of cell bodies.

plaster of Paris. *(plae'-ster uhv pae'-ris)*
A common name for gypsum.

plate heat-exchanger. *(pleit' heet iks-chein'-jer)*
A type of heat exchanger consisting of a series of alternating flat and undulated plates.

Plato. *(plei'-d:o)*
A saccharometer that expresses the specific gravity as the weight of extract in a 100-gram solution at a temperature of 64 °F (17.5 °C). This percentage is designated degrees Plato. The original saccharometer was devised by Balling in 1843, however his tables were slightly erroneous and were later corrected by Dr. Plato for the German Imperial Commission (Normal-Eichungskommission). Abbrev: °P. **See also:** Balling; Belgian degree; Régie; specific gravity.

Conversion of Degrees Plato to Degrees Balling

°P	°B	°P	°B	°P	°B	°P	°B
1	0.97	6	5.92	11	10.90	16	15.95
2	1.95	7	6.90	12	11.90	17	16.95
3	2.92	8	7.90	13	12.90	18	17.95
4	3.91	9	8.90	14	13.94	19	18.95
5	4.91	10	9.90	15	14.95	20	19.97

Plimsol line. *(plim[p]'-sel layn* [can also be: plim-sol', -sal])*
In England, a line on beer glasses to indicate a full measure. Etym: After Samuel Plimsoll.

plumule. *(ploo'-myool)*
Synonym for acrospire.

plunger. *(pluhn'-jer)*
Hand-held, pumplike device used to insert a cork into a bottle neck.

pneumatic malting. *(n[y]oo-ma'-d:ik mohl-ting)*
A method of germinating barley in bulk in thermostatically controlled and ventilated boxes or drums. It was invented by Dr. Baud at the Tourtel Brewery in Tantonville, France. Also in France, Nicholas Galland patented one of the first germination boxes in the 1970s. **See also:** box malting; drum malting; Saladin box.

pocket. *(pa'-kit)*
A long, large canvas sack containing 50–150 kilograms of loose, dry hops.

polish, to. *(pa'-lish, too)*
To brush the malt free of dust and other foreign particles.

Polyclar. *(pa'-lee-klar)*
A plastic-based protein- and polyphenol-reducing agent.

polymer. *(pa'-lee-mer)*
A compound molecule formed by the joining of many smaller identical units. For example, polyphenols formed from phenols, and polypeptides formed from peptides.

polyphenol. *(pa-lee-fee'-nol)*
A complex organic compound partly responsible for chill haze in beer.

polysaccharide. *(pa-lee-sae'-kuh-rayd)*

A complex carbohydrate consisting of ten or more monosaccharide units joined together by the expulsion of a water molecule. Includes: starch, cellulose, and dextrins.

polyvinylpolypyrrolidone. *(pa-li-vay'-nel-puh-ro'-li-don)*

A plastic-based fining agent also known as Polyclar.

pombé. *(pom-bei')*

1. A beery drink made from millet in Guinea, Africa. It is drunk during ceremonies and purification rites; the alcoholic sensation derived from it is believed to be a sacred means of rejecting disorder in the soul and of attaining a rebirth in serenity. *Pombé* is prepared by women as follows: After having been steeped, germinated, and sundried, the red grains of millet (sorghum) are crushed into a flour, mixed with water and gombo stems, and simmered in large clay pots for an entire day. The brew is then drawn into a second vessel and boiled overnight. The next morning, more flour and water are added, and the brew is drawn again on the following day, and medicinal or magical herbs are added. Pombé, when ready, is slightly hazy, yellow, and foamy, rich in vitamin B, and low in alcohol. **Syn:** *tan; pombo.* **2.** In Rwanda and Uganda, a type of beer prepared from banana juice. It is prepared by women from bananas that are neither too ripe nor too green (the first mature too quickly and the second do not contain enough sugars). The bananas are peeled and buried in sand for three days, then they are placed on a cow hide, covered with branches, and trampled. The juice is put in pots that are heated; herbs are added for flavoring. The pombé is later drawn in wooden pots that have been rubbed with burnt sorghum flour. A yeasty product is then prepared from sorghum or millet. Fermentation takes forty-eight hours at a temperature that should be as constant as possible.

pony. *(po'-nee)*

1. A small liquid measure that is 1/5 of a pint. **2.** In New South Wales, a small 5-ounce beer glass. **3.** In Victoria and Western Australia, a 4-ounce glass.

pony keg. *(po-nee kehg)*

A 1/4-barrel (.29-hectoliter) keg.

Poperinge. *(po'-puh-ring-e)*

A variety of hops from Flanders.

Poperinge Hoppefeesten. *(po'-puh-ring-e hoh'-pe-fei-sten)*
A hop festival held every third year in Poperinge, Belgium. The festival begins with a folkloric procession of young hops, children dressed in red and yellow (the colors of the city) and wearing hats resembling hop flowers. It is followed by a hop-picking contest and beer-drinking festivities.

porcupine. *(por'-kyuh-payn)*
See: Armstrong rake.

porridge. *(poh'-rij)*
A brewer's name for mash. In France it is sometimes called *salade*.

porter. *(por'-d:er)*
A moderately bitter, very dark, almost black, and mildly alcoholic top-fermented beer first brewed in Shoreditch, London, in 1730 by a man named Ralph Harwood as a substitute for a then-popular mix of ale, beer, and twopenny called three-heads. It was then called entire and was advertised as being richer and more nourishing than ale and was intended for porters, carters, and other heavy laborers who would find in it the strength to accomplish tasks that no spirit drinker could perform. It was nicknamed porter's ale and, eventually, simply porter. Its dark color was derived from roasted, unmalted barley and sometimes a dash of licorice. In the British Isles, porter was overtaken in popularity by bitter stout in the nineteenth century, and the last porter was brewed in Dublin in 1973. Porter is still brewed today, mostly by bottom fermentation, in Germany, North and South America, Africa, China, Denmark, Hungary, Poland, and Russia. Its alcohol content varies between 5 and 7.5 percent by volume.

Porter Gaff. *(por'd:er gaef')*
A cocktail consisting of porter (or stout) and lemonade.

porter's ale. *(por'-d:erz eiyl')*
See: porter.

posset. *(pa'-sit)*
A traditional English drink made from hot milk curdled with ale, wine, or other liquor, sweetened with sugar, and flavored with spices. There are numerous recipes, one of which suggests mixing 1 liter of hot ale flavored with sugar, powdered ginger, grated nutmeg, and 1 liter of hot milk. **Syn:** ale posset.

post-off discount. *(post' af dis'-kawnt)*
A reduction in price given by a brewer to a wholesaler or retailer.

pot. *(pat)*
In Queensland and Victoria, a beer glass generally of 10-ounce capacity. In Western Australia the same term applies to glasses of 10-, 15-, or 20-ounce capacities.

potable water. *(po'-d:uh-bel wa'-d:er)*
Synonym for drinking water.

pot ale. *(pat' eiyl')*
Synonym for spent grains.

potential alcohol. *(po-tehn'-chel ael'-kuh-hohl)*
An estimate of the final alcohol content of a beer based on the original gravity or the measured sugar content prior to fermentation.

pothouse. *(pat'-haws)*
An obsolete name for a low-grade tavern or ale house. Also spelled: pot-house.

powdery mildew. *(paw'-duh-ree mil'-doo)*
Synonym for hop mold.

ppm.
Abbreviation for parts per million; the measurement is defined as volume or weight.

precipitate. *(pree-si'-puh-teyt)*
A solid compound formed by the reaction of compounds in a solution.

precipitation. *(pree-si-puh-tei'-shen)*
A clarification process that coagulates impurities, causing them to sink.

precursor. *(pree-kuhr'-ser)*
A substance from which another substance is derived in chemical reactions.

premium. *(pree'-mee-uhm)*
A marketing term used by brewers to qualify the top of their product line.

preservative. *(pree-zuhr'-vuh-d:iv)*
A chemical substance added to beer to slow down or prevent oxidation, deterioration, or infection.

preservative value. *(pree-zuhr'-vuh-d:iv vael'-yoo)*
The antiseptic or preservative value of hops as calculated by the formula PV equals 10 (a + b − a / 3). It was found that the preservative value of alpha acids (a) was three times as great as that of beta acids (b − a / 3). Because the antiseptic potency of alpha and beta acids depends largely upon the pH of the medium and other factors, this formula is not recognized internationally. Abbrev: P.V. or PV.

pressure regulator. *(preh'-sher rey'-gyuh-ley-d:er)*
A device for controlling the pressure in beer containers.

pressure relief valve. *(preh'-sher ree-leef' vaelv)*
Pressure-sensing valve used to prevent explosion of overpressurized tank. It can also prevent implosions.

pressurization. *(preh-sher-ri-zei'-shen)*
The process of controlling the tightness of casks and kegs by pressurizing them and soaking them in water.

pricking. *(pri'-king)*
The natural process by which beer gradually turns sour through the action of *Acetobacter* on alcohol.

pricked beer. *(prikt' beeyr')*
Beer turned sour or that has acquired a vinegar smell and taste.

Pride of Ringwood. *(prayd' uhv ring'-wud)*
A variety of hops grown in Australia and Idaho containing 5.5–7 percent alpha acids.

prima melior. *(pree'-ma mei'-lee-or)*
First quality, or the strongest, beers brewed in medieval monasteries (AD 853) to be served to the fathers and distinguished guests. Second quality beers, called *secunda* or *cervisia*, were for laymen; and *tertia*, or third quality, were for travelers and pilgrims. This tradition has survived in some Belgian abbeys where three strengths of beer are brewed and classified accordingly as single, double, or triple. **Syn:** *celia.*

primary. *(pray'-meh-ree)*
Short for primary fermentation bin.

primary attenuation. *(pray'-meh-ree uh-teh-nyuh-wei'-shen)*
The attenuation measured at the end of primary fermentation.

primary fermentation. *(pray'-meh-ree fuhr-mehn-tei'-shen)*
The first stage of fermentation carried out in open or closed containers and lasting from two to seven days during which time the bulk of the fermentable sugars are converted to ethyl alcohol and carbon dioxide gas. **Syn:** principal fermentation; initial fermentation.

primary fermentation bin. *(pray'-meh-ree fuhr-mehn-tei'-shen bin)*
Synonym for primary fermenter.

primary fermenter. *(pray'-meh-ree fuhr-mehn'-ter)*
A vessel in which primary fermentation is carried out. **Syn:** primary fermentor; primary fermentation bin; primary; primary fermentation vessel.

primary fermentor. *(pray'-meh-ree fuhr-mehn'-ter)*
Orthographic variant for primary fermenter.

priming. *(pray'-ming)*
The addition of small amounts of fermentable sugars (preferably corn sugar or syrup) to fully fermented beer before bottling to induce a renewed fermentation in the bottle and thus carbonate the beer. **See also:** dry priming; overpriming.

priming solution. *(pray'-ming suh-loo'-shen)*
A solution of sugar in water added to aged beer at bottling to induce a second fermentation (bottle conditioning).

priming sugar. *(pray'-ming shu'-ger)*
Corn or cane sugar added in small amounts to bulk beer prior to racking or to each bottle prior to capping to induce a new fermentation in the bottle and thus create carbonation. Homebrewers use about 3/4–1 cup of sugar per 5-gallon batch of beer.

Primus, Jean. *(pree'-mus, zha~)*
See: Gambrinus.

principal fermentation. *(prin[t]'-suh-pel fuhr-mehn-tei'-shen)*
Synonym for primary fermentation.

private label beer. *(pray'-vit lei'-bel beeyr')*
Any beer brewed by a local brewer for a private entrepreneur, a large-scale retailer, or independent distributor. Examples: Billy Beer (after Billy Carter), Nude Beer, and New Amsterdam Amber Beer. More commonly known as contract-brewed beer.

Progress. *(pra'-grehs)*
A variety of hops cultivated in the United Kingdom and containing 5–7 percent alpha acids.

Prohibition. *(pro-[h]uh-bi'-shen)*
A law instituted by the Eighteenth Amendment (after the Volstead Act) on January 18, 1920, forbidding the sale, production, importation, and transportation of alcoholic beverages in the United States of America. It was repealed by the Twenty-first Amendment on December 5, 1933.

Prohibition Bureau. *(pro-[h]uh-bi'-shen byu'-ro)*
A federal government agency established in 1920 to enforce the National Prohibition Act.

Prohibition-days beer. *(pro-[h]uh-bi'-shen deiz beeyr')*
Beer made during the Prohibition era from odd recipes calling for such ingredients as potato peels, raisins, and baker's yeast.

Prohibition era. *(pro-[h]uh-bi'-shen eh'ruh)*
The thirteen years, ten months, and eighteen days (January 16, 1920 to December 5, 1933) during which the Eighteenth Amendment was in force.

Prohibition-style beer. *(pro-[h]uh-bi'-shen stay[e]l beeyr')*
In homebrewing, refers to a poor or mediocre beer made by amateur techniques and low-grade products.

propylene glycol alginate. *(pro'-puh-leen glay'-cohl ael'-ji-neit)*
A foam-stabilizing additive, the modified extract of a seaweed, usually added at a rate of about 160 parts per million (0.0160 percent) in some commercial beers.

protease. *(pro'-d:ee-eiz)*

A malt enzyme that develops in barley during germination and is capable of degrading complex proteins into polypeptides and amino acids.

protein. *(pro'-teen)*

A complex organic compound found in animal and plant tissues containing carbon, hydrogen, oxygen, nitrogen, and sulfur. All proteins are composed of large configurations of twenty amino acids. Proteins are responsible for the head retention and body of beer and partially for its haziness.

proteinaceous layer. *(pro-tee-nei'-shuhs lei'-yer)*

Synonym for aleurone layer.

proteinase. *(pro-tee-neys)*

The enzyme that works to break large protein molecules down into medium-sized proteins. It is less thermolabile than peptidase so it works at higher temperatures where peptidase is soon denatured.

protein coagulation. *(pro'-teen ko-[w]ae'-gyuh-ley-shen)*

The tendency of proteins to become insoluble and either remain in suspension or precipitate as a clot or curd. This occurs when solutions of water-soluble proteins are heated, during wort boiling, to a temperature at which the proteins become denatured. Protein coagulation is desirable because it helps remove higher molecular-weight proteins that can lead to chill haze in the finished beer. The coagulation should not be too complete, however, because higher molecular-weight proteins also contribute to the body of the beer.

protein content. *(pro'-teen kan'-tehnt)*

The percentage of the malt grain, which is protein.

protein rest. *(pro'-teen rehst)*

A stage of the mashing process during which complex proteins are decomposed by proteolytic enzymes to progressively less complex fractions. The stability of finished beer is largely established during the protein rest. Nutrients required for proper fermentation also are developed during this process. The proteolytic enzymes become active at temperatures from 113–140 °F (45– 60 °C). The protein rest should be employed for a period of twenty to thirty minutes when using undermodified malts.

proteolysis. *(pro-d:ee-a'-luh-sis)*
The hydrolysis of a protein molecule into amino acids by proteolytic enzymes.

proteolytic enzyme. *(pro-d:ee-uh-li'-d:ik ehn'-zaym)*
An enzyme that hydrolyzes complex proteins into simpler soluble bodies.
See also: amylolytic enzyme.

provisie. *(pgho-vi-zee')*
A brown beer brewed in Oudenaarde, Belgium. It is aged for a minimum of two years and a maximum of twenty-five years and contains about 6 percent alcohol by volume.

Pseudoperonospora humuli. *(su-do-puh-ra-no-spo'-ruh hyoo'-myuh-lay)*
Scientific name for downy mildew.

Psylloides attenuata. *(si'-loy-deez uh-teh-nyuh-wa'-d:uh*)*
Scientific name for the hop flea beetle.

P.U.
Abbreviation for Pasteurization Unit. Also spelled: PU.

pub. *(puhb)*
A synonym for public house.

pubgoer. *(puhb'-go-wer)*
One who frequents public houses.

public house. *(puhb'-lik haws)*
In England, an establishment where alcoholic beverages are sold and consumed. **Syn:** pub.

publican. *(puh'-bli-ken)*
The owner or manager of a pub.

pull date. *(pul' deit)*
The deadline after which unsold beer should be removed from the shelf and recalled to the company (usually around sixty days).

pulp filter. *(puhlp fil'-ter)*
Synonym for mass filter.

pulque. *(pool'-kei)*

An alcoholic beverage obtained in Mexico and some parts of Central America by fermenting the juice (called *aguamiel*, honey water) of an agave cactus (Amaryllidaceous family) of the maguey type, especially *Agave atrovirens*, *A. potatorum*, *A. americana, and A. tequilana*. It has an alcoholic content of 6–7 percent alcohol by volume. Tequila and mescal, sometimes called *pulque* brandies, are produced by distilling pulque.

pulque curado. *(pool'-kei koo-ra'-do)*

Pulque mixed with fruit juices, especially pineapple.

puncheon. *(puhn'-chen)*

A large cask varying in size according to commodity: 72 imperial gallons (± 325 liters) for beer, 120 imperial gallons (545 liters) for whisky or brandy, and 114 imperial gallons (518 liters) for rum.

punt. *(puhnt)*

The hollow at the bottom of a bottle. **Syn:** kick.

purchase. *(puhr'-chis)*

The name sometimes given to the thumbpiece on a tankard.

Pure. *(pyoor)*

A variety of hops organically grown in the United Kingdom and containing approximately 5.5 percent alpha acids.

purity. *(pyu'-ruh-d:ee)*

Synonym for brilliance.

purity law. *(pyu'-ruh-d:ee loh')*

See: Reinheitsgebot.

Purl. *(puhr[e]l)*

1. A type of mild ale prepared from plant roots, herbs, and spices. **2.** Early Purl, a drink consisting of hot ale, wormwood, sugar, and gin, was taken in England in the 1800s as a morning appetizer. **Syn:** Dog's Nose.

P.V.

Abbreviation for preservative value. Also spelled: PV.

PVPP.

See: polyvinylpyrrolidone.

pyment. *(pi-mehnt')*

1. A variety of melomel prepared by fermenting a must of honey, grape juice, and water. **2.** Honey-sweetened wine. Sometimes spelled: pymeat. Also called: pyment-clarre.

quaff. *(kwaf)*
> To drink deeply.

quart. *(kwohrt)*
> A liquid measure. **See also:** imperial quart; U.S. quart.

quarte. *(kaght'-[e])*
> An Old French measure for liquids with a capacity of 46 cubic inches, or 1.863 liters. Also spelled: *carte*.

quartern. *(kwar'-tern)*
> The fourth part of various units of measure.

quas(s). *(kvas)*
> Orthographic variant for *kvas(s)*.

quiet process. *(kway'-et pra'-sehs)*
> **See:** Burton Union System.

R.
Abbreviation for Régie (°Régie).

rack, to. *(raek, too)*
To transfer beer from one vessel into another or into bottles and casks while leaving the dregs at the bottom of the first container.

racker. *(rae'-ker)*
An apparatus for racking.

racking. *(rae'-king)*
The process of transferring fermented beer from the maturation vat into packaging containers—bottles, cans, casks, kegs.

racking back. *(rae'-king baek')*
An open tank in which green beer is held for a short period before being transferred to the barrels.

racking cock. *(rae'-king kak')*
A two-holed nozzle on isobarometric (counterpressure) bottle fillers; it is inserted in the mouth of the bottle to pour the beer while evacuating the air. A third hole creates a counterpressure of air prior to the flow of beer.

racking gravity. *(rae'-king grae'-vuh-d:ee)*
The specific gravity at which green beer is put into barrels or bottles, usually a few degrees higher than final gravity.

racking square. *(rae'-king skwehr')*
A large holding vessel from which beer is racked.

racking tube. *(rae'-king toob')*
In homebrewing, a U-shaped tube of rigid plastic with an inlet approximately 1.5 inches above the bottom and used with a siphon to draw beer from the fermenter or storage vessel while leaving the dregs behind.

radicle. *(rae'-di-kel)*
Root. The lower part of the anis of an embryo seedling; the root part; often the hypocotyl (part of the anis or stem), sometimes together with the root; a rudimentary root. **See also:** malted couche; rootlets.

Radlermass. *(ghad'-ler-mas)*
In Germany, a mix of beer and lemonade. The term means cyclists' beer. **See also:** Russ.

raisonable. *(ghei-soh-na'-ble)*
In France, a 1-liter beer glass.

rauchbier. *(ghawk'-beegh)*
In Germany, an amber or brown bottom-fermented beer produced by a few breweries in the city of Bamberg in northern Bavaria. Its unique roasted or smoked flavor results from the use of malts that are dried over an open-fire of moist beechwood logs, a technique dating back, according to some researchers, to 1678. **Syn:** Bamberg beer; Bamberger *rauchbier;* smoked beer.

raw sugar. *(roh' shu'-ger)*
Brown unrefined sugar crystals covered with a film of syrup.

reagent. *(ree-ey'-jint)*
A substance involved in a reaction that identifies the strength of the substance being measured.

real ale. *(reeyl' eiyl')*
In England, unpasteurized, cask-conditioned draft ale that completes its maturation in the pub cellar as opposed to pasteurized, filtered, and chilled kegged ale. Real ale is served at cellar temperature, ideally 60 °F (13.3 °C).

real attenuation. *(reeyl' uh-teh-nyuh-wei'-shen)*
The attenuation of beer devoid of alcohol and carbon dioxide. The carbon dioxide is evaporated, and the alcohol is removed by distillation. In the brewing industry only apparent attenuation measures the progress of fermentation.

Formula: $A = (B - b) / B \times 100$
A = real attenuation
B = original gravity in °B or °P
b = specific gravity of beer devoid of alcohol and carbon dioxide

real extract. *(reeyl' ehk'-straekt)*
This is the gravity of the actual residual extract in fermented beer. It can be measured with a hydrometer by first boiling off the alcohol in fermented beer and replacing the volume lost with distilled water.

recrating machine. *(ree-krei'-d:ing muh-sheen')*
Synonym for crater.

red mead. *(rehd' meed)*
A variety of melomel prepared by fermenting a must of honey, red currants, and water.

red mold. *(rehd' mohld')*
Synonym for hop mold.

reducing valve. *(ri-doo'-sing vaelv')*
A valve to control the pressure on a fluid, liquid, or gas.

refrigerator. *(ree-fri'-juh-rey-d:er)*
Common name for a simple cold water–based brewery wort cooler, not true refrigeration in the modern sense of the word.

Régie. *(gheh-zhee'*)*
In France, a measure of the density of wort. The legal density is defined as the ratio of the mass of a given volume of liquid (usually 50 centimeters cubed) at 59 °F (15 °C) to that of the mass of an equal volume of water at 39.2 °F (4 °C) (1 liter of water equals 1 kilogram). The Régie density is obtained by moving the comma of the legal density two digits to the right; hence, a legal density of 1,045 equals 4.5 °Régie (°R). Formula: °R equals (legal density – 1,000) × 100. One °Régie equals 2.6 °Balling. **See also:** *bière.*

regional specialty brewery. *(ree'-juh-nel speh'-shil-tee broo'-[e]-ree)*
A brewery that produces more than 15,000 barrels of beer annually, with its largest-selling product a specialty beer.

regulator. *(rey'-gyuh-ley-d:er)*
A device used to control and measure gas flow from tank to gas line.

regulator-carbonator. *(reh'-gyuh-ley-d:er kar-buh-nei'-ter)*
A type of carbonator used in the carbonated beverage industry to ensure a regulated ratio of carbon dioxide gas and sugar.

Reinheitsgebot. *(ghayn'-hayts-ge-bot')*
A German law of which the title signifies "pledge of purity" or "order of purity." This purity law governs the production and quality of beer in Germany. Inspired by an earlier law instituted in by Duke Albert IV 1487, William VI, the elector of Bavaria, decreed in 1516 that only water, malted barley, malted wheat, and hops could be used to make beer. Yeast was not included but taken for granted. This law was ruled to be protective in 1987 and was repealed, allowing beers with adjuncts to be brewed and sold in Germany. However, all German brewers signed a collective agreement to continue to adhere to the Reinheitsgebot.

Reinheitsgebot-pure. *(rayn'-hayts-ge-bot'-pyoor')*
In homebrewing, refers to a beer made from the four basic ingredients, namely, malted barley or malted wheat, water, hops, and yeast—without the addition of adjuncts or chemical additives.

repitch, to. *(ree-pich', too)*
To add yeast to induce a renewed fermentation. **See:** re-yeasting.

reproduction phase. *(ree-pruh-duhk'-shen feiz')*
The period following the lag phase during which the yeast cells divide at a constant rate and the cell count doubles at each generation in regular increments of time. The optimal temperature for most yeast reproduction is 86 °F (30 °C); however, it varies dramatically with the type of yeast strain. **Syn:** logarithmic phase; exponential phase.

reputed pint. *(ri-pyoo'-d:id paynt')*
1. In Britain, a half bottle (1/12 of an imperial gallon, or 0.38 liter). **2.** In South Australia, a beer glass with a capacity of 15 ounces.

reputed quart. *(ri-pyoo'-d:id kwohrt)*
In British measure equal to 1/6 of an imperial gallon (0.75 liter).

residual extract. *(ri-sij'-[e]-wel ehk'-straekt)*
The residual gravity as determined by evaporating one-third of the volume of the beer, thus eliminating all the alcohol and carbon dioxide, and readjusting the sample to its original volume with the addition of distilled water.

resin. *(reh'-zin)*
The gummy organic substance produced by certain plants and trees. Humulone and lupulone, for example, are bitter resins produced by the hop flower.

resinification. *(reh-zin-nuh-fi-kei'-shen)*
The oxidation and polymerization of humulone (alpha acid) and lupulone (beta acid) during the storage of hops. The crystalline bitter acids gradually lose aroma, bittering, and antiseptic power, and are eventually transformed into hard resins that are useless to the brewing process. **See also:** hard resins; soft resins.

resin scum. *(reh'-zin skuhm')*
The brownish substance found on the froth of beer during primary fermentation.

respiration. *(reh-spuh-rei'-shen)*
The absorption of oxygen and production of carbon dioxide by germinating barley that is caused by the activity of the embryo and the rest of the aleurone. A lack of oxygen during steeping results in the formation of anaerobic substances such as ethanol, lactic acid, and esters.

respiratory phase. *(rehsp'-[e]-ruh-to-ree feiz')*
The second aerobic stage of the fermentation process immediately following the lag period, so called because the yeast draws oxygen from the wort to oxidize a variety of acid compounds. During this stage, six-carbon sugar (glucose) is first converted into three-carbon acid (pyruvic acid), causing a significant drop in pH; the pyruvic acid is then reduced to activated acetic acid (acetyl CO-A), followed immediately by the Krebs cycle. **See also:** fermentation phase; Krebs cycle; lag period.

rest. *(rehst)*
Mash rest. Holding the mash at a specific temperature to induce certain enzymatic changes.

rest beer. *(rehst beeyr')*
Unracked beer and sediments at the bottom of a storage tank.

retorrification. *(ri-toh-ri-fuh-key'-shen)*
The act of warming the grist prior to mashing in order to reduce the differential between strike heat and initial heat.

returnable. *(ri-tuhr'-nuh-bel)*
Describes packaging material that may be returned, refunded, and reused.

reverse osmosis. *(ri-vuhrs' az-mo'-sis)*
A filtration method that uses pressure to push water and other very small molecules through a membrane with fine pores. Larger molecules are excluded. A good method for removing inorganic contaminants (metals, chloride, nitrates), but when used in conjunction with a carbon filter it also removes organics. A reverse osmosis system is rather expensive and generates a large volume of waste water.

re-yeasting. *(ree-yee'-sting)*
Inducing a secondary fermentation during maturation by adding a little yeast to a brew still containing fermentable sugars but lacking live yeast cells.

rhodomel. *(ro'-duh-mehl)*
Mead made with attar, a rose-petal distillate.

rice. *(reis)*
Grain of the cereal grass plant *Oryza sativa*. As an adjunct, rice is appreciated for its 70 percent starch, the highest starch level of any cereal. Its moisture content is around 11–13 percent, and it has a low protein level of 7–9 percent. Rice may be added to the mash to increase its starch content and correct an excess of protein. In the United States the addition of 40–50 percent rice is not uncommon whereas in Europe a ratio of 10–20 percent is more frequent.

rice beer. *(reis beeyr')*
Synonym for *saké*.

rice wine. *(reis wayn')*
Synonym for *saké*.

RIMS. *(rimz)*
Recirculating infusion mash system.

rinsing machine. *(rin'-sing muh-sheen')*
A machine for rinsing bottles and casks after washing.

roast, to. *(rost, too)*
To expose to fire.

roasted barley. *(ro'-stid bar'-lee)*
Unmalted barley that has been kilned to a dark brown color similar to that of chocolate or black malt but with a different, coffeelike flavor.

roasted malt. *(ro'-stid mohlt')*
Malt made from barley heated in a sequence of stages starting at 320 °F (160 °C), then 419 °F (215 °C), and finally 437 °F (220–225 °C). The malt acquires a brilliant external appearance while the endosperm becomes black. Roasted malt is used to flavor stout and dark beers.

rocky heads. *(ra'-kee hehdz')*
See: *kraeusen.*

roller mill. *(ro'-ler mil)*
Synonym for grinder.

ropy fermentation. *(ro'-pee fuhr-mehn-tei'-shen)*
A viscous gelatinous blob, or "rope," from bacterial contamination usually resulting from a *Pediococcus* infection.

roquille. *(gho-kee'-ye)*
An Old French (in Paris) capacity measure for liquids equal to 1/32 of a pint.

root beer. *(root' beeyr')*
A nonalcoholic beverage flavored with oil of wintergreen and oil of sassafras.

rootlets. *(root'-lits)*
The seminal roots that grow in a tuftlike formation on germinating barley. **Syn:** malt sprouts. **See also:** coombs; couch; culms; kaulms; matted couche; radicle.

rose hips. *(roz' hips)*
Versatile fruit/herb used in wines and specialty beers.

rotary sparger. *(ro'-d:uh-ree spar'-jer)*
A hydraulically operated apparatus fitted in the lauter tun for spraying hot water on the mash.

round. *(rawnd)*
A name given in the eighteenth century to vertical, cylindrical, wooden tuns each holding 300 gallons.

rouser. *(raw'-zer)*
Synonym for brewer's paddle.

rousing. *(raw'-zing)*
The action of stirring thoroughly the contents of a vat, tank, or cask, usually as an aid to fermentation.

ruh. *(roo[h]')*
A term once used to describe the process (or period) of cold secondary fermentation or maturation in bottom-fermented beer.

ruh beer. *(roo[h]' beeyr')*
Bottom-fermented beer ready for lagering.

runchera. *(run'-chei'-ruh)*
See: *chicha.*

run off. *(ruhn' af)*
The act of emptying a vessel, usually the mash tun.

runoff. *(ruhn'-af)*
The liquid that is separated from the spent grains during lautering. Also called: runnings; wort; sweet wort; sweet liquor.

Russ. *(ghoos)*
In Germany, a mix of wheat beer and lemonade. **See:** Radlermass.

Russian stout. *(ruh'-shen stawt')*
In Britain, a very strong stout brewed originally from 1780 to World War I by the London-based Anchor Brewery (now part of Courage) for exportation to St. Petersburg in Russia. Present-day Russian stout, brewed by Courage, is nonpasteurized and matured in casks for two months and afterward bottle-aged

for one full year before it is marketed. It is brewed from an original wort gravity of 1101.8 and contains about 10.5 percent alcohol by volume. **Syn:** imperial Russian stout; imperial stout.

rye. *(ray)*
Grain from the cereal plant *Secale cereale.*

rye malt. *(ray mohlt')*
Malt derived from rye. It lends a distinct flavor to beers even when used in small quantities.

Ss

Saaz. *(tsots)*

A variety of hops grown in Bohemia in western Czechoslovakia with 3–5 percent alpha acids and in Oregon with 4–6 percent alpha acids. It is the traditional flavoring hop for Pilsener-type beers.

saccharase. *(sae'-kuh-reis)*

Synonym for invertase.

saccharification. *(sae-kuh-re-fi-kei'-shen)*

The natural process through which malt starch is converted into fermentable sugars, mainly maltose.

saccharification rest. *(sae-kuh-re-fi-kei'-shen rehst)*

A stage of the mashing process during which complex glucose chains are broken down into fermentable sugars. Saccharification is accomplished by alpha-amylase and beta-amylase acting in concert to reduce complex glucose chains. Alpha-amylase is most active at temperatures between 131 and 158 °F (55 and 70 °C). Beta-amylase is most active at temperatures between 113 and 149 °F (45 and 65 °C). This stage of mashing requires a temperature range between 145 and 158 °F (63 and 70 °C). Higher mash temperatures produce more full-bodied worts because beta-amylase becomes deactivated sooner at higher temperatures. Lower mash temperatures yield more fermentable sugars. Rest durations vary with temperature. At higher temperatures, a twenty- to forty-minute rest will accomplish conversion. At lower temperatures, a rest of forty-five minutes to two hours is required.

saccharifying enzyme. *(sae-kuh'-ri-fay-ing ehn'-zaym)*

Synonym for beta-amylase.

saccharometer. *(sae-kuh-ra'-muh-d:er)*

A type of hydrometer for measuring the sugar concentration of a solution by determining the specific gravity. The reading shows the percentage extract by weight, which is converted into percentage by volume by multiplying the reading by the specific gravity or by finding the equivalent volume in tables computed by Balling and Plato.

Saccharomyces. *(sae-kuh-ro-may'-seez)*

A genus of the Ascomycetes class of yeasts, subfamily Saccharomycetoideae. All species of this genus have the common property of generating ethyl alcohol from sugar, but are differentiated by their ability to ferment the carbohydrates: galactose, maltose, sucrose, melibiose, lactose, raffinose, and starch. Etym: So named by the German chemist Mayer in 1830 when he first isolated yeast under a microscope. *Saccharomyces* is a scientific translation of an earlier expression, sugar mushrooms, given to yeast by Schwann. **See also:** *zuckerpilz.*

Saccharomyces carlsbergensis. *(sae-kuh-ro-may'-seez karlz-buhr-gehn'-sis*)*

Scientific name for bottom-fermenting yeast.

Saccharomyces cerevisiae. *(sae-kuh-ro-may'-seez cehr-[e]-vee'-see-ei*)*

Scientific name for top-fermenting yeast.

Saccharomyces uvarum. *(sae-kuh-ro-may'-seez yoo'-vuh-rem)*

Scientific name for bottom-fermenting yeast.

saccharose. *(sae'-kuh-ros)*

Synonym for sucrose.

saccharum. *(sae'-kuh-rem)*

A brewer's name for invert sugar.

sack mead. *(saek meed)*

Mead made with a high proportion of honey to water, producing a very strong beverage.

sack metheglin. *(saek meh-theh'-glin)*

Sweet-tasting metheglin.

sage ale. *(seij' eiyl')*

Misnomer for an infusion of sage leaves formerly used in the seventeenth century for medicinal purposes.

sahti. *(saeh'-tee)*

A type of homemade beer brewed in Finland from a mix of barley and rye malts, flavored with hops and juniper berries, and partially filtered using straw and branches. *Sahti* may contain up to 10 percent alcohol by weight.

Saint Arnold(us). *(seint ar-nohld'-[uhs])*

See: Saint Arnou.

Saint Arnou. *(English: seint ar-noo'; French: sae~ agh-noo')*

The patron saint of brewers, born in 580 in the Chateau of Lay-Saint-Christophe in the Old French diocese of Toul, north of Nancy. He married Doda with whom he had many sons, two of whom were to become famous: Clodulphe, later called Saint Cloud, became bishop of Metz (658–696); and Anchise, who married Begga, daughter of Pépin de Landen and mother of Charlemagne. St. Arnou, was acclaimed bishop of Metz in 612, a role he assumed for fifteen years and ten days after which he retired to a monastery near Remiront where he died on August 16, 640. In 641 the citizens of Metz requested that the body be exhumed from Saint Mont and be ceremoniously carried to Metz where he was to be buried in the Church of the Holy Apostles. It was during this voyage that a miracle took place in a town called Champigneulles. The tired porters and followers stopped for a rest and a drink. Regretably there was only one mug of beer to be shared, but that mug never went dry and filled everyone else's mug. Also spelled: Saint Arnoul(d); Saint Arnold(us); sometimes Saint Arnou le Lorrain in distinction from Saint Arnou de Oudenaarde.

Saint Bartholomew. *(seint bar-thoh'-luh-myoo)*

Patron saint of mead whose birthday is celebrated on August 23.

Saint Margaret's ale. *(seint marg'-[e]-rits eiyl')*

A misnomer for water.

saison. *(sei-zo~')*

An amber- or copper-colored top-fermented beer from Walloon, Belgium, and France once brewed in the summertime (April through May) from a high-gravity wort and drunk four to six months later, but now it is available year-round. *Saison* is naturally conditioned in 1-liter and 750-milliliter bottles. It has a fruity flavor and an alcohol content of about 4.5 percent alcohol by weight (5.6 percent by volume).

sakazuki. *(sa-ka-zoo-kee*)*

A small porcelain bowl for drinking *saké.*

saké. *(sa-kei)*

A traditional Japanese fermented drink made from rice. Contrary to popular belief, *saké* is not a spirit (it is not distilled) nor is it a wine (it is not macerated), but rather a special type of beer brewed from a cereal base. The rice is washed, steamed, and fermented with a yeastlike fungus (*Aspergillus orgyzae*) that acts both as a saccharifier and fermenter. Primary fermentation takes from thirty to forty days, after which more rice and water are added to generate a secondary fermentation lasting eight to ten days. A special yeast, *Saccharomyces saké,* is sometimes added to activate fermentation. The alcohol content varies between 14 and 17 percent by volume. Saké is colorless, slightly hazy, lacks carbonation, and is served warm (100 °F, ± 37.8 °C). Etym: From Osaka, Japan. **Syn:** (Japanese) rice wine; (Japanese) rice beer. **See also:** *amasaké; sakazuki; shirosaké; shoto saké; tokkori.*

Saladin box. *(sae'-luh-din baks')*

A pneumatic germination system invented by Jules Alphonse Saladin in France in the 1880s. The term is now synonymous with germination box.

salt. *(sohlt)*

1. Common name for sodium chloride, or table salt. **2.** Any compound produced by the reaction of an acid with an alkali. (Example: calcium chloride.)

saltwater. *(sohlt'-wa-d:er)*

Synonym for brine. Also spelled: salt-water.

salty. *(sohl'-tee)*

An undesirable taste in beer caused by salt.

sang-lo. *(zang-lo'*)*

A type of rice beer made in China during the Tang dynasty (618–907) and later. *Sang-lo* was a regional beer produced in the southern region of Su-chou.

Sanke tap. *(saeng'-ke taep)*

Universal, ball-style tap head for commercial-style kegs.

sarsaparilla. *(saes-[e]-puh-ri'-luh)*

A dried root that can improve mouthfeel and head retention of a beer. It has been identified as a possible carcinogen by the U.S. Food and Drug Administration. It is also used in the making of some carbonated, nonalcoholic beverages.

saturate, to. *(sae'-choo-reit, too)*
To carbonate a liquid to its limit capacity. **Syn:** to carbonate.

saturation. *(sae-chuh-rei'-shen)*
1. Synonym for carbonation. **2.** Carbonation to the limit capacity of a liquid under specific conditions of temperature, pressure, and sugar content. Water, for example, can dissolve 6.8 grams/liter of carbon dioxide at 50 °F (10 °C) and 2 kilograms per square centimeter of pressure. Most beers contain between 4.5 and 5 grams/liter of carbon dioxide.

saturator. *(sae'-chuh-rei'd:er)*
Synonym for carbonator.

Savinja Goldings. *(suh-vin'-yuh gohl'-dingz)*
A variety of hops grown in Yugoslavia containing 6–7 percent alpha acids.

scale. *(skey[e]l)*
A device used for measuring specific quantities of a substance by weight. A grain scale should be graduated in increments of 1/8–1/4 of a pound. A scale used for measuring hops and water treatments should have gram graduations. A scale for lab use should have .01–.00001 graduations.

schankbier. *(shank'-beegh)*
In Germany, the weakest category of beers prepared from wort gravities of 7–8 °B and containing 2–3 percent alcohol by weight. **See also:** *bier; starkbier; vollbier.*

schechar. *(shei-khar)*
Orthographic variant for *shekar.*

schenelle. *(sheh-neh'-le)*
A very tall, slender tankard of stone- or earthenware with a slightly tapered body and a cover fitted with a thumbpiece.

schooner. *(skoo'-ner)*
1. A tall beer glass with a capacity of 15 ounces. **2.** In South Australia, a schooner applies to a glass of only 9 ounces.

Schultheiss Berliner Weisse. *(shul'-tays begh-lee'-ner vay'-se)*
See: Berliner *weisse.*

schwarzbier. *(shvaghts'-beegh)*
A dark brown or black-colored lager beer.

Scotch ale. *(skach' eiyl)*
A top-fermented beer of Scottish origin but now also produced in Belgium and France with an alcohol content of 7 or 8 percent by volume. Scotch ales are traditionally strong, very dark, thick, and creamy. One particular example is brewed by Peter Maxwell Stuart in his castle at Traquair (twenty miles south of Edinburgh) and is available on location from May to September. In Scotland, the pub expression for such a beer is "wee heavy," which also is the brand name of such an ale produced by Fowler's brewery.

scotches. *(ska'-chis)*
Wooden wedges used to prevent beer casks from moving. Also known as chocks.

screw cap. *(skroo' kaep)*
A type of beer-bottle stopper to be twisted on or off rather than pried off like a crown cork.

screw stopper. *(skroo' sta'-per)*
A type of sealing stopper first introduced in 1885, now largely superseded by crown corks.

scum. *(skuhm)*
The white froth that forms at the surface of the primary fermentation vessel.

scurvy grass ale. *(skuhr'-vee graes eiyl')*
1. A medicinal drink formerly prepared by adding an infusion of watercress to ale. It was believed to guard against scurvy. **2.** An infusion of watercress.

scutellum. *(skyoo-teh'-lem)*
The shield-shaped sheet of tissue (cotyledon) separating the embryo of the barley grain from the endosperm.

sealed bottle. *(seeyld' ba'-d:el)*
A bottle that is hermetically capped.

seasonal beers. *(seez'-[e]-nel beeyrz')*
Special beer styles brewed for a specific season such as Oktoberfest.

secondary. *(seh'-ken-deh-ree)*
Synonym for secondary fermenter.

secondary attenuation. *(seh'-ken-deh-ree uh-teh-nyuh-wei'-shen)*
The attenuation measured at the end of secondary fermentation.

secondary fermentation. *(seh'-ken-deh-ree fuhr-mehn-tei'-shen)*
1. The second, slower stage of fermentation carried out in closed containers at 39–46 °F (4–8 °C) for top-fermenting beers and at 32–36 °F (0–2 °C) for bottom-fermenting beers and lasting from a few weeks to many months, depending on the type of beer. **2.** A renewed fermentation in bottles or casks produced by priming or re-yeasting.

secondary fermentation bin. *(seh'-ken-deh-ree fuhr-mehn-tei'-shen bin')*
Synonym for secondary fermenter.

secondary fermenter. *(seh'-ken-deh-ree fuhr-mehn'-ter)*
Any closed container in which secondary fermentation is allowed to occur. **Syn:** secondary fermentation bin; secondary.

secondary fermentor. *(seh'-ken-deh-ree fuhr-mehn'-ter)*
Orthographic variant for secondary fermenter.

secondary tank. *(seh'-ken-deh-ree taengk)*
See: conditioning tank.

second running. *(seh'-kend ruh'-ning)*
Synonym for second wort.

second wort. *(seh'-kend wuhrt')*
The wort obtained by sparging the spent grains. **Syn:** second running; spargings. **See also:** first wort.

sediments. *(seh'-d:uh-ments)*
The refuse of solid matter that accumulates at the bottom of fermenters and conditioning vessels. **Syn:** settlings.

seidel. *(zay'-del)*
A large German beer tankard with a capacity exceeding 1 pint.

sekkar. *(shei-khar)*
Orthographic variant of *shekar*.

Select. *(si-lehkt')*
A variety of hops cultivated in the Germany containing 4–5 percent alpha acids.

sérieux. *(sei-ghee-yue')*
In France, a beer glass for the "serious" drinker, with a capacity of 2 liters.

serving tank. *(ser'-ving taengk)*
See: conditioning tank.

set mash. *(seht' maesh')*
A condition that occurs during lautering when the wort is drained too quickly and a bed (fine powder mixed with grain husks) collapses and packs into a tight mass, preventing the flow of the wort. **Syn:** stuck mash; dead mash.

settlings. *(seht'-lingz)*
Synonym for sediments.

settling tub. *(seht'-ling tuhb)*
A vessel in which fermentation is first started in commercial breweries.

Shandy (Gaff). *(shaen'-dee [gaef])*
1. Originally, a drink made of beer and ginger, ginger beer, or ginger ale. **2.** A mix of beer and lemonade, sometimes called Lemon Shandy. **See also:** Panaché; Radlermass; Russ.

sheet filter. *(sheet fil'-ter)*
A plate and frame filter that uses single-direction, reusable cellulose sheets.

shekar. *(shei-khar)*
1. A Hebrew word meaning to be or become inebriated as cited in Isaiah 5:11. **2.** A beery drink made from corn, dates, and honey and drunk by Sem, Noah's eldest son. Also spelled: *shecar; sekkar; schechar*.

shelf-keeping unit. *(shehlf kee'-ping yoo'-nit)*
See: SKU.

shelf life. *(shehlf layf')*
The length of time that a bottle or can of beer can be left on a shelf before spoiling. A pasteurized beer has a greater life expectancy than an unpasteurized one; the same is true of dark beers versus pale beers, or beers of high alcoholic content as opposed to lighter ones, and of heavily hopped beers more than milder ones. Beers kept cold also survive longer. Unpasteurized draft beer should be drunk within thirty days at the most whereas pasteurized bottled or canned beer may be stored up to sixty days. Additives are often used to prolong the shelf life of packaged beer. **Syn:** beer life; life expectancy. **See also:** pull date.

shelf talker. *(shehlf ta'-ker)*
Shelf-mounted promotional signage often used by retailers of beer, wine, and other alcoholic beverages.

shimeyane. *(shee-mei-ya-nei)*
An alcoholic beverage produced in South Africa by fermenting brown sugar, brown bread, and malted corn.

shirosaké. *(shee-ro-sa-kei*)*
A weak, colorless *saké* (± 5 percent alcohol by volume).

shive. *(shayv)*
1. A circular wooden bung for casks. **2.** A small hole pierced in the wooden bung (or shive) of a cask into which the publican or cellarman inserts a wooden peg to control the escape of gas. **Syn:** spile.

shot and a beer. *(shat' end uh beeyr')*
A small glass of liquor chased with a tall glass of beer.

shoto saké. *(sho-to sa-kei*)*
A Japanese drink made by fermenting sugarcane juice.

show mead. *(sho meed)*
The Old English term for a fermented mixture of honey and water.

shu. *(shoo*)*

A type of millet beer made in China during the Han dynasty (200 BC) at the beginning of the Chinese Empire. **See also:** *chiu; li; pei; sang-lo; t'ien tsiou.*

sicera. *(si'-seh-ruh*)*

A strong hopped drink (*Cicera ex lupulis confectam*) made by the Jewish people during their captivity in Babylon. It was believed to immunize against leprosy.

sieve, to. *(siv, too)*

In malting, to separate grains according to size by means of a sieve having apertures of known size. **Syn:** to bolt.

sight glass. *(sayt glaes)*

Small section of glass pipe placed along piping to allow brewer to view liquid being transferred. Sometimes used to measure volume in a vessel.

sikaru. *(see-ka-roo)*

The name given to "grain wine" on Mesopotamian clay tablets (circa 8000–4000 BC) found during the archeological excavations at Sumer. Sumer once stretched between two rivers, the Tigris and the Euphrates, in what is Iraq today. *Sikaru* was made by steeping a bread made from malted barley in water for three to four days and was drunk with a straw or reed. The brewery was called Bit Sikari, and the brewer was Pa-e-bi. The ale houses were managed by women called *tsabitu*. Sixteen varieties of beer were produced in both pale and dark colors; eight were made from spelt (an early form of wheat), five from barley, and three from a mix of spelt and barley. Sikaru was flavored with spices, especially cinnamon. The same term was later used in Babylonia as late as 562 BC. **See also:** *bi-se-bar.*

Sike's hydrometer. *(sayks hay-dra'-muh-d:er)*

A hydrometer invented in 1816 by Bartholomew Sike, a British excise officer, for measuring the alcoholic strength of beverages, especially spirits, giving readings from 70 over proof to zero.

silica gel. *(si'-li-kuh jehl')*

A hard, amorphous, granular form of hydrated silica used to adsorb nitrogen matter in beer.

sima. *(see'-muh)*

Mead in Finnish.

single-gauge regulator. *(sing'-gel-geyj reh'-gyuh-ley-d:er)*
A regulator that measures only in-line pressure.

single-stage fermentation. *(sing'-gel-steij' fuhr-mehn-tei'-shen)*
In homebrewing, complete fermentation carried out in a single container that is fitted with a fermentation lock as opposed to two-stage fermentation that takes place in a primary fermenter before being transferred to a secondary fermenter.

single-stage fermenter. *(sing'-gel-steij' fuhr-mehn'-ter)*
In homebrewing, a wide-mouthed container made of food-grade plastic and fitted with an airtight cover and removable cap for inserting a fermentation lock, usually with a capacity of 7 or 8 U.S. gallons (5.8–6.7 imperial gallons).

siphon. *(say'-fen)*
In homebrewing, clear plastic tubing 4–6 feet long with an inside diameter of about 3/8 of an inch used to draw beer from one container to another.

siphon clamp. *(say'-fen klaemp')*
A spring device made of steel or plastic (nylon) used in homebrewing to crimp the siphon and thus easily start and stop the drawing process.

Siris. *(see-ris)*
The daughter of Ninkasi. In ancient Sumer, this female (sometimes male) deity personified the beer itself.

six-rowed barley. *(siks'-rod' bar'-lee)*
A variety of barley having three rows of fertile spikelets at each node on which six rows of grains are ultimately formed. Because it has proportionally more husk material and a less well-developed grain than two-rowed barley, it yields less extract. Scientific name: *Hordeum hexastichum*. **Syn:** six-row barley; winter barley.

skeachen. *(skee-a-khen)*
A Scottish ale of the fourteenth century.

skim, to. *(skim, too)*
To remove the froth or scum that forms at the top of the fermentation vat.

skimming. *(ski'-ming)*

1. Removing the scum on the surface of the first head of the fermenting brew. **2.** Recovering the top-fermenting yeast at the surface of the wort prior to pouring off. **See also:** crop.

skimming oar. *(ski'-ming or')*

An instrument used to remove the yeast at the surface of the fermentation vessel. **See also:** parachute.

skimmings. *(ski'-ming[g]z)*

The floating dust, light corns, and awns at the surface of the steeping liquor.

skirt. *(skuhrt)*

The wavy contour of a crown cork that is pressed around the mouth of the bottle.

SKU.

Abbreviation for shelf-keeping unit, it refers to the type of packaging in which a product is contained.

slaked lime. *(sleykt laym)*

Calcium hydroxide. Used to precipitate bicarbonate from water.

slotting fees. *(sla'-d:ing feez)*

Fees charged by retailers for allocating shelf space to a specific brand of merchandise. Slotting fees are currently legal in the United States for food items but illegal for alcoholic beverages.

small ale. *(smohl' eiyl')*

An obsolete term once used in England to describe an ale with low alcoholic strength.

small beer. *(smohl' beeyr')*

1. In early England, a weak beer probably made from the washings of the mash as opposed to strong beer that was made from the first runnings. In fourteenth-century England, small beer sold for 1 pence and was called penny ale whereas the stronger version was known as better beer. **2.** In early America, a beer of low-alcohol content for daily consumption. George Washington had a recipe for "small beer." **3.** In Queensland, Australia, a 5-ounce beer glass. **4.** Generally speaking, a weak or diluted beer.

smoked beer. *(smokt' beeyr')*
See: *rauchbier.*

smoked malt. *(smokt' mohlt')*
Malt that has been dried over an open fire. It imparts a smoky flavor to beers and is traditionally used in German-style *rauchbier.*

smooth. *(smoodh)*
Giving a pleasant, creamy sensation.

Society for the Preservation of Beers from the Wood. *(so-say'-uh-d:ee fohr dhuh preh'zer-vei'-shen uhv beeyrz' fruhm dhuh wud')*
A British association of beer enthusiasts that, in 1973, gave rise to the Campaign for Real Ale (CAMRA).

soft resins. *(sohft' reh'-zinz)*
One of the two fractions secreted by the lupulin gland during the development of the hop cones. Soft resins are composed mainly of about 45 percent alpha acids (alpha resins or humulones) and 25 percent beta acids (beta resins or lupulones). Extracted from hops during the boiling stage, they contribute most of the nine hundred bittering substances in beer. The alpha acids are substantially isomerized to iso-alpha-acids whereas some of the beta acids are oxidized to bitter materials such as humulones. **Syn:** bitter resins. **See also:** hard resins; hop oils.

soft water. *(sohft' wa'-d:er)*
Water devoid of calcium and magnesium salts.

SOL.
Abbreviation for colloidal solution (one that flows), a liquid in which solid particles of colloidal dimensions are suspended. **See also:** gel.

solubilization. *(sa-lyuh-be-li-zey'-shen)*
Dissolution of matter into solution.

solute. *(sal'-yoot)*
The dissolved component of a solution whose physical state does not change, or the component that is present in a smaller quantity than the solvent.

solution. *(suh-loo'-shen)*
Homogenous mixture of compounds.

solvent. *(sal'-vent)*

Usually a liquid that is capable of dissolving one or more other substances and is present in greater quantity than the solute in a solution.

solventlike. *(sal'-vent-layk)*

Flavor and aromatic character similar to acetone or lacquer thinner, often due to high fermentation temperatures.

sor. *(zohr*)*

Hungarian for beer.

sora. *(so'-ruh)*

A beer made from maize in Peru prior to the arrival of the Conquistadores. It was apparently much stronger than *chicha* and was not available to the common *mojica*.

sorghum. *(sohr'-gem)*

A cereal grain from various grasses (*Sorghum vulgare*), also known as *kafir* corn in South Africa, where a sorghum beer is produced.

sorghum beer. *(sohr'-gem beeyr')*

Synonym for *kafir* beer.

soubya. *(soo-bee-ya)*

Egyptian rice beer.

sour. *(saw[e]r)*

A taste perceived on the sides of one's tongue as produced with lemon juice.

souring. *(saw'-[e]-ring)*

The spoiling of beer caused by bacterial contamination.

sour mash. *(saw[e]r' maesh')*

In beer brewing, a procedure in which all or part of the mash is allowed to sit for a time (approximately ten hours) in order to promote the bacterial formation of acids in the production of beers in which sour flavors are intended. Alternately, the mash can be inoculated with a culture to receive the same results.

sowens. *(so'-wenz)*

Seventeenth-century Scots name for the hopped beers of Denmark.

Spalt. *(shpehlt)*

A variety of hops cultivated in Germany containing 3.5–4.5 percent alpha acids.

Spalt Select. *(spohlt si-lehkt')*

A variety of hops cultivated in the United States containing 3–6 percent alpha acids.

sparge, to. *(sparj, too)*

To spray hot water on the spent grains after mashing.

sparge arm. *(sparj arm)*

A rotating perforated pipe that sprays hot liquor over the mash, or goods, during sparging.

sparger. *(spar'-jer)*

A device used to deliver an evenly dispersed spray of water over the grain bed in the lauter tun. This device can be a perforated pipe, a sprinkler head attached to a piece of tubing, a watering-can diffuser, or a manufactured sparging unit. It is used to wash the soluble sugars from the grain bed. A fine spray is employed to make sure the grain bed is not disturbed during sparging.

sparging. *(spar'-jing)*

In mashing, an operation consisting of spraying the spent grains of the mash with hot water to retrieve the liquid malt sugar remaining in the grain husks. To prevent the mash from packing, the sparging volume of water must equal the volume of wort coming out at the base of the mash tun, thus maintaining a constant level. Also, by maintaining the level of hot water above the filter bed, the oxidation of the tannin in the husks is reduced considerably. **See also:** lautering; set mash.

spargings. *(spar'-jingz)*

Synonym for second wort.

sparging water. *(spar'-jing wa'-d:er)*

The fine spray of hot water used for sparging, the temperature of which must be the same as that of the mashing liquor.

sparkle, to. *(spar'-kel, too)*

To foam or bubble.

sparkler. *(spar'-kler)*
Adjustable nozzle fitted to a beer pump. It is used to control the amount of head on a pint.

sparklet cartridge. *(spark'-lit kar'-trij)*
A nonrefillable carbon dioxide cartridge used with pressurized beer kegs to maintain a constant pressure while the keg is emptied.

sparkling. *(spark'-ling)*
Effervescence caused by fermentation.

sparkling ale. *(spark'-ling eiyl')*
In Adelaide, Australia, a top-fermented beer similar to Britain's pale ale. Also a U.S. term for a class of ales brewed mostly before Prohibition to compete with lagers.

sparkling mead. *(spark'-ling meed)*
A mead made effervescent by a secondary fermentation in the bottle.

Spaten water. *(shpa'-ten wa'-d:er)*
Water from the artesian wells of the Spaten brewery in Munich. An analysis of those waters, among the most famous in the world, conducted in 1880, gave the following composition in grams per liter: 0.12 carbonate of lime, 0.077 carbonate of magnesia, 0.057 sodium carbonate, 0.009 potassium sulfate, 0.003 lime sulfate, 0.019 sodium nitrate, 0.014 silica, 0.001 iron and aluminum oxides, 0.022 organic matters, and 0.002 sodium chloride. **See also:** brewing water.

Special "B"malt. *(speh'-shel bee mohlt')*
An dark caramel malt that imparts a distinctive but intense toasted malt flavor. Also called: Belgian Special "B."

special beer. *(speh'-shel beeyr')*
Any beer that is produced by spontaneous fermentation. (Examples: *gueuze, lambic, faro.*)

special bitter. *(speh'-shel bi'-d:er)*
Bitter ale prepared from an original wort gravity of 1.038–1.045. It is intermediate in strength and flavor to ordinary and strong bitters. **Syn:** best bitter. **See also:** bitter.

specific gravity. *(spi-si'-fik grae'-vuh-d:ee)*

A measure of the density of a liquid or solid as compared to that of water, which is given the value 1.000 at 39.2 °F (4 °C). For the sake of accuracy, the specific gravity of liquids should always be measured as closely as possible to that temperature. The specific gravity is a dimensionless quantity (with no accompanying units) because it is expressed as a ratio in which all dimensions cancel. Abbrev: SG; s.g.

speise. *(shpay'-ze)*

A German word that literally means food. This term refers to the wort or other priming sugar used to carbonate a top-fermented beer.

spelt. *(spehlt)*

1. A primitive species of wheat, the grains of which do not thresh free of the chaff. **2.** *Triticum spelta*, a hybrid of wheat and barley grown to some extent in Germany and Switzerland. **3.** A local name for *emmer* (*Triticum dicoccum*)—a wheat species having a spike broken up into segments and grains that do not thresh free of the chaff. They are tetraploid wheats. Also spelled: speltz.

spent grains. *(spehnt' greynz')*

The refuse of grain husks remaining in the mash tun after lautering. They contain about 25 percent protein and are useful as a nitrogenous addition to cattle fodder. **Syn:** draff; brewer's grains.

spent hops. *(spehnt' haps')*

The refuse of hops remaining after the boiling. They are compounded with ferrous sulfate and other mineral salts and used as artificial horticultural fertilizers.

Spezyme. *(speh'-zaym*)*

A group of four enzymes, Spezyme BBA, Spezyme AA, Spezyme GA (glucoamylase), and Spezyme IGI (immobilized glucose isomerase), developed by Powell & Scholefield Laboratories in England and manufactured by the Finnsugar Group, a Finland sugar corporation. Spezyme BBA, a beta-amylase extracted from barley, is used in the brewing industry to standardize or raise the diastatic power of diastatic malt extracts. Spezyme AA, an endo-amylase derived from a selected strain of *Bacillus subtilis*, readily hydrolyzes gelatinized starch into soluble dextrins. It is used in the traditional cooking process of whole grains when an additional beta-glucanase activity is desired. Spezyme GA, a glucoamylase, is used in the brewing industry to produce low-carbohydrate beer. **See also:** Supavit Z.

Sphaerotheca mucalaris. *(sfi-ro-thee'-kuh myoo-kuh-la'-ris)*
Scientific name for a hop mold.

spigot. *(spi'-git)*
1. A device for regulating the flow of beer from a cask or barrel. 2. A tap for a cask.

spile. *(spayl)*
The hole atop of a beer cask. **Syn:** shive.

spitzmalz. *(shpits'-mohltz)*
German for pointed malt; a hard malt that is made from barley and has barely germinated.

split. *(split)*
Synonym for nip.

spreader. *(spreh'-d:er)*
An apparatus that spreads out the flow of malted barley evenly over the mill rollers.

spring barley. *(spring' bar'-lee)*
Barley sown in spring.

spruce beer. *(sproos' beeyr')*
1. Traditionally, a beery beverage produced in North America and northern Europe by fermenting molasses and other sugars with the exudate of spruce trees or a decoction of the buds and cones of such trees, sometimes with malt. 2. Danzig spruce beer; a black beer produced in Danzig by fermenting the sap and young shoots of the black spruce tree (*Picea nigra*) with a sugary wort of molasses or maple sugar. **Syn:** black beer.

square. *(skwehr)*
A vessel.

squares. *(skwehrz)*
Brewers' term for a square fermentation vessel.

SRM.
Abbreviation for Standard Reference Method. One of two different analytical methods of describing beer color developed by comparing with a reference. The

second method uses EBC (European Brewery Convention) units. Degrees SRM, approximately equivalent to degrees Lovibond, are used by the ASBC (American Society of Brewing Chemists) whereas degrees EBC are European units.

stacking. *(stae'-king)*
The action of piling casks one tier above the other.

stale ale. *(steiyl' eiyl')*
In sixteenth-century England, the name given to one-year-old ale.

stale flavor. *(steiyl' flei'-ver)*
Synonym for off-flavor.

stale yeast. *(steiyl' yeest')*
A yeast containing dead cells resulting in a slow-starting fermentation or no fermentation at all.

standard mash. *(staen'-derd maesh')*
A mash made in a brewer's laboratory using specified amounts of water and malt. Also called: congress mash.

starch. *(starch)*
Any of a group of carbohydrates or polysaccharides secreted in the form of granules by certain cereals, composed of about one-quarter amylose (inner shell) and three-quarters amylopectin (outer shell). Starch hydrolyzes to yield dextrins and maltose through the action of amylases. Barley starch is enclosed in the endosperm and constitutes 63–65 percent of the weight of two-rowed barley and about 58 percent of the weight of six-rowed barley. **See also:** amylopectin; amylose.

starch test. *(starch' tehst')*
A simple test to ascertain if all the malt starch has been converted to maltose. It consists of adding a drop of tincture of iodine to a drop of cold wort on a clean white saucer. If the color remains iodine-brown, the starch conversion is complete whereas a blue or purplish blue coloration is indicative of the presence of starch and that mashing must continue. Since iodine is toxic, the test sample must not be returned to the mash. **Syn:** iodine test; iodine starch test.

starkbier. *(shtaghk'-beegh)*

In Germany, one of the three legal categories for beers comprising those brewed from an original gravity of at least 16 °B and containing no less than 5 percent alcohol by weight. **See also:** *bier; schankbier; vollbier.*

starter. *(star'-d:er)*

A separate batch of fermenting yeast added to the bitter wort once it has cooled down to 70 °F (21 °C). In homebrewing, it is prepared by pitching yeast in a quart of wort cooled to about 75 °F (24 °C), preferably one or two days in advance.

starting gravity. *(star'-d:ing grae'-vuh-d:ee)*

Synonym for original gravity.

starting specific gravity. *(star'-d:ing spi-si'-fik grae'-vuh-d:ee)*

Synonym for original gravity.

stave. *(steiv)*

Each of the thin, curved pieces of wood that, when assembled, constitute a cask or barrel.

stavewood. *(steiv'-woud)*

Synonym for caskwood.

steam beer. *(steem' beeyr')*

A beer produced by hybrid fermentation using bottom yeast fermented at top yeast temperatures (60–70 °F, 15–20 °C). Fermentation is carried out in long, shallow, panlike vessels called clarifiers followed by warm conditioning at 50–55 °F (10–12 °C) and *kraeusening.* This style of beer is indigenous to the United States and was first produced in California at the end of the nineteenth century (during the gold rush) where temperatures were too warm for proper fermentation of bottom yeasts. At one time there were as many as twenty-seven breweries making steam beer in San Francisco. Today it is brewed by the Anchor Steam Brewing Company under the registered tradename of Steam Beer, a highly hopped, amber-colored, foamy beer containing 3.8 percent alcohol by weight (4.74 percent by volume). Etym: Named after the hissing sound produced by the pressure released when a cask is tapped.

steam heater. *(steem' hee'-d:er)*

An apparatus that produces warm or hot air.

steep, to. *(steep, too)*
To soak barley in water for 40–120 hours during which time it absorbs the moisture and oxygen required for the embryo to germinate.

steep. *(steep)*
Synonym for steeping tank.

steeping. *(stee'-ping)*
The action of soaking hard dry barley in water in a steeping tank for approximately 40–80 hours and sometimes up to 120 hours under controlled conditions of temperature (55–59 °F, 13–15 °C), humidity (from 10–15 percent to 45–50 percent), and oxygenation, in order to soften it. Steeping is best carried out in stages separated by air rests. A typical steeping schedule would be twelve hours at 59 °F (15 °C) followed by twelve hours air rest then another sixteen-hour steep. Barley is considered to be sufficiently steeped when the moisture content has reached 42–44 percent. Sometimes steeping is called wetting. **See also:** oversteeping.

steeping copper. *(stee'-ping ka'-per)*
A large closed vessel used for mashing or boiling.

steeping tank. *(stee'-ping taengk)*
A cylindro-conical tank for steeping barley. **Syn:** steeping vat; steep tank; steep.

steeping vat. *(stee'-ping vaet)*
Synonym for steeping tank.

steep liquor. *(steep' li'-ker)*
The chalky, alkaline water used for steeping.

steep tank. *(steep' taengk)*
Synonym for steeping tank.

stein. *(shtayn)*
A German earthenware drinking vessel with a capacity, in Munich, of 50 centiliters, 1 liter, or 3 liters.

steinie. *(steh-nee'*)*
In France, a 1-liter family-size bottle for beverages such as cider, lemonade, and beer.

stemware. *(stehm'-wehr)*
A generic term for drinking glasses that have a stem. Contrary to barware, stemware in used exclusively at the dining table. There are five different glasses: goblet, wine, sherbet or champagne, cocktail, and cordial.

step infusion. *(stehp in-fyoo'-zhen)*
A temperature-controlled mash procedure, often called a temperature program mash, that employs multiple temperature rests. With this mashing method, the temperature of the mash is changed by applying heat or introducing hot water to produce the desired temperature increase. Typically, this method of mashing employs a protein rest and a saccharification rest.

sterilant. *(steh'-ruh-lent)*
Synonym for sterilizing agent.

sterile. *(steh'-ril)*
Free of living organisms, especially microorganisms—bacteria, molds, and yeasts.

sterile beer. *(steh'-ril beeyr')*
Ultra-filtered beer from which all living organisms, including yeasts, have been removed or destroyed.

sterilizer. *(steh'-ruh-lay-zer)*
An apparatus for sterilizing objects by means of dry heat, steam, or boiling water.

sterilizing agent. *(steh'-ruh-lay-zing ei'-jent)*
Any substance that will kill all forms of microbial life, including bacteria and other infective organisms. Homebrewers can prepare a sterilant by one of two methods: (1) adding 2 teaspoons of potassium sulfite or sodium sulfite (metabisulfite) to 1 quart of water. A pinch of citric acid helps to activate the release of the sulfur dioxide; or (2) adding 2 teaspoons of household chlorine bleach to 1/2 a gallon (2 quarts) of water. In both cases the sterilant must be thoroughly rinsed out with hot water after use. **Syn:** sterilant.

Stiftsbräu. *(shtifts'-broy)*
See: abbey beer.

stillage. *(sti'-lij)*
A brick, wooden, or metal structure that supports casks of beer in the pub cellar.

stillion. *(stil'-yen)*

An X-shaped cradle, similar to a sawhorse, on which wooden casks and barrels are rested during maturation to prevent separation of the staves under pressure.

stingo. *(sting'-go)*

A strong ale or beer.

stinking water. *(steengk'-ng wa'-d:er)*

See: *waipiro.*

stirring spoon. *(stuh'-ring spoon')*

Synonym for brewer's paddle.

stirrup cup. *(stuhr'-uhp kuhp')*

A drinking vessel or cup similar in shape to a rhyton. Such a cup was given to a man mounted on a horse upon his departure or arrival from a long journey. It is often shaped like the head of a hound, fox, or fish or like a clenched fist.

stock ale (or beer). *(stak' eiyl [beeyr'])*

An ale brewed very strong to be stored for a long period of time.

stone ale. *(ston' eiyl')*

An ale once brewed at the Monastery of Stone in Staffordshire, England.

stopper. *(sta'-per)*

A general name for any type of closing or capping device for bottles and casks. Bottle caps are classified into in three main categories based on the type of closure: crown corks, screw stoppers, and wire-on stoppers.

stoppered. *(sta'-perd)*

Fitted with a stopper.

storage. *(sto'-rij)*

Synonym for secondary fermentation or maturation.

storage cellar. *(sto'-rij seh'-ler)*

A refrigerated room, originally a cellar, where beer is stored while undergoing secondary fermentation.

storage tank. *(sto'-rij taengk)*
A vessel or tank in which beer is stored prior to racking.

stout. *(stawt)*
In Britain, a very dark top-fermented beer made from pale malt and 7–10 percent roasted, unmalted barley, often with the addition of caramel malt or sugar. Stout was first introduced by Guinness as an extra stout (higher gravity) version of their plain porter. The new stout was darker, richer, hoppier, and more alcoholic than porter, which it gradually overtook in popularity until porter disappeared completely. Today, a distinction is drawn between sweet and dry stout. Although both are highly hopped (600–700 grams per hectoliter), sweet stout is less bitter than the dry version. Their alcohol contents are both about 5 percent by volume. Etym: Probably from stout ale or stout porter. **Syn:** bitter stout. **See also:** dry stout; porter; Russian stout; sweet stout.

strain, to. *(strein, too)*
To pump or pour a solution through a permeable material to remove solid matter.

strainer. *(strei'-ner)*
Synonym for hop back.

straining. *(strei'-ning)*
The action of passing a solution through a screen to separate solid matter from the liquid. In homebrewing, a nylon sieve, a muslin bag, or a nylon mesh straining bag may be used.

strength. *(strehng[k]th)*
1. The alcohol content of a beer. **2.** The specific gravity of the wort prior to fermentation. **3.** The degree of bitterness of a beer.

strike heat. *(strayk heet')*
The maintained temperature of the mash liquor prior to the grist addition.

strike temperature. *(strayk tehmp'-[e]-ruh-chur)*
The water temperature at mashing-in; generally somewhat higher than the target mash temperature to compensate for heat uptake by the grist.

Strisselspalt. *(shtghi'-sel-shpehlt)*
A variety of hops containing approximately 2.7 percent alpha acids.

strobile. *(stra'-bil)*
The flower or cone of the hop plant. **Syn:** hop cone; hop flower.

strong beer. *(strohng' beeyr')*
Full-strength beer as opposed to small beer.

strong bitter. *(strohng' bi'-d:er)*
Synonym for extra special bitter.

stubbie. *(stuh'-bee)*
A type of beer bottle once popular in the United States however is now practically obsolete.

stuck fermentation. *(stuhk' fuhr-mehn-tei'-shen)*
Fermentation that has stopped prematurely, that is, before the final gravity has been reached. In homebrewing, this phenomenon may be caused by a weak starter, the destruction of yeast cells by unwashed sterilant, wort that is too hot, or fermentation temperatures that are too low.

stuck mash. *(stuhk' maesh')*
Synonym for set mash.

stuykmanden. *(steek-man'-den)*
In Belgian brewing, a big basket made of wicker or, in later times, copper that was lowered onto the surface of the mash through the top of the mash tank, where it acted as a strainer and allowed the liquid portion of the mash to filter through.

style. *(stay[e]l)*
The whole sum of flavor and other sensory characteristics by which individual beers may be placed in categories for purposes of comparison. Beers of the same style have the same general flavor profile.

Styrian Goldings. *(sti'-ree-en gohl'-dingz)*
A variety of hops grown in Yugoslavia containing 5–7 percent alpha acids.

Submarino. *(sub-ma-ree'-no)*
A variant of the drink called Depth Charge prepared in Mexico by immersing a shot glass full of tequila in a glass of beer.

substrate. *(suhb'-streit)*

A chemical substance upon which an enzyme acts. The suffix *-ase* denotes an enzyme that acts upon a particular substrate; for example, invertase inverts sucrose, maltase hydrolyzes maltose, and lactase hydrolyzes lactose. Some enzymes, however, have been known for so long that their original name has been retained, such as pepsin.

Sucellus. *(soo-seh'-luhs*)*

The god of brewing and coopering in ancient Gaul. He is represented alongside the goddess of mead with a pitcher in one hand and a mallet in the other.

sucrase. *(soo'-kreis)*

Synonym for invertase.

sucrose. *(soo'-kros)*

A double sugar obtained from sugarcane and sugar beets. It is not directly fermentable by yeast and must first be hydrolyzed to glucose and fructose by the enzyme invertase secreted by the yeast. **Syn:** cane sugar; beet sugar; table sugar; household sugar; saccharose.

Süddeutsches weizenbier. *(zue'-doy-ches vay'-tsen-beegh)*

Synonym for *weizenbier.*

suds. *(suhdz)*

1. Slang for beer. **2.** Suds factory, a brewery.

sugar. *(shu'-ger)*

1. A generic name for a class of carbohydrates including fructose, glucose, maltose, and lactose. **2.** Without qualification it invariably refers to sucrose.

sugar beet. *(shu'-ger beet)*

A beet, *Beta vulgaris,* cultivated for its high sugar content (15–20 percent).

sugarcane. *(shu'-ger-kein)*

A tall stout grass, *Saccharum officinarum,* grown in warm climates and cultivated extensively for its high sugar content, which—among its other uses— is a rich source of fermentable sugar.

sugaring. *(shug'-[e]-ring)*

Adding sugar to the wort to increase its sugar content and, consequently, the alcoholic strength of the resulting beer.

sulfuring. *(suhlf'-[e]-ring)*
Treating with sulfur dioxide.

sulfurlike. *(suhl'-fer-layk)*
Reminiscent of rotten eggs or burnt matches; a by-product of some yeasts.

sun flavor. *(suhn' flei'-ver)*
An off-taste in beer caused by exposure of the beer to sun or light rays.
Syn: sunstruck.

sunstruck. *(suhn'-struhk)*
Synonym for sun flavor or lightstruck.

Supavit Z. *(soo'-puh-vit zee [zed])*
A yeast nutrient developed by the Powell & Scholefield Laboratories in England, the result of research work into the action of zinc ions on the fermentation of wort by yeast. It is used in the brewing industry to correct any zinc deficiency in the wort while at the same time providing the vitamins, amino acids, and trace elements essential to counteract sluggish fermentation.

sweet. *(sweet)*
Possessing a taste of sugar; the opposite of dry.

sweet gale. *(sweet gey[e]l)*
A fragrant herb sometimes used in holiday-style beers. Also called: bog myrtle; myrica gale.

sweet mead. *(sweet meed)*
A sweet-tasting mead, containing a certain amount of unfermented sugars, as opposed to dry mead.

sweet orange peel. *(sweet o'-rinj pee[e]l)*
A sweet-flavored spice sometimes used in Belgian strong ales.

sweet stout. *(sweet stawt)*
The English version of stout as opposed to the dry stout of Ireland. It is slightly less alcoholic than dry stout and often has lactose added to increase the sweetness. Sweet stout is typified by Mackeson Stout. **Syn:** milk stout.
See also: stout.

sweet wort. *(sweet wuhrt')*
The sugary liquid obtained by mashing and sparging malt.

swimmer. *(swi'-mer)*
Synonym for attemperator.

swing stopper. *(swing sta'-per)*
Synonym for wired-on stopper.

swing-top. *(swing tap)*
A reusable bottle cap, usually ceramic with a rubber gasket, held in place by a metal wire, called a bail.

TA.
Abbreviation for titratable acidity.

table sugar. *(tei'-bel shu'-ger)*
Synonym for sucrose.

table tent. *(tei'-bel tehnt)*
Freestanding tabletop display, usually made of folded card stock, used in restaurants to promote food and beverages.

takju. *(tyak'-joo*)*
A type of rice beer brewed in Korea. Also spelled: *yakju.*

Talisman. *(tae'-lis-men)*
A variety of hops grown in Washington containing 7.5–9 percent alpha acids and about 4.5 percent beta acids.

talla. *(da-luh*)*
A type of beer produced in Ethiopia by fermenting roasted barley, millet, or maize and flavored with the twigs and leaves of a local tree. *Talla* (or *dalla*) also was prepared in Abyssinia from barley and *dagussa* (*Pennisetum spicatum*). Barley grains were buried between leaves in a trench of dry soil for three days, unearthed and fashioned into a broad flat cake called *bekel*, which would later be diluted with water and added to a mix of ground barley and *mascilla* (white sorghum) to induce fermentation. The mixture was again diluted, boiled, and fermented for about ten days. It was flavored, prior to fermentation, with powdered *giscio* (*geshu*) leaves.

tan. *(tan)*
Synonym for *pombé.*

Tango. *(taeng'-go [French: tae~-go'])*
In France, a mix of pale beer and grenadine syrup.

tank. *(taengk)*
A large storage vessel or container for holding liquids.

tankard. *(taeng'-kerd)*
A tall drinking jug on a flat or short molded base with a hinged or removable cover and a single handle used for drinking beer in northern Europe since the Middle Ages.

tannic. *(tae'-nik)*
Synonym for astringent.

tannic acid. *(tae'-nik ae'-sid)*
Synonym for tannin.

tannin. *(tae'-nin)*
Any of a group of organic compounds contained in certain cereal grains and other plants. Hop tannins have the ability to help in the precipitation of haze-forming protein materials during the boiling (hot break) and cooling (cold break) of the wort. Tannin is mainly present in the bracts and strigs of the hop cone and imparts an astringent taste to beer. Also called "hop tannin" to distinguish it from tannins originating from malted barley. The greater part of the tannin content of the wort is derived from malt husks, but malt tannins differ chemically from hop tannins. Nontechnical term used for phenols. **Syn:** tannic acid. **See also:** phenols.

tanzemann. *(tan'-tse-man)*
A Swiss drinking vessel made of sculptured wood depicting a peasant (which forms the stem) with a basket (which forms the bowl) on his or her back. The same vessel is called Buttenmann in Germany.

tap, to. *(taep, too)*
1. To place a tap in the opening of a cask or keg. **2.** To draw beer from a cask or keg.

tap. *(taep)*

1. A device for regulating the flow of liquids from a keg or cask. **2.** On tap; draft beer.

tap water. *(taep wa'-d:er)*

Synonym for drinking water.

tapioca. *(tae-pee-o'-kuh)*

Cassava starch produced by the tuberous roots of the cassava, or manioc, plant. It is rarely used as an adjunct because its starch has an alkaline reaction that impairs the quality of beer.

taproom. *(taep'-room)*

A room in a tavern where draft beer is served.

Target. *(tar'-git)*

A variety of hops cultivated in the United Kingdom and containing 8–9.5 percent alpha acids.

tart. *(tart)*

Taste sensation caused by acidic flavors.

tartaric acid. *(tar-tae'-rik ae'-sid)*

A component of acid blend frequently used in wine- or meadmaking.

taste test. *(teist' tehst')*

A test carried out in industry to evaluate a new product or changes in an existing product, and usually held by a panel of experts or consumers.

tavern. *(tae'-vern)*

1. Historically, a place where wine was sold as opposed to an ale house, which served beer. **2.** Today, a drinking establishment where, until recently, only beer was served and only men were allowed. **See also:** *brasserie.*

taverner. *(tae'-ver-ner)*

The owner of a tavern. In early England, taverns were owned by vintners who were allowed to sell wine only. In 1635 a law was passed allowing them to also sell ale, beer, food, and tobacco. **Syn**: tavern keeper.

tavern keeper. *(tae'-vern kee'-per)*
The owner or licensee of a tavern.

TCA cycle. *(tee-cee-ei say'-kel)*
Abbreviation for tricarboxylic acid cycle, a synonym for citric acid cycle.

t-cork. *(tee-kohrk)*
A plastic-topped cork that can be easily reinserted into a bottle.

TCW.
Abbreviation for thousand-corn weight.

tej. *(teyj)*
Mead in Ethiopian.

temporary hardness. *(tehmp'-[e]-reh-ree hard'-nis)*
A form of hardness in water caused by the presence of soluble bicarbonates of calcium and magnesium. Temporary hardness, contrary to permanent hardness, is removable by boiling to precipitate the carbonates.

terminal extract. *(tuhr'-mi-nel ehk'-straekt)*
The density of the fully fermented beer.

terminal gravity. *(tuhr'-mi-nel grae'-vuh-d:ee)*
Synonym for final specific gravity.

tertiary fermentation. *(tuhr'-shee-eh-ree fuhr-mehn-tei'-shen)*
Renewed fermentation carried out in bottles for the purpose of conditioning.

testing jar. *(teh'-sting jar)*
Synonym for hydrometer jar.

test tube. *(tehst' toob)*
Synonym for hydrometer jar.

Tettnang. *(teht'-nang)*
A variety of hops grown in the Lake Constance region in Germany containing 3–5 percent alpha acids and also grown in Idaho, Washington, and Oregon containing 4–6.5 percent alpha acids and 4.5–6.5 percent beta acids.

texture. *(tehks'-cher)*
Synonym for mouthfeel.

thermometer. *(thuhr-ma'-me-d:er)*
A device for measuring temperature. Thermometers specifically designed for brewers (and winemakers) are normally calibrated from 14–230 °F (-10–110 °C). They are filled with alcohol rather than mercury so that if they break they will not contaminate the beer (the broken glass can be recovered through a filter). In homebrewing, a cheese or milk thermometer with a scale ranging from 32–212 °F (0–100 °C) is adequate. **See also:** centigrade; Fahrenheit.

thermophilic. *(thuhr-muh-fi'-lik)*
Heat loving; bacteria operating at unusually high temperatures.

thermostat. *(thuhr'-muh-staet)*
An automatic device used to regulate temperature.

thin. *(thin)*
Describes a beer lacking fullness of palate or body.

thinning the piece. *(thi'-ning dhuh pees')*
In traditional floor malting, reducing the thickness of the germinating barley to control the temperature by allowing a greater amount of heat to escape. **See also:** piece.

thousand-corn weight. *(thaw'-zend kohrn' weit')*
The average weight of 1,000 (and sometimes 5,000) corns of barley as determined on a dry weight basis, usually around 35–45 grams. The greater the weight, the higher the extract yield.

Two-rowed barley: %E = 84.5 – 0.75 P + 0.1 G
Six-rowed barley: %E = 80 – 0.75 P + 0.1 G
%E = percentage of extract
P = percentage of protein
G = 1,000 corn weight in grams

The protein content of barley varies from 8–16 percent, but maltsters usually prefer samples containing 9–11 percent. Abbrev: TCW.

three-heads. *(three'-hehdz)*

In England, a mix of beer, ale, and twopenny. It was the precursor of porter.

three-point-two beer. *(three'-poynt-too' beeyr')*

In the United States, beer not exceeding 3.2 percent alcohol by volume. Also spelled: 3.2 beer. **See also:** Cullen Act.

three-tier system. *(three'-tee[e]r sis'-tem)*

A beer distribution system mandated in some states following Prohibition. It stipulates that beer must go from a brewery to a wholesaler before being distributed to retailers.

thumbpiece. *(thuhm'-pees)*

The projecting knob attached to the hinged lid of a covered vessel (flagon or tankard) that, when pressed with the thumb, holds the lid open for drinking. Also spelled: thumb-piece. **Syn:** billet; lever. **See also:** purchase.

Thunaeus test. *(tu-nei'-uhs tehst')*

A laboratory test to determine the germinative capacity of barley by immersing the grains in 0.75–1 percent (alcohol by weight) hydrogen peroxide. The number of grains to have chitted after three days are counted. Nongerminated grains are peeled and encouraged to germinate in wet sand or wet filter pads. The total number of grains to have germinated after both treatments constitutes the germinative energy.

tied house. *(tayd' haws')*

In England, a system by which a pub or inn is tied to a single brewery by mutual agreement.

t'ien tsiou. *(tee'-en tsee'-oo*)*

The name given to millet beer in Chinese texts dating back to 2000 BC. *T'ien tsiou* is green beer not yet clarified and not fully fermented whereas *tsiou* is a fully fermented and clarified beer. **See also:** *chiu; li; shu.*

tileque. *(ti-lei'-kee*)*

See: *kuchasu.*

tiswin. *(tiz-ween')*

A beerlike beverage once made from corn, wheat, jimson, and water by the Apache Indians. Its production was outlawed by the government in 1885. *Tiswin* was made as follows: Dry corn was soaked overnight, then laid on yucca leaves spread over holes in the ground and covered with gunnysack. It was sprinkled with water daily for about one week until germination was complete and the sprouts had grown 2 inches long. The corn was then spread in the sun to partially dry and was later ground and mixed into a dough weighing about 10 pounds. About 4 gallons of water were then added to the dough, which was boiled in an earthenware vessel to about half its original content, after which jimson weeds were added. Lost water was replaced and the mixture boiled again until reduced by half. After straining, ground wheat was added, and the liquid was fermented overnight to be drunk the following morning. **Syn:** *tulipai* (yellow water); *oafka*.

titratable acidity. *(tay-trey'-tuh-bel uh-si'-d:uh-d:ee)*
A common term among winemakers that refers to the amount of acid titrated against a known standard base. Abbrev: TA.

titration. *(tay-trey'-shen)*
Measurement of a substance in solution by addition of a standard disclosing solution to initiate an indicative color change.

TNBS method. *(tee en bee ess meh'-thuhd)*
Abbreviation for 2,4,6-trinitrobenzene-1-suphonic acid. A rapid colorimetric procedure commonly used for the estimation of amino nitrogen, where side-chain and end-group amino nitrogen present in peptides and proteins is measured in addition to that in amino acids.

toasted malt. *(to'-stid mohlt')*
Pale malt kilned for ten to fifteen minutes at 350 °F (176.6 °C) to impart a toasted aroma to beer.

tokkori. *(to-ko-ree)*
In Japan, a bottle for warming *saké*.

Tomboy. *(tam'-boy)*
A mixed drink prepared in a highball glass (8 ounces) by adding 1/2 a cup of chilled tomato juice to 1/2 a cup of cold beer.

tonne. *(tuhn)*
A wooden cask with a capacity of 2.2 barrels.

top fermentation. *(tap' fuhr-mehn-tei'-shen)*
One of the two basic fermentation methods characterized by the tendency of the yeast cells to rise to the surface during fermentation. Primary fermentation generally occurs at 59–77 °F (15–25 °C) and lasts for about one week.

top-fermented beer. *(tap'-fuhr-mehn'-tid beeyr')*
Synonym for ale.

top-fermenting ale yeast. *(tap'-fuhr-mehn'-ting eiyl' yeest')*
Synonym for top-fermenting yeast.

top-fermenting yeast. *(tap'-fuhr-mehn'-ting yeest')*
One of the two varieties of brewer's yeast, so called because it rises to the surface of the wort during fermentation. It cannot ferment below 55 °F (13 °C) and works best at temperatures of 59–77 °F (15–25 °C). The maximum growth temperature for *Saccharomyces cerevisiae* is 99.5–106.6 °F (37.5–39.8 °C). Compared to bottom-fermenting yeast, ale yeast ferments more rapidly and has a higher alcohol tolerance; however, it does not metabolize trisaccharides as efficiently, which means that it yields sweeter beers. **Syn:** *Saccharomyces cerevisiae;* ale yeast; top yeast; top-fermentation yeast; top-fermenting ale yeast.

topping-up. *(ta'-ping uhp')*
In homebrewer's parlance, adding water after primary fermentation to fill the secondary fermenter, thus reducing the surface area exposed to oxygen.

topuy. *(to-poo-ee*)*
A rice beer brewed in the Philippines.

top yeast. *(tap' yeest')*
Synonym for top-fermenting yeast.

torrified wheat. *(toh'-ruh-fayd [h]weet)*
Wheat that has been heated quickly at high temperature, causing it to puff up, rendering it easier to mash.

total hardness. *(to'-d:el hard'-nis)*
The sum of temporary and permanent hardness.

Tradition. *(truh-di'-shen)*

A variety of hops cultivated in Germany containing 5–7 percent alpha acids, and in the United States containing 4.5–6.5 percent alpha acids.

Trappist beer. *(trae'-pist beeyr')*

Any beer brewed in one of the six remaining brewing abbeys, five of which are in Belgium and one is in the Netherlands. Trappist beers are top fermented, golden-to-deep hued (amber or brown) and fairly strong, ranging from 5.7–12 percent alcohol by volume (4.6–9.6 percent alcohol by weight); they are fruity and often bittersweet; they are bottle-conditioned by priming and re-yeasting. The origin of Trappist beers dates back to the Middle Ages when epidemics were spread by contaminated water. Monasteries located on the traveling route to pilgrimage areas provided travelers with food, shelter, and a hygenic beverage free of pathogenic microbes. There were many abbeys all over Europe; Germany alone accounted for close to five hundred. In Belgium, two orders brewed beer: the Benedictines and the Cistercians. After the revolution, only the Trappists (Cistercians of strict observance) continued to brew beer. There are five brewing abbeys left in Belgium: (1) Chimay (also known as Abbaye de Notre-Dame-de-Scourmont), located near the French border in the province of Hainaut, was founded in 1850. The brewery, built in 1863, produces three distinct qualities distinguished by the color of the bottle caps: Red, White, and Blue. Red Cap, an amber-colored beer with a thick, dense foam, averages 6–6.2 percent alcohol by volume (4.8–5 percent alcohol by weight). It is also sold in tall bottles (*bouteilles bordelaises*) sealed with champagne corks. White Cap is slightly stronger with an alcohol content of 7.55 percent by volume (6 percent alcohol by weight). Blue Cap is stronger yet, with 8.75 percent alcohol by volume (7 percent alcohol by weight); it is vintage dated and reaches peak maturity after two years. (2) Orval (also known as Villiers-devant-Orval) is situated in the province of Luxembourg near the French border. It was founded in 1070 by Benedictine monks from Calabre who were replaced in the twelfth century by monks from Trèves. The present abbey was constructed between 1926 and 1948, and the brewery was built in 1931. It produces a well-hopped amber-colored beer of 5.7 percent alcohol by volume (4.5 percent alcohol by weight). (3) Rochefort, the Abbaye Notre Dame de St. Rémy, is located near Dinant in the province of Namur. It is closed to the public, and the production is limited (20–25 hectoliters per year). Three qualities are produced, 6°, 8°, and 10° Belgian, the last being the darkest. (4) St. Sixtus, the Abbaye de St. Sixte, located at Westvleteren in the province of West Flanders, was established in 1831. Their production is limited (3,000 hectoliters per year), and their beers are sold on the premises only. Three qualities are produced: 10°, 20°, and 25 °Balling (6.2°, 8°, and 10.5–11.0 °Belgian) called Abt, Extra, and Special. St. Sixtus beers also are produced commercially by the Brasserie Saint

Bernard in Watou of which Prior 8° is the best known. (5) Westmalle, the abbey's brewery, Notre Dame du Sacré-Coeur, located in the province of Antwerp, was established in 1836. It produces three beers: a tripple (or tripel), a golden-hued, creamy beer of 8 percent alcohol by volume (6.4 percent alcohol by weight); a double (or dubbel), a darker, sweeter, and less alcoholic beer containing 6 percent alcohol by volume (4.8 percent alcohol by weight); and a simple, which is drunk by the monks themselves and not available commercially. Other Belgian monastic orders such as Affligem, Tangerloo, Maredsous, and Lesse no longer brew their own beer but have licensed commercial breweries to do so. In the Netherlands, the Trappist abbey of Our Lady of Koningshoven, located near Tilburg in North Brabant, operates a brewery called Schaapskooi (or Skaapskoi, meaning sheep den) in conjunction, originally, with Artois but now with Skol. The monks brew three beers: a double (5.2 percent alcohol by volume), a triple (6.4 percent alcohol by volume), and a quadrupel (8 percent alcohol by volume). **See also:** abbey beer.

treacle. *(tree'-kel)*
British molasses.

tricarboxylic acid cycle. *(tray-kar-bak-si'-lik ae'-sid say'-kel)*
Synonym for citric acid cycle. Abbrev: TCA cycle.

tri-clamp or tri-clover. *(tray-klaemp, tray-klo'-ver)*
Clamp used to attach hoses and other fittings to brewing vessels.

tripel. *(tghee'-pel)*
A strong Belgian ale characterized by a pale color, sweet flavor, and high alcohol content.

trisaccharides. *(tray-sae'-kuh-raydz)*
Sugars formed from the combination of three monosaccharides.

trojniack. *(troy'-nee-aek*)*
A slightly sweet mead made in Poland by fermenting a must of 1 part honey and 2 parts water with a special strain of Malaga yeast. It averages 12.5 percent alcohol by volume and is aged for three years. Also spelled: *trojniak*.

trub. *(troob)*
Suspended particles caused by the precipitation of proteins, hop alpha acids, and tannins during the boiling and cooling stages of the wort. **See also:** cold break; hot break; tannin.

trumpet. *(truhm'-pit)*
Funnel-shaped device.

tsabitu. *(tsa-bee-too)*
The name given to ale wives in ancient Sumer. **See also:** *sikaru.*

tsiou. *(tsee[e]w)*
See: *t'ien tsiou.*

tub. *(tuhb)*
A large open vessel for holding liquids, originally made of wood but now made of metal or plastic.

tulipai. *(too-lee-pay'*)*
A synonym for *tiswin,* meaning yellow water.

tun. *(tuhn)*
1. A large vessel for holding liquids. **2.** A measure of capacity for holding liquids, equal to 250 wine gallons.

tunnel pasteurization. *(tuh'-nel paes[h]-chuh-ri-zei'-shen)*
A method of pasteurization for bottled and canned beer. It consists of a tunnel-like apparatus in which the bottles are sprayed with hot water (pre-heating and pasteurizing, twenty minutes at 140 °F, 60 °C) and later with cold water (pre-cooling and cooling). The entire process takes about an hour and the output ranges from 2,000–60,000 bottles (or cans) per hour. **See also:** flash pasteurization.

tun room. *(tuhn room)*
The part of a brewery where fermentation takes place.

tuplak. *(toop'-lak*)*
In Czechoslovakia, a boot-shaped glass used on festive occasions and at beer-drinking contests.

tuppenny. *(tuhp'-[e]-nee)*
Orthographic variant for twopenny.

turbidity. *(tuhr-bi'-d:uh-d:ee)*
Cloudiness in a beer. **See also:** chill haze; haze.

turner. *(tuhr'-ner)*
A tool for turning the malt and separating matted rootlets. **Syn:** malt oar; malt turning device. **See also:** couche; malted couche; malt plow.

Twenty-first Amendment. *(twehn'-tee fuhrst uh-mehnd'-ment)*
See: Prohibition.

twopenny. *(too'-peh-nee)*
A pale, small beer sold in England in the eighteenth century at 4 deciliters per quart or 2 deciliters per pint. Also spelled: tuppenny or two-penny.

two-rowed barley. *(too'-rod' bar'-lee)*
A variety of barley (*Hordeum distichum*) on which only the central spikelet in each triad is fertile, forming two rows of grains each. It is the variety most appreciated for brewing because its corn is better developed and the husk is thinner. **Syn:** two-row barley; spring barley; Chevalier barley.

two-stage fermentation. *(too'-steij fuhr-mehn-tei'-shen)*
Fermentation carried out in two containers, one for the primary and another for the secondary, as opposed to single-stage fermentation. **Syn:** double-stage fermentation.

tyg. *(tig)*
A communal drinking vessel made of pottery (slipware) with four to six handles, used at convivial gatherings.

U.K. gallon. *(yoo key′ ga′-len)*
Synonym for imperial gallon. **See also:** gallon.

ullage, to. *(uh′-lij, too)*
1. To calculate the headspace (airspace) in a cask or barrel. **2.** To refill a cask or bottle.

ullage. *(uh′-lij)*
1. The empty space at the top of a bottle, cask, or barrel between the liquid and the top of the container. In standard-size bottles, the headspace is usually 1–1.5 inches. An excess volume of air will accelerate oxidation and cause aerobic bacteria to sour the beer. **Syn:** headspace; airspace. **2.** The space measured in terms of the volume of liquid required to fill the container to capacity. **3.** The dregs (or liquid) left in a cask after leakage or racking.

ullaged. *(uh′-lijd)*
Describes a container short of its full measure.

Ultra. *(uhl′-truh)*
A variety of hops cultivated in the United States containing 2–4.5 percent alpha acids.

underback. *(uhn′-der-baek)*
A vessel underneath the mashing tun where the mash is poured.

undercarbonated. *(uhn′-der-kar′-buh-nei-d:id)*
Describes a beer lacking carbonation or effervescence. In homebrewing this is easily remedied by adding more priming sugar.

underletting. *(uhn'-der-leh-d:ing)*
The process of heating the mash by introducing hot water through the bottom of the mash tun.

unhopped. *(uhn-hapt')*
Synonym for nonhopped.

union. *(yoo'-nyen)*
See: Burton Union System.

uni-tank. *(yoo'-ni taengk)*
Brewing vessel used as both a fermenting and conditioning tank.

units of bitterness. *(yoo'-nits uv bi'-d:er-nis)*
See: I.B.U.

unload, to. *(uhn-lod', too)*
To remove the steeped barley from the steeping tank.

undermodified malt. *(uhn'-der-ma'-d:uh-fayd' mohlt')*
Malt of high amylase strength containing large amounts of unconverted protein because the germinating barley has been dried and kilned before the proteinase enzymes were able to fully convert the protein fraction.

underoxygenated. *(uhn'-der-ak'-si-ji-nei'-d:id)*
Describes an undersaturated wort, that is, one containing less than 9 parts per million of oxygen, in which the yeast reproduces with difficulty.

unpitching. *(uhn-pi'-ching)*
The action of removing old pitch from inside a cask or barrel. **Syn:** depitching.

ur-. *(ugh)*
A German prefix, an abbreviated form of *urtyp*, meaning original type, used to denote a beer brewed according to the original style.

U.S. gallon. *(yoo ehs' ga'-len)*
See: gallon.

U.S. quart. *(yoo ehs' kwohrt')*
A capacity measure of 57.75 cubic inches (0.9463 of a liter).

vacuum pump. *(vae'-kyoom puhmp')*
An apparatus consisting of a cylindro-conical vessel through which a flow of air is pumped to remove dust particles on the barley grains.

valence. *(vey'-len[t]s)*
The degree to which an ion or radical is able to combine directly with others.

vase. *(veis)*
A hollow vessel used for holding liquids.

vat. *(vaet)*
A large vessel for holding liquids during fermentation. Often called: tun.

VDK (vicinal diketones 2,3). *(vis'-[e]-nel day-kee'-tonz)*
Family of compounds that includes pentanedione and diacetyl, two closely related fermentation by-products with strong aromas and/or flavors.

vegetable gelatin. *(vehj'-[e]-tuh-bel jeh'-luh-tin)*
Synonym for agar-agar.

ventilation. *(vehn-tuh-ley'-shen)*
Synonym for airing.

venting. *(vehn'-ting)*
The act of allowing excess carbon dioxide to escape from a cask of beer prior to serving.

vessel. *(veh'-sil)*
A hollow receptacle for holding liquids.

VGA.
A variety of hops cultivated in the United States containing approximately 6.9 percent alpha acids.

Vienna. *(vee-eh'-nuh)*
1. An amber-colored, bottom-fermented beer originally brewed in Austria where it is now rare and known as Spezial to differentiate it from the classic version. Vienna-style lagers, still brewed in South America and Mexico, are amber-colored, lightly hopped, malty, and fairly strong (± 4.4 percent alcohol by weight or 5.5 percent by volume). **2.** A term often synonymous with Märzen.

Vienna malt. *(vee-eh'-nuh mohlt')*
Malt dried at a slightly higher temperature than pale lager malt; however, its main distinction is in the unique germination process used before drying. A beer made with Vienna malt will be deep gold to copper in color.

vieux lambic. *(vee-oe' lam'-beek)*
Old *lambic,* or lambic aged three years in a cask and one year in a bottle.

vinous. *(vay'-nuhs)*
Reminiscent of wine.

viscosity. *(vis-ka'-si-d:ee)*
Of glutinous consistency; the resistance of a fluid to flow. The body of a beer.

vitamin C. *(vai'-d:uh-min see)*
Synonym for ascorbic acid.

vitner's hose. *(vint'-nerz hoz)*
Insulated hose used to transfer liquids. Its heat tolerance makes it favorable for transferring hot wort.

volatiles. *(va'-luh-taylz)*
The volatiles in beer are divided into seven groups: alcohols (higher alcohols or fusel alcohols), esters, carbonyls, organic acids, sulfur compounds, amines, and phenols. These volatiles are responsible for most of the flavors found in beer.

vollbier. *(fohl'-beegh)*

One of the three legal categories for beers in Germany, comprising those of medium strength brewed from an original gravity of 11–14 °B and containing 3.5–4.5 percent alcohol by weight. **See also:** *bier; schankbier; starkbier.*

vorlauf. *(fogh'-lawf)*

German term for recirculation of wort through the grain bed.

v/v.

Abbreviation for volume per volume as in percentage volume of alcohol per volume of solution. **See also:** alcohol by volume.

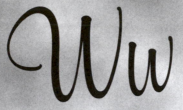

waghebaert. (va'-gheh-behght*)
    A type of strong beer brewed in Brussels in the fifteenth century.

waipiro. (wa-ee-pee-ro*)
    The Maori people used this word, meaning stinking water, to describe a brew prepared by Captain James Cook at Dusky Sound, New Zealand, in 1773. This beer was made by boiling the small branches of the *manuka* and the *rimu* trees (which he describes as spruce and tea plants) for three to four hours and adding molasses and yeast.

wallop. (wah'-luhp)
    British slang (cockney) for mild beer.

wash beer. (waesh' beeyr')
    Synonym for distiller's beer.

wassail bowl. (wa'-sel bol')
    In 1732 Sir Watkin W. Wynne presented the famous silver gilt bowl, which had a liquid capacity of 10 gallons, to Jesus College of Oxford. The recipe for the wassail, or swig, made at the college on St. David's Day consisted of 1/2 a pound of sugar put into the bowl with 1 pint of warm beer poured over the sugar. The dispenser then grated nutmeg and some ginger into the bowl, added 4 glasses of sherry and 5 additional pints of beer, stirred well, and sweetened to taste. He then covered the mixture and let it stand for two or three hours, after which he was required to put three or four slices of toast into it—and then it was ready to be served. If preparing wassail today, one might also add two or three slices of lemon and a few lumps of loaf sugar rubbed on the peel of a lemon for extra flavor.

water. *(wa'-d:er)*

One of the four ingredients of beer. The only requirements for water used in brewing is that it be drinkable and nonchlorinated. Chemically speaking, brewing water should be nonalkaline and of a certain hardness, prerequisites easily attained with the proper treatment.

water hardeners. *(wa'-d:er hard'-[e]-nerz)*

Mineral elements such as gypsum, Epsom salt, table salt, or Burton salts added to water that is soft or neutral to render it hard.

water hardness. *(wa'-d:er hard'-nis)*

The degree of hardness of water caused by the presence of mineral elements dissolved into it. It is expressed, in metric usage, in parts of calcium carbonate per million parts of water; in England, in Clark degrees water hardness is valued as 1 part of calcium carbonate per 70,000 parts of water; in France, a degree of hardness is 1 milligram of calcium carbonate per 1,000 liters of water; in Germany it is valued as 1 milligram of calcium oxide per 1,000 liters of water. The German figure, when multiplied by 17.9, gives parts per million of calcium carbonates. **Syn:** hardness of water. **See:** brewing water; hard water; permanent hardness; soft water; temporary hardness.

Degrees of Water Hardness

Grain per:	ppm	U.S. gal	°Clark	°French	°German
1 ppm	—	0.0583	0.07	0.1	0.056
1 grain per U.S. gal	17.1497	—	1.2	1.7149	0.958
1 °Clark	14.3	0.833	—	1.43	0.8
1 °French	10.0	0.583	0.7	—	0.56
1 °German	17.9	1.044	1.43	1.78	—

water lock. *(wa'-d:er lak')*

Synonym for fermentation lock.

water quality. *(wa'-d:er kwa'-li-d:ee)*

Refers to biological, chemical, and mineral content and properties of water. The quality of water has an impact on the quality and taste of a specific beer type. To this end the modern brewer can adjust, alter, or correct the chemical composition of water by adding or subtracting elements or mineral salts to the required optimal standards. Generally speaking, dark beers are made from soft to neutral water whereas pale beers are made from hard to neutral water. **See also:** water treatment.

water seal. *(wa'-d:er seeyl')*
 Synonym for fermentation lock.

water sensitivity. *(wa'-d:er sehn[t]-suh-ti'-vuh-d:ee)*
 See: dormancy.

water treatment. *(wa'-d:er treet'-ment)*
 Altering the characteristics and composition of water by mechanical or chemical means. In homebrewing, hard water is softened by boiling for about twenty minutes and racking, and soft water is hardened by the addition of calcium sulfate (gypsum) and magnesium sulfate (Epsom salt). Half a teaspoon of each to every gallon (4.5 litres) is a good recipe.

weeping barrel. *(wee'-ping bae'-rel)*
 A brewer's term for a leaking wooden barrel or cask caused by separation of the staves.

Weihenstephan. *(vay'-en-shteh-fehn)*
 The oldest brewery in the world. Now a brewery and brewing school located just outside Munich.

weissbier. *(vays'-beer)*
 In Germany, a generic term for wheat beers. The term is more often synonymous with Berliner *weisse* than with its southern counterpart, Süddeutsches *weizenbier*. *Weisse* means white, but such beers are usually very pale gold with a white foam. They are sometimes referred to as weisse beer in English literature. Also spelled: *weisse bier*. **See also:** lager weisse; wheat beer.

weizen. *(vay'-tsen)*
 See: *weissbier*.

weizenbier. *(vay'-tsen-beegh)*
 In Germany, a generic name for top-fermented wheat beers, especially those of the south (mainly Bavaria, Munich, and Baden-Württemberg), sometimes called Süddeutsches *weizenbier* to distinguish from those of northern Germany, which are referred to as Berliner *weisse* or simply *weissbier*. Compared to the northern Berliner weisse, weizenbier has a much higher wheat-to-barley ratio (1:1 to 2:1 as opposed to 1:3), a higher density (12–14 °B as opposed to 7–8 °B), and a higher alcohol content (+ 5 percent by volume as opposed to 3–4 percent). Weizenbier is also fuller flavored but less acidic. It is bottle-conditioned and is available in two forms: with yeast

sediments (*weizen mit hefe* or *hefeweizen[bier]*) or without (*hefefreiweizen[bier]*), both of which are often preferred with a slice of lemon. In Bavaria, wheat beer also is known as Bayerischer *weize*. **Syn:** Süddeutsches weizenbier. **See also:** wheat beer.

weizenbock. *(vay'-tsen-bohk)*
In Germany, a wheat beer of *bock* strength, that is, 5 percent alcohol by weight (6.25 percent alcohol by volume).

wet kit. *(weht' kit')*
A homebrewing kit containing a syrupy concentrate of wort as opposed to a dry kit, which contains flour.

wetting. *(weh'-d:ing)*
A rare synonym for steeping.

WGV.
Abbrevaition for Whitbread Golding Variety. A variety of hops cultivated in the United Kingdom and containing 5.5–8.5 percent alpha acids.

wheat. *([h]weet)*
A cereal from any of the grasses of the genus *Triticum*. There are thousands of varieties, divided into two categories: *Triticum vulgare* (or *Triticum aestivum*), or soft wheat, and *Triticum durum*, or hard wheat (also called durum wheat). **See also:** adjunct.

wheat beer. *([h]weet beeyr')*
Any beer containing a high proportion of malted wheat. Such beers are now produced only in Germany and Belgium. Belgian wheat beers include *blanche de* Hoegaarden, blanche de Louvain, and *lambic*. German wheat beers are classed in two categories: the *weissbier*, or Berliner *weisse*, of northern Germany, and the *weizenbier*, or Süddeutsches weizenbier, of southern Germany (mostly Bavaria and Baden-Württemberg). All wheat beers are top fermented and many are bottle-conditioned by the addition of yeast. The Belgian wheat beers contain 30–50 percent wheat, the Berliner weisse 25–30 percent, and the Bavarian weizenbier contains 50 percent or more.

wheat malt. *([h]weet mohlt')*
Malted wheat. It can constitute up to 60 percent of the mash for some wheat beers. Used in small quantities, it aids in head retention without imparting significant changes in flavor.

whicked weed. *(wi'-kid weed')*
A depreciatory name given to hops by English ale brewers in the fifteenth century.

whirlpool. *([h]wuhrl'-pool)*
An apparatus for the clarification of beer consisting of a large cylindrical tank about as tall as it is broad. The wort is introduced at high speed (8–12 meters per second) through a pipe set tangentially at about midpoint in the vertical wall. As the wort comes to rest in the tank, the trub, or hot break, deposits as a cone at the bottom by a process of sedimentation. The whirlpool often is used in conjunction with a hop separator.

white ale. *([h]wayt' eiyl')*
An medicinal concoction once prepared in Devon and Cornwall by mixing beer and rum with eggs, salt, and flour.

white beer. *([h]wayt' beeyr')*
Synonym for *witbier.*

white mold. *([h]wayt' mohld')*
Synonym for hop mold.

Whitsan church ale. *([h]wit'-sen chuhrch' eiyl')*
Synonym for Whitsun ale.

Whitsontide ale. *([h]wit'-sen-tayd eiyl')*
Synonym for Whitsun ale.

Whistun ale. *([h]wit'-sen eiyl')*
A church ale and feast in sixteenth- and seventeenth-century England. Also called: Whitsontide ale or Whitsan church ale.

whole hops. *(hol' haps')*
Synonym for loose hops.

Wieze Oktoberfesten. *(vee'-ze ohk-to'-begh-feh'-sten*)*
A beer festival held annually in Belgium since 1956 from September 30 to October 15.

wild beer. *(way[e]ld' beeyr')*
A beer fermented by wild yeasts. **Syn:** gushing beer.

wild yeast. *(way[e]ld' yeest')*
   1. Any airborne yeast. 2. In the fermenting wort, any yeast other than the cultured strain used for fermentation (*Saccharomycae cerevisiae* or *Saccharomycae carlsbergensis*).

Willamettes. *(wi-lae'-mits)*
   An U.S. variety of hops developed to improve the low acreage yield of Fuggles and increase its alpha-acid content. It is grown in Oregon with a 5–6 percent alpha acid content.

winter barley. *(win'-ter bar'-lee)*
   A synonym for barley sown at the end of autumn.

winy. *(way'-nee)*
   Sherrylike flavor; can be caused by warm fermentation or oxidation in very old beer.

witbier. *(vit'-beegh)*
   See: Hoegaardse *wit* and Leuvense wit.

withering. *(wi'-dhu-ring)*
   Blowing dry air into barley after germination is complete to decrease the ratio of humidity in the green malt.

wood alcohol. *(wud' ael'-kuh-hohl)*
   Synonym for methyl alcohol.

wood chips. *(wud' chips)*
   Synonym for clarifying chips.

woodruff. *(wud'-ruhf)*
   An herb with a vanillalike scent used to flavor some wines.

wood strips. *(wud' strips)*
   Synonym for clarifying chips.

work, to. *(wuhrk, too)*
   To ferment.

wort. *(wuhrt')*
The bittersweet sugar solution obtained by mashing the malt and boiling in the hops before it is fermented into beer. **See also:** bitter wort; sweet wort.

wort boiler. *(wuhrt' boy'-ler)*
Synonym for brew kettle.

wort chiller. *(wuhrt' chi'-ler)*
An apparatus used in homebrewing to cool the wort rapidly.

wort cooler. *(wuhrt' koo'-ler)*
Synonym for wort receiver.

wort copper. *(wuhrt' ka'-per)*
Synonym for brew kettle.

wort gelatin. *(wuhrt jeh'-luh-tin)*
Culture medium made up from wort as a nutrient source and gelatin to solidify it; for surface-culturing yeast.

wort kettle. *(wuhrt' keh'-d:el)*
Synonym for brew kettle.

wort receiver. *(wuhrt' ri-see'-ver)*
A cooling vessel into which the wort is poured after straining the hops. **Syn:** wort cooler.

wort straining. *(wuhrt' strei'-ning)*
The process of straining the wort through a filter.

w/v.
Abbreviation for weight per volume as in percentage weight of alcohol per volume of solution. **See also:** alcohol by volume; alcohol by weight.

Wye Target. *(way' tar'-git)*
A variety of hops grown in England containing 10–11 percent alpha acids.

yakju. *(yak'-joo*)*
An orthographic variant for *takju.*

yard of ale. *(yard uhv eiyl')*
A 3-foot-long horn-shaped drinking glass that holds about a quart of beer and consists of a long fluted neck resting on a globular bottom similar in shape to a coach horn. It was originally intended to be drained at a single draught. **Syn:** ale yard; yard of beer; long glass.

yeast. *(yeest')*
Microscopic, unicellular, fungi of the genus *Saccharomyces,* distinct from bacteria because they possess a true nucleus. Yeasts are classed depending on their ability to sporulate and the method of sporulation. Brewing yeasts are classed into three categories: bottom-fermenting yeast, or *Saccharomyces carlsbergensis,* reclassified *Saccharomyces uvarum;* top-fermenting yeast, or *Saccharomyces cerevisiae;* and wild yeasts, such as *Saccharomyces candida* and other species. Each category is further subdivided into strains. Because yeasts belong to the plant family, they are named according to the International Code of Botanical Nomenclature; each yeast is known by a binomial combination, the first name being that of the genus, the second that of the species. More than five hundred types of yeasts have been isolated, not including the numerous wild strains. The rate of reproduction of yeasts in wort varies with the temperature and reaches a maximum at about 86 °F (30 °C). The reproduction rate of *Saccharomyces cerevisiae* is greater than that of *Saccharomyces uvarum* at high temperatures, and the opposite holds at lower temperatures. Brewer's yeasts are sensitive to heat and may be killed by exposure to temperatures of 125.6 °F (52 °C) or above for ten minutes or more. During the fermentation process, yeast converts the natural malt sugars into equal parts of alcohol and carbon dioxide gas. Yeast was first viewed under a microscope in 1680

by the Dutch scientist Antonie van Leeuwenhoek; later, in 1867, Louis Pasteur discovered that yeast cells lack chlorophyl and that they could develop only in an environment containing both nitrogen and carbon. **See also:** bottom-fermenting yeast; lag phase; reproduction phase; top-fermenting yeast.

yeast back. *(yeest' baek')*
A large open vessel, usually with a capacity of 80–500 hectoliters (1,800–11,000 gallons), in which top yeast recovered from the fermentation vessel is stored. **See also:** parachute.

yeast bite. *(yeest' bayt)*
A brewer's term describing a sour, bitter taste in beer.

yeast energizer. *(yeest' eh-ner-jay'-zer)*
A vitamin and mineral supplement for brewing yeast used to accelerate its growth.

yeast extract. *(yeest' ehk'-straekt)*
Yeast nutrient. Yeast extract is the contents of the yeast cell. Yeast is cultured specifically for this purpose and is centrifuged, separating the cell wall skeletons (also called hulls or ghosts) from the extract.

yeast food. *(yeest' food')*
Synonym for yeast nutrients.

yeast head. *(yeest' hehd')*
The yeast-containing froth at the surface of top-fermenting ale at the end of primary fermentation. It is sometimes recovered by skimming or suctioning and used for pitching further worts.

yeast hulls. *(yeest' huhlz)*
Skeletons of a yeast cell wall. Also called: ghosts.

yeasting. *(yee'-sting)*
Synonym for pitching.

yeast nutrients. *(yeest' noo'-tree-ents)*
1. The elements essential to the life and growth of yeast cells, which include oxygen, carbon, nitrogen, phosphorus, sulfur, various minerals, and certain vitamins, all of which are normally present in aerated wort. Carbon is obtained

from glucose, galactose, fructose, sucrose, maltose, maltotriose, maltulose, and maltotriulose; nitrogen is obtained from ammonium salts, amino acids, and small peptides; phosphorus is obtained from phosphates; sulfur comes from inorganic sulfate or sulfite, thiosulfate, methionine, or glutathione. **2.** An additional dose of proteinous compounds and phosphates to ensure that the yeast remains healthy throughout fermentation. If the wort contains less than 60 percent malt or consists of malt extract, additional nutrients may be required. **Syn:** yeast food.

yeasty. *(yee'-stee)*
Yeastlike flavor; a result of yeast in suspension or beer sitting too long on sediment.

yellow water. *(yeh'-lo wa'-d:er)*
Synonym for *tiswin*. **See also:** *tulipai.*

yield. *(yee[e]ld')*
See: yield of extract.

yield difference. *(yee[e]ld' dif'-[e]-rehn[t]s)*
Difference in yield of extract in the laboratory and in a brewery for a given malt. Extract values are determined in a laboratory and are regarded as the greatest possible yield because the sample grist is very fine and the rest at saccharification temperature is long. Brewery grist is coarser and saccharification rests are shorter, so the extract yield of a malt in a brewery is less than it is in the lab. Modern breweries are able to realize a yield difference that is within 1 percent of the lab value. For example, if the lab extract value is 80 percent dry weight, the brewery should have a yield that is 79 percent or slightly higher.

yield of extract. *(yeeyld' uhv ek'-straekt)*
The percentage of extractable dry matter in the grist, that is, the total amount of dry matter that passes into solution in the wort during mashing.

Yorkshire stone square. *(yohrk'-sher ston' skwehr)*
An open fermentation vessel with a capacity of 36 hectoliters (28 barrels) unique to the town of Tadcaster in Yorkshire. It was originally made of stone and later of slate, and consists of two separate sections divided by a deck. The wort is fermented in the main (lower) compartment, and the yeast rises over the deck through a manhole that has a 5-inch (15-centimeter) flange. The beer drains back through pipes while the yeast settles and is skimmed off.

zitos. *(dzee'-tohs)*
The modern Greek name for beer. **See also:** *zythos*.

zithum. *(zi'-dhem)*
Orthographic variant for *zythum*.

zuckerpilz. *(tsu'-ker-pilts)*
An early name, meaning sugar fungus, given to yeast by Kützing and Schwann around 1837.

zur. *(tsoor*)*
Synonym for *kiesel*.

zurkel. *(tsoogh'-kel)*
German term for a valve used to dispense beer samples. Also called: *zwickel*.

zymase. *(zay'-meis)*
A complex of enzymes in yeast that are responsible for alcoholic fermentation by converting glucose to alcohol and carbon dioxide gas. Etym: So named by Eduard Buchner in 1897.

zymocides. *(zay'-muh-saydz)*
A component of certain yeast strains that serve as poisons to other strains of yeast.

zymology. *(zay-ma'-luh-jee)*
The science or study of fermentation. **Syn:** zymurgy.

zymometer. *(zay-ma'-muh-d:er)*
An instrument for measuring the degree of fermentation.

zymosis. *(zay-mo'-sis)*
Fermentation.

zymotechnics. *(zay-mo-tehk'-niks)*
The science of producing as well as controlling fermentation. **Syn:** zymurgy.

zymurgy. *(zay'-mer-jee)*
The title of a magazine (*Zymurgy®*) published by the American Homebrewers Association. **Syn:** zymology.

zythos. *(zue'-tos)*
The Greek name for barley wine, from the Egyptian word *zythum.*

zythum. *(zay'-them)*
An old name for barley wine (beer) made in Pharaoh's Egypt in the Nile Delta. A third-century BC papyrus describes the making of barley wine as follows: Six-rowed barley is mixed with water and baked into a bread, which is afterward broken, crushed, and diluted in date juice and water. The mixture then undergoes crude filtration and fermentation. *Zythum* was flavored with juniper berries, powdered ginger, hops, black cumin, saffron, and other herbs. *Dizythum* was said to have been a more potent drink; *carmi* was a palace variety; and *busa* was the familial beer. **Also spelled:** *zithum; zythem.*

Thermometer Scales

The two most commonly used temperature scales in brewing and malting are the traditional Fahrenheit (°F) scale and the metric centigrade (°C) scale. These scales are based on the freezing and boiling point of pure water.

Freezing point: 0 °C   32 °F
Boiling point: 100 °C   212 °F

Conversion Formulas
°F = (°C × 9/5) + 32 or (°C × 1.8) + 32
°C = (°F − 32) × 5/9 or (°F − 32) / 1.8

Temperature Conversion Table

°F	°C	°F	°C	°F	°C	°F	°C	°F	°C	°F	°C	°F	°C
32	0	58	14	84	29	110	43	136	58	162	72	188	87
33	1	59	15	85	29	111	44	137	58	163	73	189	87
34	1	60	16	86	30	112	44	138	59	164	73	190	88
35	2	61	16	87	31	113	45	139	59	165	74	191	88
36	2	62	17	88	31	114	46	140	60	166	74	192	89
37	3	63	17	89	32	115	46	141	61	167	75	193	89
38	3	64	18	90	32	116	47	142	61	168	76	194	90
39	4	65	18	91	33	117	47	143	62	169	76	195	91
40	4	66	19	92	33	118	48	144	62	170	77	196	91
41	5	67	19	93	34	119	48	145	63	171	77	197	92
42	6	68	20	94	34	120	49	146	63	172	78	198	92
43	6	69	21	95	35	121	49	147	64	173	78	199	93
44	7	70	21	96	36	122	50	148	64	174	79	200	93
45	7	71	22	97	36	123	51	149	65	175	79	201	94
46	8	72	22	98	37	124	51	150	66	176	80	202	94
47	8	73	23	99	37	125	52	151	66	177	81	203	95
48	9	74	23	100	38	126	52	152	67	178	81	204	96
49	9	75	24	101	38	127	53	153	67	179	82	205	96
50	10	76	24	102	39	128	53	154	68	180	82	206	97
51	11	77	25	103	39	129	54	155	68	181	83	207	97
52	11	78	26	104	40	130	54	156	69	182	83	208	98
53	12	79	26	105	41	131	55	157	69	183	84	209	98
54	12	80	27	106	41	132	56	158	70	184	84	210	99
55	13	81	27	107	42	133	56	159	71	185	85	211	99
56	13	82	28	108	42	134	57	160	71	186	86	212	100
57	14	83	28	109	43	135	57	161	72	187	86		

Conversion Factors

To convert:	To:	Multiply by:
British barrels	British gallons	36
	cubic feet	5.779568
	cubic meters	0.1636591
	liters	163.6546
	U.S. barrels	1.3725
British firkins	British pints	72
	British gallons	9
	cubic centimeters	40,914.79
	cubic feet	1.444892
	U.S. firkins	1.2000949
	liters	40.91364
British gallons	British barrels	0.027777
	British firkins	0.111111
	British ounces (fluid)	160
	British quarts	4
	cubic centimeters	4,546.087
	cubic feet	0.160544
	cubic inches	277.4193
	cubic meters	0.004546
	liters	4.54596
	U.S. ounces (fluid)	153.7215
	U.S. gallons	1.20095
British gallons/second	cubic centimeters/second	4,546.087

To convert:	To:	Multiply by:
British ounces (fluid)	cubic centimeters	28.41305
	cubic inches	1.733387
	British gallons	0.00625
	milliliters	28.41225
	U.S. ounces (fluid)	0.9607594
British pints	British gallons	0.125
	British gills	4
	British ounces (fluid)	20
	British quarts	0.5
	cubic centimeters	568.26092
	liters	0.568245
	U.S. gills	4.903797
	U.S. pints	1.200949
British quarts	British gallons	0.25
	cubic centimeters	1,136.522
	cubic inches	69.35482
	liters	1.13649
	U.S. gallons	0.032056
	U.S. quarts	1.200949
Centigrade (°C)	Fahrenheit (°F)	$(°C \times 9/5) + 32$
Centigrams	grains	0.15432
	grams	0.01
Centiliters	cubic centimeters	10
	cubic inches	0.6102545
	liters	0.01
	U.S. ounces (fluid)	0.33815
Centimeters	feet	0.03281
	inches	0.3937
	meters	0.01
	microns	10,000
	millimeters	10

To convert:	To:	Multiply by:
Centimeters/minute	inches/minute	0.3937
Centimeters/second	feet/minute	1.969
	feet/second	0.03281
	meters/minute	0.6
	meters/second	0.01
Cubic centimeters	British gallons	0.000218997
	British gills	0.00739
	British quarts	0.00087988
	British ounces (fluid)	0.03519
	cubic feet	0.000035314
	cubic inches	0.06102
	cubic millimeters	1,000
	liters	0.001
	milliliters	1
	U.S. drams	0.27051
	U.S. gallons	0.00026417
	U.S. gills	0.0084535
	U.S. ounces (fluid)	0.033814
	U.S. pints	0.00211337
	U.S. quarts	0.0010567
Cubic feet	British gallons	6.229
	British ounces (fluid)	966.6143
	cubic centimeters	28,316.847
	cubic meters	0.028317
	cubic inches	1,728
	liters	28.3168
	U.S. gallons	7.481
	U.S. pints	59.844256
	U.S. quarts	29.922078
	U.S. ounces (fluid)	957.50649
Cubic inches	British barrels	0.000797
	British gallons	0.0036
	cubic centimeters	16.38706
	cubic feet	0.00058
	cubic meters	0.0000163

To convert:	To:	Multiply by:
	cubic millimeters	16,387.06
	liters	0.01639
	U.S. gallons	0.004329
	U.S. pints	0.034632
	U.S. quarts	0.017316
	U.S. ounces (fluid)	0.554
Cubic meters	British barrels	6.11
	British gallons	219.9692
	cubic feet	35.3147
	cubic inches	61,023.74
	liters	1,000
	U.S. barrels	8.3864145
	U.S. gallons	264.17205
	U.S. pints	2,113.3764
	U.S. quarts	1,056.6882
	liters	1,000
Cubic millimeters	cubic inches	0.000061
Drams (avoirdupois)	grains	27.3437
	grams	1.7718
	drams (apothecaries)	0.455729
Drams (apothecary)	drams avoirdupois	0.2194286
	pounds avoirdupois	0.008571429
	pounds troy	0.010416667
	ounces troy	0.125
	ounces avoirdupois	0.1371429
	pennyweight	2.5
Fahrenheit (°F)	centigrade (°C)	$(°F \times 5/9) - 32$
Feet	centimeters	30.48
	inches	12
	meters	0.3048
	millimeters	304.8
	mils	12,000

To convert:	To:	Multiply by:
Feet/minute	centimeters/second	0.508
	meters/second	0.00508
	meters/minute	0.305
	miles/hour	0.011364
Feet/second	centimeters/second	30.48
	meters/minute	18.288
	meters/second	0.3048
Firkins	See U.S. firkins and British firkins.	
Gallons	See U.S. gallons and British gallons.	
Grains avoirdupois	grains troy	1
Grains troy	grains avoirdupois	1
	drams (apothecaries)	0.01666
	drams (avoirdupois)	0.03657
	grams	0.0647989
	milligrams	64.7989
	ounces apothecaries	0.002083
	ounces avoirdupois	0.0022857
	ounces troy	0.002083
	pennyweight	0.0416667
	pounds avoirdupois	0.0001428
	pounds troy	0.0001736
	scruples	0.05
Grams	decigrams	10
	drams avoirdupois	0.5643
	drams apothecary	0.2572
	grains	15.43235
	kilograms	0.001
	milligrams	1,000
	ounces avoirdupois	0.03527
	ounces troy	0.03215
	pennyweight	0.64301
	pounds avoirdupois	0.00204

To convert:	To:	Multiply by:
	pounds troy	0.002679
	scruples	0.77162
Hectoliters	cubic feet	3.531566
	liters	100
	U.S. gallons	26.41794
	U.S. ounces (fluid)	3,381.497
Hundredweight (long)	kilograms	50.80235
Hundredweight (short)	kilograms	45.35924
Imperial (measures)	See British (measures).	
Inches	centimeters	2.54
	feet	0.083333
	meters	0.0254
	microns	25,400
	millimeters	25.4
	mils	1,000
Kilograms	British gallons	0.2199
	British quarters (long)	0.078736522
	cubic centimeters	1,000
	cubic inches	61.023
	drams avoirdupois	564.4
	grains	15,432.358
	grams	1,000
	hundredweight (long)	0.01968
	hundredweight (short)	0.02204
	ounces avoirdupois	35.2739
	ounces troy	32.15074
	pounds avoirdupois	2.20462
	pounds troy	2.6792
	pennyweight	643.015
	scruples	771.61792
	tons (long)	0.009842

To convert:	To:	Multiply by:
	tons (metric)	0.001
	tons (short)	0.0011023
	U.S. gallons	0.26417
Kilometers	feet	3,280.84
	yards	1,093.6133
Liters	British gallons	0.21997
	British gills	7.03902
	British ounces (fluid)	35.196
	British pints	1.795756
	British quarts	0.8798775
	centiliters	100
	cubic centimeters	1,000
	cubic feet	0.03532
	cubic inches	61.0255
	cubic meters	0.001
	drams	270.5179
	milliliters	1,000
	U.S. gallons	0.26417205
	U.S. gills	8.4535058
	U.S. ounces (fluid)	33.8147
	U.S. pints	2.1133764
	U.S. quarts	1.0567
Liters/minute	cubic feet/minute	0.0353147
	cubic feet/second	0.000588578
Liters/second	cubic feet/minute	2.11888
	U.S. gallons/minute	15.850342
	U.S. gallons/second	0.2641723
Meters	centimeters	100
	feet	3.28084
	inches	39.37008
	kilometers	0.001
	millimeters	1,000

To convert:	To:	Multiply by:
Meters/second	feet/second	3.281
	feet/minute	196.86
Microinches	microns	0.0254
Microns (micrometer)	centimeters	0.0001
	inches	0.000039
	microinches	39.37008
	millimeters	0.001
	mils	0.03937
Milligrams	centigrams	0.1
	drams apothecaries	0.0002572
	drams avoirdupois	0.000564
	grains	0.015432
	grams	0.001
	avoirdupois	0.00003527
	ounces apothecaries	0.00003215
	pennyweight	0.000643
	scruples	0.0007716
Milliliters	British ounces (fluid)	0.035196
	British pints	0.001759804
	cubic centimeters	1
	cubic inches	0.06102
	cubic milliliters	1,000
	liters	0.001
	U.S. drams	0.2705198
	U.S. gills	0.008453742
	U.S. ounces (fluid)	0.0338149
	U.S. pints	0.002113436
Millimeters	centimeters	0.1
	cubic centimeters	1.000028
	cubic inches	0.061025
	feet	0.00328
	inches	0.03937

To convert:	To:	Multiply by:
	meters	0.001
	microns	1,000
	mils	39.37
Mils	centimeters	0.00254
	inches	0.001
	microns	25.4
	millimeters	0.0254
Ounces (fluid)	*See British ounces (fluid) and U.S. ounces (fluid).*	
Ounces avoirdupois	centigrams	2,834.9527
	cubic centimeters	28.35
	cubic inches	1.73
	drams (avoirdupois)	16
	grains	437.5
	grams	28.3495
	kilograms	0.02835
	ounces troy	0.911458
	pennyweight	18.22917
	pounds avoirdupois	0.0625
	pounds troy	0.07595
	scruples	21.871
Ounces troy	centigrams	3,110.3481
	drams avoirdupois	17.5543
	drams apothecaries	8
	grains	480
	grams	31.103481
	kilograms	0.03110348
	ounces avoirdupois	1.09714
	milligrams	31,103.481
	pennyweight	20
	pounds avoirdupois	0.06837
	pounds troy	0.08333
	scruples	24

To convert:	To:	Multiply by:
Parts per million	grains per U.S. gallons	0.0584
	grams per U.S. gallon	0.0038
	grams per liter	0.001
	ounces per barrel	0.0042
	milligrams per liter	1
Pints	*See British pints and U.S. pints.*	
Pounds avoirdupois	British quarts	0.399
	cubic centimeters	453.59
	cubic feet	0.016
	drams avoirdupois	256
	grains	7,000
	grams	453.5924
	kilograms	0.4535924
	ounces avoirdupois	16
	ounces troy	14.5833
	pennyweight	291.667
	pounds troy	1.21528
	scruples	350
	U.S. quarts	0.4793
Pounds troy	drams apothecaries	96
	drams avoirdupois	210.65
	grains	5,760
	grams	373.24177
	kilograms	0.3732417
	ounces apothecaries	12
	ounces avoirdupois	13.1657
	ounces troy	12
	pennyweight	240
	pounds avoirdupois	0.822857
	scruples	288
Quarts	*See British quarts and U.S. quarts.*	

To convert:	To:	Multiply by:
Revolutions/minute	revolutions/second	0.01667
Revolutions/second	revolutions/minute	60
Scruples	drams apothecaries	0.33333
	drams avoirdupois	0.73142
	grains	20
	grams	1.29597
	ounces apothecaries	0.04166
	ounces avoirdupois	0.0457
	ounces troy	0.04166
	pennyweight	0.8333
	pounds apothecaries	0.003472
	pounds avoirdupois	0.002857
	pounds troy	0.003472
Square centimeters	square feet	0.001076
	square inches	0.155
	square meters	0.0001
	square millimeters	100
	square mils	155,000.31
Square feet	square centimeters	929.03
	square inches	144
	square meters	0.0929
Square inches	square centimeters	6.4516
	square feet	0.00694
	square meters	0.000645
	square millimeters	645.16
Square meters	square centimeters	10,000
	square feet	10.7639
	square inches	1,550
Square millimeters	square centimeters	0.01
	square feet	0.00001
	square inches	0.00155

To convert:	To:	Multiply by:
Tons (long)	kilograms	1,016.047
	ounces avoirdupois	35,840
	pounds apothecaries	2,722.22
	pounds avoirdupois	2,240
	pounds troy	2,722.22
	tons (metric)	1.01605
	tons (short)	1.12
Tons (metric)	kilograms	1,000
	ounces avoirdupois	35,273.96
	pounds apothecaries	2,679.2289
	pounds avoirdupois	2,204.6226
	pounds troy	2,679.2289
	tons (long)	0.9842
	tons (short)	1.10231
Tons (short)	kilograms	907.185
	ounces avoirdupois	32,000
	pounds apothecaries	2,430.555
	pounds avoirdupois	2,000
	pounds (troy)	2,430.555
	tons (long)	0.89286
	tons (metric)	0.90718
U.S. firkins	British firkins	0.8326747
	cubic feet	1.203125
	liters	34.06775
	U.S. barrels	0.29464286
	U.S. pints	72
U.S. gallons	British gallons	0.83267
	cubic centimeters	3,785.412
	cubic feet	0.13368
	cubic inches	231
	cubic meters	0.003785
	liters	3.7854
	U.S. ounces (fluid)	128
	U.S. pints	8
	U.S. quarts	4

To convert:	To:	Multiply by:
U.S. gallons/hour	liters/hour	3.7854118
U.S. gallons/second	cubic centimeter/second	3,785.4118
	cubic feet/minute	8.020833
	liters/minute	227.1183
U.S. ounces (fluid)	British ounces (fluid)	1.040843
	cubic centimeter	29.57373
	cubic inches	1.8046875
	liters	0.0295727
	U.S. gallons	0.0078125
	U.S. gills	0.25
	U.S. pints	0.0625
	U.S. quarts	0.03125
U.S. pints	British pints	0.8326747
	cubic centimeters	473.17647
	cubic feet	0.01671
	cubic inches	28.875
	liters	0.4731632
	milliliters	473.1632
	U.S. gallons	0.125
	U.S. ounces (fluid)	16
	U.S. gills	4
	U.S. quarts	0.5
U.S. quarts	British quarts	0.8326747
	cubic centimeters	946.35295
	cubic feet	0.03342
	cubic inches	57.75
	liters	0.9463264
	U.S. gallons	0.25
	U.S. gills	8
	U.S. ounces (fluid)	32
	U.S. pints	2
Yards	meters	0.9144

Conversions between U.S. and U.K. Liquid Measurements

The U.K. gallon is also called the British gallon, the British imperial gallon, the imperial gallon, and, in Canada, the Canadian gallon.

To obtain the weight of U.S. gallons, multiply the specific gravity by 8.337.

To find the U.S. gallon capacity of a rectangular tank, multiply the length (in inches) by the width and the resulting figure by the depth. Divide this figure by 231 (1 gallon equals 231 cubic inches).

To find the U.S. gallon capacity of a cylindrical tank, first measure the cubic inch content by multiplying the diameter (in inches) by itself (square the diameter) and multiply the resulting figure by 0.7854 and the one after that by the depth. This gives the cubic inch content which, divided by 231, gives the gallon capacity.

	U.S. Gallons to:		U.K. Gallons to:	
Gallons	Liters	U.K. gal	Liters	U.S. gal
1	3.7854	0.83270	4.5460	1.20092
2	7.5708	1.66539	9.0919	2.40183
3	11.3562	2.49809	13.6379	3.60275
4	15.1416	3.33079	18.1839	4.80367
5	18.9271	4.16348	22.7298	6.00458
6	22.7125	4.99618	27.2758	7.20550
7	26.4979	5.82888	31.8217	8.40642
8	30.2833	6.66158	36.3677	9.60734
9	34.0687	7.49427	40.9137	10.80825
10	37.8541	8.32697	45.4596	12.00917

Liters to U.S. and U.K. Gallons

Liters	U.S. gal	U.K. gal
1	0.26417	0.21998
2	0.52843	0.43995
3	0.79252	0.65993
4	1.05669	0.87990
5	1.32086	1.09988
6	1.58503	1.31985
7	1.84920	1.53983
8	2.11338	1.75980
9	2.37755	1.97978
10	2.64172	2.19975

Fluid Ounces to Centiliters— Centiliters to Fluid Ounces

cl	fl oz	fl	cl
1	0.35196	1	2.8412
2	0.7039	2	5.6824
3	1.0559	3	8.5237
4	1.4078	4	11.3649
5	1.7598	5	14.2061
6	2.1118	6	17.0473
7	2.4637	7	19.8886
8	2.8157	8	22.7298
9	3.1676	9	25.5710
10	3.5196	10	28.4122

Conversion of Alcohol Percentages by Volume (V/V) to Alcohol Percentages by Weight (W/W)

V/V	W/V	V/V	W/V
1.0	0.79	3.0	2.38
1.1	0.87	3.1	2.46
1.2	0.95	3.2	2.54
1.3	1.03	3.3	2.62
1.4	1.11	3.4	2.70
1.5	1.19	3.5	2.78
1.6	1.27	3.6	2.86
1.7	1.35	3.7	2.94
1.8	1.43	3.8	3.02
1.9	1.51	3.9	3.10
2.0	1.59	4.0	3.18
2.1	1.67	4.1	3.26
2.2	1.75	4.2	3.34
2.3	1.82	4.3	3.42
2.4	1.90	4.4	3.50
2.5	1.98	4.5	3.58
2.6	2.06	4.6	3.66
2.7	2.14	4.7	3.74
2.8	2.22	4.8	3.82
2.9	2.30	4.9	3.90

V/V	W/V		V/V	W/V
5.0	3.98		8.0	6.40
5.1	3.98		8.1	6.48
5.2	4.14		8.2	6.56
5.3	4.22		8.3	6.64
5.4	4.30		8.4	6.72
5.5	4.38		8.5	6.80
5.6	4.46		8.6	6.88
5.7	4.54		8.7	6.96
5.8	4.62		8.8	7.04
5.9	4.70		8.9	7.12
6.0	4.78		9.0	7.20
6.1	4.87		9.1	7.29
6.2	4.95		9.2	7.37
6.3	5.03		9.3	7.45
6.4	5.11		9.4	7.53
6.5	5.19		9.5	7.61
6.6	5.27		9.6	7.69
6.7	5.35		9.7	7.77
6.8	5.43		9.8	7.85
6.9	5.51		9.9	7.93
			10.0	8.02
7.0	5.59			
7.1	5.67			
7.2	5.75			
7.3	5.83			
7.4	5.91			
7.5	5.99			
7.6	6.07			
7.7	6.15			
7.8	6.24			
7.9	6.32